CHRISTIAN THEOLC

SERIES ED

Timothy Gorringe Serene

CHRISTIAN THEOLOGY IN CONTEXT

Any inspection of recent theological monographs makes plain that it is still thought possible to understand a text independently of its context. Work in the sociology of knowledge and in cultural studies has, however, increasingly made obvious that such divorce is impossible. On the one hand, as Marx put it, 'life determines consciousness'. All texts have to be understood in their life situation, related to questions of power, class, and modes of production. No texts exist in intellectual innocence. On the other hand, texts are also forms of cultural power, expressing and modifying the dominant ideologies through which we understand the world. This dialectical understanding of texts demands an interdisciplinary approach if they are to be properly understood: theology needs to be read alongside economics, politics, and social studies, as well as philosophy, with which it has traditionally been linked. The cultural situatedness of any text demands, both in its own time and in the time of its rereading, a radically interdisciplinary analysis.

The aim of this series is to provide such an analysis, culturally situating texts by Christian theologians and theological movements. Only by doing this, we believe, will people of the fourth, sixteenth, or nineteenth centuries be able to speak to those of the twenty-first. Only by doing this will we be able to understand how theologies are themselves cultural products—projects deeply resonant with their particular cultural contexts and yet nevertheless exceeding those contexts by being received into our own today. In doing this, the series should advance both our understanding of those theologies and our understanding of theology as a discipline. We also hope that it will contribute to the fast developing interdisciplinary debates of the present.

Kierkegaard

Thinking Christianly in an Existential Mode

Sylvia Walsh

OXFORD
UNIVERSITY PRESS

OXFORD
UNIVERSITY PRESS

Great Clarendon Street, Oxford OX2 6DP

Oxford University Press is a department of the University of Oxford.
It furthers the University's objective of excellence in research, scholarship,
and education by publishing worldwide in

Oxford New York

Auckland Cape Town Dar es Salaam Hong Kong Karachi
Kuala Lumpur Madrid Melbourne Mexico City Nairobi
New Delhi Shanghai Taipei Toronto

With offices in

Argentina Austria Brazil Chile Czech Republic France Greece
Guatemala Hungary Italy Japan Poland Portugal Singapore
South Korea Switzerland Thailand Turkey Ukraine Vietnam

Oxford is a registered trade mark of Oxford University Press
in the UK and in certain other countries

Published in the United States
by Oxford University Press Inc., New York

First published 2009

British Library Cataloguing in Publication Data
Data available

Library of Congress Cataloging in Publication Data
Data available

Typeset by SPI Publisher Services, Pondicherry, India
Printed in Great Britain
on acid-free paper by
CPI Antony Rowe, Chippenham, Wiltshire

ISBN 978–0–19–920835–7 (hbk)
978–0–19–920836–4 (pbk)

1 3 5 7 9 10 8 6 4 2

In memory of

Edna Hatlestad Hong

(1913–2007)

Christian Author and Kierkegaard Translator

Preface

Kierkegaard was first and foremost a Christian thinker, yet his specifically Christian writings are still relatively unfamiliar to many scholars and general readers, with the result that the attack on the established church of his time for which he is most famous has sometimes been regarded as anti-Christian. Nothing could be further from the truth. Not since Luther has there been a Protestant thinker who has so uncompromisingly sought to define and present Christianity in its utmost integrity, casting into reflection the ideality of Christianity and what it means to be a Christian in the strictest sense in the interest of reintroducing authentic Christianity as an existential possibility for every individual in the modern age.

This study seeks to sift out the distinctive areas and nature of Kierkegaard's contributions, both critical and constructive, to modern Christian theology within an existential mode of thinking Christianly that characterizes his theological reflection and method of communication. While it is possible to understand Kierkegaard's construal of Christianity without reference to his life and the age in which he lived, it is impossible to read him properly without some knowledge of his life and the historical, philosophical, theological, and social contexts of his authorship. Chapter 1 will set the stage for reading Kierkegaard in context by presenting a biographical overview of his religious upbringing and theological education, the major intellectual influences and events in his life, and the nature and phases of his writings as they unfolded in the intellectual and historical milieu of his time. There has been a tendency of late to 'localize' Kierkegaard by emphasizing the Danish context of his authorship, but it must also be viewed in the broader arena of European intellectual and sociopolitical developments in the first half of the nineteenth century. Chapter 2 will flesh out Kierkegaard's distinctive understanding of Christianity as an 'existence-communication' and the existential mode of theological reflection appropriate to it in contrast to objective ways of doing theology in the modern age which in his view had turned Christianity into a doctrine, thereby falsifying the relation of both believers and nonbelievers to it. Chapters 3–7 will then focus on Kierkegaard's understanding of a number of theological concepts and issues that constitute some of his most original and most important contributions to Christian thought.

Kierkegaard was a dialectical thinker *par excellence*, construing Christianity as combining gospel and law, grace and works, leniency and rigour, positive and negative existential qualifications in a distinctive form of dialectic which he calls 'inverse dialectic' or 'the dialectic of inversion', according to which 'the essentially Christian is always the positive which is recognizable by the negative' (*JP* i. 760; iv. 4680; v. 5997, translation modified). Inverse dialectic pervades Kierkegaard's understanding of Christianity and Christian existence, so that an awareness of it is essential for a proper understanding of his theology. We shall have occasion in the chapters ahead to see more clearly how it functions in his thought.

Kierkegaard was also a master prose stylist and poetic writer, employing an array of pseudonyms, literary genres, and imaginative figures to present his own views as well as some with which he disagreed. No one can possibly express his thought as well as Kierkegaard himself does. Consequently, Kierkegaard and his pseudonyms will frequently be allowed to speak for themselves in this study. Readers encountering Kierkegaard for the first time can thus enjoy a taste of his artistry as a writer as well as his genius as a Christian thinker and hopefully acquire an appetite for more. No attempt has been made to alter the sometimes patriarchal character of Kierkegaard's language, which reflects the linguistic practice and social structure of his time. But I have taken the liberty of amending, where justified, the standard translations of terms that are gender neutral rather than masculine in Danish.

I wish to thank Princeton University Press for permission to reprint from the following works by Søren Kierkegaard:

- *The Concept of Anxiety*. © 1980 Princeton University Press.
- *Concluding Unscientific Postscript to Philosophical Fragments* (2 vols.). © 1992 Princeton University Press.
- *Philosophical Fragments/Johannes Climacus* © 1985 Princeton University Press.
- *Practice in Christianity*. © 1991 Howard V. Hong (published by Princeton University Press).
- *The Sickness unto Death* © 1980 Howard V. Hong. Published by Princeton University Press, 1983 paperback edition.
- *Works of Love*. © 1995 Postscript, Inc. Published by Princeton University Press, 1998 paperback edition.

Thanks are also due to the Stetson University Interlibrary Loan Services for their help in securing resources for the preparation of this book. My indebtedness to my husband, Robert L. Perkins, is immeasurable, as he has been a constant support and constructive critic for this and all my academic projects.

S. W.

Contents

Abbreviations

References to Kierkegaard's works and papers in English and Danish are cited in parentheses in the text using the following list of abbreviations together with volume and page numbers or, for Kierkegaard's papers, entry numbers.

BA	*The Book on Adler* (1995), ed. and tr. Howard V. Hong and Edna H. Hong (Princeton: Princeton University Press).
C	*The Crisis and a Crisis in the Life of an Actress*. See *CD*.
CA	*The Concept of Anxiety* (1980), ed. and tr. Reidar Thomte in collaboration with Albert B. Anderson (Princeton: Princeton University Press).
CD	*Christian Discourses* and *The Crisis and a Crisis in the Life of an Actress* (1997), ed. and tr. Howard V. Hong and Edna H. Hong (Princeton: Princeton University Press).
CI	*The Concept of Irony* together with 'Notes on Schelling's Berlin Lectures' (1989), ed. and tr. Howard V. Hong and Edna H. Hong (Princeton: Princeton University Press).
COR	*The Corsair Affair* (1982), ed. and tr. Howard V. Hong and Edna H. Hong (Princeton: Princeton University Press).
CUP	*Concluding Unscientific Postscript to 'Philosophical Fragments'*, i–ii (1992), ed. and tr. Howard V. Hong and Edna H. Hong (Princeton: Princeton University Press).
EO	Either/or, i–ii (1987), ed. and tr. Howard V. Hong and Edna H. Hong (Princeton: Princeton University Press).
EPW	*Early Polemical Writings* (1990), ed. and tr. Julia Watkin (Princeton: Princeton University Press).
EUD	*Eighteen Upbuilding Discourses* (1990), ed. and tr. Howard V. Hong and Edna H. Hong (Princeton: Princeton University Press).
FSE	*For Self-Examination* and *Judge for Yourself!* (1990), ed. and tr. Howard V. Hong and Edna H. Hong (Princeton: Princeton University Press).
FT	*Fear and Trembling* (2006), ed. C. Stephan Evans and Sylvia Walsh, tr. Sylvia Walsh (Cambridge: Cambridge University Press).
JC	*Johannes Climacus*. See *PF*.
JFY	*Judge for Yourself!* See *FSE*.
JP	*Søren Kierkegaard's Journals and Papers*, i–vii (1967–78), ed. and tr. Howard V. Hong and Edna H. Hong, assisted by Gregor Malantschuk (Bloomington, Ind., and London: Indiana University Press).
KJN	*Kierkegaard's Journals and Notebooks*, i. (2007), ed. Niels Jørgen Cappelørn, Alastair Hannay, David Kangas, Bruce H. Kirmmse, George Pattison,

Vanessa Rumble, and K. Brian Söderquist (Princeton: Princeton University Press).

LD — *Letters and Documents* (1978), tr. Hendrik Rosenmeier (Princeton: Princeton University Press).

PC — *Practice in Christianity* (1991), ed. and tr. Howard V. Hong and Edna H. Hong (Princeton: Princeton University Press).

PF — *Philosophical Fragments* and *Johannes Climacus* (1985), ed. and tr. Howard V. Hong and Edna H. Hong (Princeton: Princeton University Press).

PV — *The Point of View: On My Work as an Author; The Point of View for My Work as an Author; Armed Neutrality* (1998), ed. and tr. Howard V. Hong and Edna H. Hong (Princeton: Princeton University Press).

R — *Fear and Trembling* and *Repetition* (1983), ed. and tr. Howard V. Hong and Edna H. Hong (Princeton: Princeton University Press).

SKP — *Søren Kierkegaards Papirer*, 2nd enlarged edn. (1968–78), ed. Niels Thulstrup, with index vols. xiv–xvi by Niels Jørgen Cappelørn (Copenhagen: Gyldendal).

SKS — *Søren Kierkegaards Skrifter* (1997–2008ff.), ed. Niels Jørgen Cappelørn, Joakim Garff, Jette Knudsen, Johnny Kondrup, and Alastair McKinnon (Copenhagen: Gads Forlag).

SKS K — *Kommentarer* to *Søren Kierkegaards Skrifter*.

SLW — *Stages on Life's Way* (1988), ed. and tr. Howard V. Hong and Edna H. Hong (Princeton: Princeton University Press).

SUD — *The Sickness unto Death* (1980), ed. and tr. Howard V. Hong and Edna H. Hong (Princeton: Princeton University Press).

SV1 — *Søren Kierkegaards Samlede Værker*, i–xiv, 1st edn. (1901–6), ed. A. B. Drachmann, J. L. Heiberg, and H.O. Lange (Copenhagen: Glydendalske Boghandels Forlag).

TA — *Two Ages: The Age of Revolution and the Present Age. A Literary Review* (1978), ed. and tr. Howard V. Hong and Edna H. Hong (Princeton: Princeton University Press).

TDIO — *Three Discourses on Imagined Occasions* (1993), ed. and tr. Howard V. Hong and Edna H. Hong (Princeton: Princeton University Press).

TM — *'The Moment' and Late Writings* (1998), ed. and tr. Howard V. Hong and Edna H. Hong (Princeton: Princeton University Press).

UDVS — *Upbuilding Discourses in Various Spirits* (1993), ed. and tr. Howard V. Hong and Edna H. Hong (Princeton: Princeton University Press).

WA — *Without Authority* (1997), ed. and tr. Howard V. Hong and Edna H. Hong (Princeton: Princeton University Press).

WL — *Works of Love* (1995), ed. and tr. Howard V. Hong and Edna H. Hong (Princeton: Princeton University Press).

1

That Single Individual

Like many young people struggling to find themselves in the modern world, Søren Aabye Kierkegaard (1813–55) at age 22 was uncertain about his purpose in life. Writing in a poetic, possibly quasi-autobiographical fashion for a projected novel while vacationing by the sea, he mused:

> What I really need is to get clear about *what I must do*, not what I must know, except insofar as knowledge must precede every act. What matters is to find my purpose, to see what it really is that God wills that *I* shall do; the crucial thing is to find a truth that is truth *for me*, to find *the idea for which I am willing to live and die*. Of what use would it be to me to discover a so-called objective truth, to work through the philosophical systems so that I could, if asked, make critical judgments about them, could point out the inconsistencies within each system; of what use would it be to me to be able to develop a theory of the state, combining the details from various sources into a whole and constructing a world I did not live in but merely held up for others to see; of what use would it be to me to be able to formulate the meaning of Christianity, to be able to explain many specific points—if it had no deeper meaning *for me and for my life*?. . . I certainly do not deny that I still accept an *imperative of knowledge* and that through it people can be influenced, but *then it must come alive in me*, and *this* is what I now recognize as the most important thing. This is what my soul thirsts for as the African deserts thirst for water.
>
> (Cf. *JP* v. 5100; *SKP* i, AA 12, translations modified)[1]

Kierkegaard found in Christianity the truth that would give meaning and purpose to his life and the idea for which he was willing to live and die. While contemplating the possible significance of his authorship years later, he wrote: 'If I were to request an inscription on my grave, I request none other than *that single individual*' (*PV* 118–19; cf. *JP* ii. 2004). The category of the single individual (*den Enkelte*) was the central category of Kierkegaard's life and thought, constituting for him 'the very principle of Christianity' and 'the one single idea' that essentially contains his whole thought (*JP* ii. 1997, 2033). As he understands it, to become the single individual is to become a whole and unified self before God, which is a possibility for every human

[1] See Fenger (1980: 81–131), and *KJN* i. 301–5 for a critical assessment of his claim that this journal entry is fictional in character.

being and our common ethical-religious task in life.[2] The category of the single individual is thus 'the category through which, in a religious sense, the age, history, the human race must go' (*PV* 118). 'The first condition of all religiousness', he claims, is to be an individual, for 'it is impossible to build up or to be built up *en masse*' (117). By the same token, 'only as an individual' can one most truly relate oneself to God (*JP* ii. 2009). Kierkegaard's own struggle to become 'that single individual' was a lifelong quest that was shaped not only by his writings, which in a very real sense constituted his own religious education and personal upbuilding, but also by the formative influences, intellectual cultivation, and significant events of his life.[3]

FORMATIVE INFLUENCES

'I Owe Everything to my Father'

Chief among the influences that figured importantly in shaping Kierkegaard's early life was his father, Michael Pedersen Kierkegaard (1756–1838), a highly successful, self-made businessman who came from peasant stock in West Jutland.[4] Shortly before his twelfth birthday Michael moved to Copenhagen to become a hosier or dry goods apprentice under a family relative and worked his way up to establish his own business by the age of 24. At age 38 he married Kirstine Nielsdatter Røyen (1757–96), the sister of his business partner, but it was a short-lived and childless marriage, as she died from pneumonia within two years. Eleven months later Michael retired from business and shortly thereafter married a maidservant in his house, Ane Sørensdatter Lund (1768–1834), who bore their first child less than five months later.[5] The shame of his premarital incontinence, a strong sense of guilt and deep remorse for having once cursed God for his hard lot as a poor shepherd boy, and the untimely deaths of five of the seven children Ane bore him, leaving only the youngest son Søren and the oldest son Peter Christian (1805–88) alive, imbued Michael Kierkegaard with a morbid melancholy that not only persisted throughout his own life but infected Søren and Peter as well (*JP* v. 5874; *PV* 79).

[2] See further Eller (1968: 101–200).

[3] For extensive biographies of Kierkegaard, see Garff (2005); Hannay (2001); Lowrie (1962).

[4] Tudvad (2004: 16–17). Kierkegaard was also deeply attached to his mother, although he never wrote about her directly in his journals or works. Upon her death, which occurred when he was only 21 years old, he visited the mother of his tutor, Hans Lassen Martensen (1808–84), who reports in his autobiography that she had never seen 'a human being so deeply distressed as S. Kierkegaard was by the death of his mother'. See Kirmmse (1996: 196).

[5] Tudvad (2004: 17–18).

According to Kierkegaard's own retrospective accounts of his childhood, his father, who was already 56 years old when Søren was born on 5 May 1813, subjected him to a very strict Christian upbringing, towards which the boy was highly ambivalent (*JP* vi. 6243; *PV* 79–80; cf. *CUP* i. 589–602). In a particularly poignant passage from his journals Kierkegaard observes: 'Humanly speaking, I owe everything to my father. In every way he has made me as unhappy as possible, made my youth incomparable anguish, made me inwardly almost scandalized by Christianity' (*JP* vi. 6167). On the one hand, his father cultivated imagination and the art of dialectic in him—capacities that would later serve him well as a thinker and writer—and instilled in him a love and veneration of Christianity that he never gave up (*JC* 118–25; *PV* 79–80). On the other hand, even though his father was 'the most affectionate of fathers', Christianity was presented to him in such a way that at times it seemed to him to be 'the most inhuman cruelty' (*JP* vi. 6167; v. 6019; *PV* 79).

Søren felt that his father had robbed him of his childhood, of the immediacy that rightfully belongs to a child: 'His fault consisted not in a lack of love but in mistaking a child for an old man' (*PV* 80; cf. *JP* vi. 6379). Søren was deprived of the opportunity to be, even to dress, like other children, leading him to declare in one of his works: 'Christianity cannot be poured into a child, because it always holds true that every human being grasps only what he has use for, and the child has no decisive use for Christianity' (*CUP* i. 590).[6] In other words, Christianity is a religion for adults, not children. Nevertheless, Kierkegaard believed that his rigorous Christian upbringing predisposed him to become a religious author and to be able to discern at an early age 'how seldom Christianity is presented in its true form' (*PV* 80). As 'fanatic' as his own Christian upbringing had been, he regarded it as far better than the 'gibberish' that often passes for Christian upbringing, and in one of his works he formulated a more adequate approach for introducing Christianity to a child (*JP* ii. 1215; *PC* 174–9).

Mynster's Sermons

A stock ingredient in Søren's Christian upbringing was the sermons of Jacob Peter Mynster (1775–1854), a curate at Our Lady's Church in Copenhagen and a popular preacher among the cultural elite of Danish society at that time. Kierkegaard's father was devoted to Mynster as a preacher and spiritual advisor, and his published sermons were regularly read at devotionals in the Kierkegaard household (*JP* vi. 6627). Søren was even

[6] See Garff (2005: 19–20); Kirmmse (1996: 151).

encouraged, on promise of a monetary reward, not only to read Mynster's sermons aloud to his father but also to write up from memory those he heard in church, which he refused to do (*JP* vi. 6355). Nevertheless, this early childhood immersion in Mynster's sermons instilled in the boy a lasting respect for the man, even though Kierkegaard later became highly critical of Mynster as Primate Bishop of the Danish People's Church, admonishing the bishop for the incongruity between his preaching and personal lifestyle and for his failure to admit publicly that the established church he represented was a watered-down version of Christianity.[7]

The Herrnhuters

Another major influence in Kierkegaard's early upbringing was his family's involvement with the Herrnhuters, a Moravian pietist group that Michael Kierkegaard joined soon after coming to Copenhagen. Although its roots go back to the Czech reformer John Hus (1374–1415) and his followers, this movement originated in the eighteenth century in the German state of Saxony through the good will of Count Nikolaus Ludvig von Zinzendorf (1700–60), a Lutheran nobleman who invited a group of Moravian refugees to form a settlement called Herrnhut (meaning 'the Lord protects') on his estate.[8] The Herrnhuters formed part of a wider pietist movement of inner religious awakening that erupted on the European continent in the seventeenth century and was popular throughout the first half of the eighteenth century. Often characterized as a 'Christianity of the heart' for its emphasis on the primacy of feeling in Christian experience, this movement was heralded by Johann Arndt's immensely popular book, *True Christianity* (1605), and received its name from a book titled *Pia Desideria* (Pious Desires), written by a German professor at the University of Halle, Philipp Jakob Spener (1635–1705).[9] Spener and another Halle colleague, August Hermann Francke (1663–1727), organized lay groups for devotional study of the Bible and cultivation of personal piety and trained ministers to revitalize the Lutheran church, which in their view emphasized doctrine over personal experience.[10]

Unlike the Halle pietists, the Herrnhuters tended to be lay-centred, mission-oriented, and separatist in organization. Although officially part of the Danish Lutheran Church, the Moravian society in Copenhagen existed alongside it. Thus the Kierkegaard family attended the Lutheran

[7] See also Tolstrup (2004); Saxbee (2003); Kirmmse (1990: 100–35).
[8] Burgess (2004: 220).
[9] Ibid. See also M. M. Thulstrup (1981); Kirmmse (1990: 29–31).
[10] Burgess (2004: 220, 222).

church on Sunday mornings for worship and went to Moravian meetings, often devoted to congregational singing, on Sunday evenings.[11] Moravian theology, with its emphasis on the suffering and crucifixion of Christ, the consciousness of sin, repentance, conversion, grace, joy, witnessing, and martyrdom for the sake of Christ, made a strong impression on young Søren and figured importantly, both pro and con, in shaping his understanding of Christianity.[12] What seems to have impressed him most about the Moravians, however, was the way they put their beliefs into practice, especially those who were willing to leave everything to preach the gospel in foreign lands and to become martyrs for their cause.[13] Their examples of dedication and discipleship stood powerfully in the background as Kierkegaard later formulated his own understanding of Christian witnessing and martyrdom.

The School of Civic Virtue

Søren's formal education commenced in 1821 when he was enrolled at the Borgerdyd School (School of Civic Virtue), a private school under the tutelage of headmaster Michael Nielsen, who had a reputation as a hard taskmaster.[14] As remembered by some of his classmates and relatives, young Søren was somewhat withdrawn yet known for the mischievous teasing and satirical remarks to which he frequently subjected people, earning him the nickname 'the Fork' at home.[15] At school he was called 'Choirboy' because of the resemblance of his dress to the outfits worn by choirboys in cathedral schools and 'Søren Sock' for the woollen stockings he wore that were emblematic of his father's occupation as a hosier.[16] Although Søren was a diligent and competent student, he did not particularly excel in his schoolwork, generally coming second or third in his class, and apparently he was not above occasionally cheating or 'peeking' as it was called at that time. He was schooled in a wide range of subjects, including history, geography, mathematics, languages (Latin, Greek, Hebrew, Danish, French, and German, but not English), composition, and religion.[17]

Balle's Catechism

One of the religious texts in which Kierkegaard was instructed as a child was Balle's *Primer*, a catechism that contained an elementary exposition

[11] Ibid. 224, 228–9, 231–5. [12] Ibid. 235–43. [13] Burgess (2006).
[14] Tudvad (2004: 168–9); Kirmmse (1996: 14). [15] Kirmmse (1996: 3–4, 6–8, 10, 151).
[16] Ibid. 7. [17] Tudvad (2004: 168–73).

of the main tenets of the Christian faith.[18] It was from this book that Kierkegaard received his first formal theological instruction. Balle's catechism was authorized for use in all Danish schools in 1794 and remained the standard text for the religious education of Danish children until 1856, when it was replaced by a new one. Structured differently from most catechisms, which are usually organized as a series of questions and answers, Balle's text was intended to be used in conjunction with Luther's *Small Catechism*.[19] It was divided into eight chapters that gave a systematic, theologically conservative, and somewhat rationalist account of the accepted doctrines of the Lutheran tradition, with particular emphasis on spelling out one's duties to God, self, and neighbour and in particular relationships (man / wife, parent / child, master / servants, authority / subjects, teachers / students).[20] The deep impression this catechism made upon Søren may be glimpsed in a poetically transmuted autobiographical account in one of his early works about a young boy who is assigned the first ten lines of Balle to be learned by heart for the next day (*EO* ii. 266–7). In this reminiscence he makes the following telling observation: 'That this event made such an impression on me, I owe to my father's earnestness, and even if I owed him nothing else, this would be sufficient to place me in an eternal debt to him' (267). Kierkegaard often incorporated autobiographical tidbits in his writings, and this was surely one of them, testifying once again to the importance of his father in structuring his early life.

UNIVERSITY YEARS

Getting Started

After completing his primary and secondary education at the Borgerdyd School, Kierkegaard took the entrance exam to Copenhagen University in October 1830 and began attending classes the next month.[21] On 1 November he was appointed to His Majesty the King's Guards but was discharged three days later by the army surgeon for being physically 'unfit for service', leaving him free to continue his higher education (*LD* 8–9). Much to the chagrin of his family, Kierkegaard lingered in the university for ten years before finally completing his degree. The university at that time was composed of four faculties: theology, law, medicine, and philosophy.[22] Before Søren could choose a primary field of study, he had to take a year of general education courses and pass qualifying exams in those subjects.

[18] N. Thulstrup (1984: 60–71).
[19] Cf. Luther (1989: 471–96).
[20] Watkin (1995: 115); N. Thulstrup (1984: 64-8).
[21] Tudvad (2004: 174).
[22] Ibid.

Acceding to his father's wish, he then enrolled in the school of theology, where he attended lectures on biblical literature, hermeneutics, exegesis, Christian dogmatics, and speculative dogmatics, as well as lectures in the school of philosophy on ancient philosophy, Christian philosophy, moral philosophy, metaphysics, aesthetics and poetics, logic, and psychology.[23] Being highly proficient in Latin, he also taught Latin for several years at the Borgerdyd School, winning acclaim from his former headmaster as a good teacher who motivated students 'to do the sort of thinking that is not merely directed at passing the examination but that will continue to have an effect in their later lives'.[24] With regard to preparing for his own examination for a degree, however, Kierkegaard confessed in a letter of 1835 that he was not making much progress because of a lack of interest, although he recognized that he 'had better dig in' for several reasons, namely because it was required for entering 'the scholarly pastures', it would be advantageous, and it would make his father happy (*JP* v. 5092).

'I Grew up in Orthodoxy'

Kierkegaard was also having doubts about Christianity at this time, as it seemed to him to have 'such great contradictions that a clear view is hindered, to say the least' (*JP* v. 5092). The Lutheran orthodox 'colossus' under which he had grown up began to totter when he started to think for himself. This colossus was built upon the Bible as the absolute standard and sole authority for all Christian teaching, the confessional writings of the early church (the Apostolic, Nicene, and Athanasian creeds), the Augsburg Confession (a comprehensive statement of the articles of the Lutheran faith adopted in 1530), and Luther's *Small Catechism* (1529), which together constituted the official writings and tenets (dogma) of the Danish Evangelical Lutheran Church as prescribed by Danish law.[25] There were also a host of theological works by Lutheran scholastic theologians of the sixteenth and seventeenth centuries who systematized Luther's teachings and engaged in doctrinal disputes and theological hairsplitting in the interest of emphasizing right belief (orthodoxy) as the basis of faith. Kierkegaard became familiar with the major dogmatic theology texts of his day while preparing for his degree.[26] But he apparently had little or no first-hand knowledge

[23] Ibid. 177–83. [24] Kirmmse (1996: 28).

[25] N. Thulstrup (1984: 32–7). The Formula of Concord (1577) was also widely adopted in German Lutheran churches but was not officially recognized in Denmark. See N. Thulstrup (1980*c*).

[26] See Barrett (2006: 155); N. Thulstrup (1978: 42–3; 1980*b*: 88.)

of Luther's writings at this stage, as they were not generally studied in the theological faculties of the time.[27] As late as 1847 Kierkegaard stated in his journal, 'I have never really read anything by Luther' (*JP* iii. 2463), although several entries in earlier years indicate that this statement should not be taken too literally (*JP* iii. 2460–2). When he did begin to dip into Luther, it was mainly Luther's sermons, not his theological works, which were read (*JP* iii. 2463–2556).

It has been plausibly argued that the thinker most influential in mediating Luther's theology to Kierkegaard was Johann Georg Hamann (1730–88), a German philosopher, theologian, and literary-social critic known as the 'Wise Man in the North'.[28] Hamann's witty, ironic, satirical, and aphoristic writing style undoubtedly left its mark on Kierkegaard, and Hamann's writings, particularly his *Socratic Memorabilia* (1759), which emphasized Socratic ignorance, faith, revelation, passion, and paradox rather than reason as the foundation for the knowledge of God, anticipated major themes in Kierkegaard's theology, leading one of Kierkegaard's biographers to declare of Hamann: 'I am inclined to say that he is the only author by whom Søren Kierkegaard was profoundly influenced.'[29]

Rationalist Theology

If Kierkegaard was in doubt about the foundations of orthodox Christianity, he was even less satisfied with the rationalist theology to which he was introduced in the lectures of Professor Henrik Nicolai Clausen (1793–1877) (*SKS* xix/1. 1–8).[30] Theological rationalism was a product of the eighteenth-century Enlightenment, which sought to subject everything to rational criticism, making reason the primary criterion for determining truth.[31] Philosophically, modern rationalism had its genesis in the thought of Descartes (1596–1650), Leibniz (1646–1715), and Spinoza (1632–77), and its terminus in the scepticism of Hume (1711–76) and the recognition of the limitations of theoretical reason by Kant (1724–1804). Theological rationalism received its impetus in the thought of John Locke (1632–1704), whose book *The Reasonableness of Christianity* (1695) gave expression in its title and content to the central tenet of the movement, and Christian Wolff (1679–1754), a Leibnizian thinker whom Kierkegaard's father especially admired and read.[32] Through the pioneering work of Wolff's successor, J. S. Semler (1725–91), and other biblical scholars such as Hermann Reimarus

[27] Hinkson (2002: 45–6). [28] Ibid. 71–6.
[29] Lowrie (1962: i. 164). See also Ringleben (2006). [30] N. Thulstrup (1982).
[31] Welch (1972: 32). [32] Hannay (2001: 37); Welch (1972: 32).

(1694–1768), theological rationalism also gave birth to modern biblical criticism.[33]

In general, theological rationalists viewed morality as the essence of religion and rejected the orthodox doctrine of original sin, believing in the basic goodness of human nature and the possibility of human progress through enlightenment and understanding. Over against positive or revealed religion they espoused natural religion, the knowledge of God through nature and the moral law within, and regarded it as being either in harmony with (Wolff) or in opposition to (Reimarus) revelation. They rejected the possibility of miracles and called into question the literal truth of the Bible by subjecting it to the emerging historical-critical methods of examination and interpretation of the time.[34] Clausen, the Danish biblical scholar under whom Kierkegaard studied, espoused a moderate form of rationalism which Kierkegaard regarded as 'second-rate' and inconsistent inasmuch as its formulations were based on scripture 'when they agree with it but otherwise not' (*JP* v. 5092; *KJN* i, AA 12). Kierkegaard also objected to the union of philosophy and Christianity,[35] particularly the notion of a 'reasonable Christianity', which in his view did not take into account the defectiveness of human cognition due to sin nor how Christianity appears to those outside of faith (*JP* iii. 3245–7; *KJN* i, AA 13, 17, 18).

Schleiermacher

A third theological position to which Kierkegaard was exposed as a university student was that of the German Reformed (Calvinist) theologian Friedrich Schleiermacher (1768–1834), whose dogmatics, *The Christian Faith* (1830), Kierkegaard read with his tutor, Hans Lassen Martensen, in the summer of 1834.[36] Martensen, a rising star soon to be appointed to the faculty of the university, met and was greatly impressed by Schleiermacher when he visited Copenhagen in 1833 (although Martensen's own theological preference soon turned to the Hegelian philosophy he encountered on a two-year study trip to Germany that commenced in autumn 1834).[37] Recognized as the father of modern theology, Schleiermacher was a seminal thinker who offered a fresh interpretation of religion and revolutionized the nature and method of doing theology in the first half of the nineteenth century. Like Kierkegaard, Schleiermacher was deeply influenced by the

[33] Welch (1972: 35). [34] Ibid. 30–40.

[35] See Barrett (2007) on the synthesis of philosophy and Christian doctrine in the standard rationalist theological textbook of the time by Karl Gottlieb Bretschneider (1776–1848).

[36] Hannay (2001: 50). [37] Schjørring (1982: 181).

Herrnhuters, having grown up in a Moravian community and attended a Moravian seminary before transferring to the University of Halle, where he was later appointed as the first university preacher before taking up a pastorate in Berlin and helping to found and teach in the university there.[38] Schleiermacher also shared Kierkegaard's dissatisfaction with theological rationalism, which led him to locate the essence of religion not in knowing or doing but in intuition and feeling, specifically the feeling of absolute dependence on God.[39]

Although Kierkegaard did not embrace Schleiermacher's theology, it has been claimed that 'of all the dogmatists [Kierkegaard] knew, he had a fundamental respect only for Schleiermacher', who is cited approvingly in several of his early writings (*CI* 59, 118, 120; *CA* 20; *SLW* 479).[40] It is quite likely that Kierkegaard was indebted to Schleiermacher for the literary idea of imaginatively constructing characters to represent different points of view in his writings, a technique he noted while reading Schleiermacher's review of the novel *Lucinde* by the German romantic writer Friedrich Schlegel (1772–1829) (*JP* iv. 3846).[41] A highly respected Plato scholar and translator, Schleiermacher also undoubtedly contributed much to the formation of Kierkegaard's lifelong love and appreciation of Socrates, who next to Jesus Christ was the main inspiration for his life.[42] While there is some complementarity between their theological views, Kierkegaard faulted Schleiermacher's early definition of religion for 'remaining in pantheism' and regarded his dogmatics as heterodox in many respects as well as genuinely orthodox and right on many points (*JP* iv. 3849, 3850; *KJN* i, DD 9, 86).[43] The main error of Schleiermacher's theology, in Kierkegaard's mature judgement, was that it treated religiousness in the sphere of being as a given condition (immediacy), whereas for Kierkegaard Christianity 'is essentially to be conceived ethically, as striving' and thus in the sphere of becoming (*JP* ii. 1096; iv. 3852–3).

Grundtvig's 'Matchless Discovery'

Another anti-rationalist theological movement in Denmark from which Kierkegaard disassociated himself early on was the cultic Christianity of Nikolai Frederik Severin Grundtvig (1783–1872) and his followers, one of whom was Kierkegaard's older brother, Peter Christian. A pastor, theologian, poet, hymnodist, educator, politician, historian, and philologist,

[38] Tice (2006: 1–16). [39] Schleiermacher (1996: 22, 29–31, 46–7; 1956: 5–18).

[40] N. Thulstrup (1978: 46); see also Crouter (2005: 98–119).

[41] Crouter (2005: 109–17). [42] Ibid. 109.

[43] See further Cappelørn *et al.* (2006); Crouter (2007); Quinn (1990).

Grundtvig was a monumental figure who exerted great influence on the development of Danish religious life and culture in the nineteenth century.[44] While serving as a Lutheran pastor in Copenhagen, Grundtvig professed to have made 'the matchless discovery' that it was not the 'dead wood' of the New Testament but the 'Living Word' of the Apostles' Creed, together with the sacraments of baptism and communion instituted by Christ, that gave birth to the Christian church and constituted the 'exclusive condition' for incorporation into its cultic community.[45] This view of the church was utterly at odds with orthodox Lutheran Christianity as well as theological rationalism, inasmuch as it replaced the authority of the Bible, whether established through revelation or through reason, with that of the church, its creed, and other symbols. Already as a university student Kierkegaard found Grundtvig's theory of the church unsatisfactory, pointing out, among other problems, different versions of the creed and the questionable status of translations of the original (*JP* v. 5089). A more incisive critique of Grundtvig was later mounted in Kierkegaard's authorship, particularly in his late writings and journals, where Grundtvig is taken to task for selfishly seeking religious freedom for himself and his adherents rather than fighting for true Christianity and for being hypocritical on the issue of the separation of church and state, which he strongly advocated but did not uphold by resigning his pastorate in the state church as a paid servant of the Crown (*TM* 207–8, 564–75).

Speculative Dogmatics

Kierkegaard's theological training culminated in an introduction to speculative dogmatics in the university lectures of his former tutor Hans Lassen Martensen and readings on the subject. Nineteenth-century German and Danish speculative dogmatics developed out of the idealist philosophy of Georg Wilhelm Friedrich Hegel (1770–1831), who sought to comprehend everything, including God or Absolute Spirit, as an encompassing whole through speculation (from the Latin *speculum*, meaning 'mirror') or the 'double mirroring' of thought and being, ideality and reality, human consciousness and ultimate reality in each other.[46] Hegel's philosophical system evolves through a necessary dialectical movement in three phases: *thesis* (the positing of a rational concept), *antithesis* (the negation of the posited concept by its opposite), and *synthesis* (the mediation or reconciliation of these polarities in a higher rational unity that simultaneously annuls and

[44] See Kirmmse (1990: 198–237); Allchin (1997); Koch (1952).
[45] Kirmmse (1990: 212–13). [46] Hodgson (2005: 7, 69, 79–81).

preserves (German: *aufheben*) both terms). Contra Kant, for whom human knowledge was limited to the sensible intuition and understanding (*Verstand*) of the phenomenal realm, Hegel envisioned the rational as the real and the real as rational, in other words, the identity of thought and being. He believed that the meaning and unity of science, history, and the products of human self-consciousness in art, religion, philosophy, and sociopolitical structures can be known and comprehended through reason (*Vernunft*), the intellectual apprehension of reality as the dialectical process by which God or Absolute Spirit progressively acquires self-consciousness or knowledge of itself in and through its divestment and self-becoming in nature and human self-consciousness. The consciousness of God as Absolute Spirit, which for Hegel culminates in philosophy rather than theology, in turn constitutes the highest realization of human self-consciousness.

There was, then, a strongly religious dimension in Hegel's philosophy that made it appealing to many Christian theologians. Indeed, for Hegel philosophy *is* theology, inasmuch as in his view they share the same content expressed in different forms (through concepts in philosophy; via representation in religion).[47] Hegel himself was a Lutheran, studied theology at the Tübingen seminary, wrote some early theological essays on Christianity, and lectured on the philosophy of religion.[48] After his death the Hegelian school divided into three factions: right-wing and centre Hegelians, made up mostly of older disciples of Hegel, and left-wing Hegelians, dubbed the 'Young Hegelians', although some on the right and in the centre were of the same generation.[49] Those on the right, such as Carl Friedrich Göschel (1784–1861), Philipp Konrad Marheineke (1780–1846), Carl Daub (1765–1836), and Johann Eduard Erdmann (1805–92), defended the compatibility of Hegelian philosophy with Christianity and continued to develop Hegel's speculative thought along theistic lines, arguing in favour of a personal God and the immortality of the soul. Those in the centre, such as Eduard Gans (1797–1839), Karl Michelet (1801–93), and Karl Rosenkranz (1805–79), continued to concern themselves with the main lines of Hegelian philosophy and the reinterpretation of religious dogma in Hegelian terms.[50] The left wing included David Strauss (1808–74), Bruno Bauer (1809–82), Ludwig Feuerbach (1804–72), Max Stirner (1806–56), Arnold Ruge (1802–80), and Karl Marx (1818–83), among others. These thinkers radically undermined Hegelian philosophy from within, converting its idealism into materialism (Marx), its theology into anthropology (Feuerbach), its objectivity into

[47] Hegel (1984–7: i. 84). [48] Crites (1998: 16–27); Hegel (1948 and 1984–7).

[49] Toews (1980: 203–54); Hodgson (2005: 15); Brazill (1970); Wood (1993*a*: 414); Strauss (1983: 43–66).

[50] Jaeschke (1990: 365–81); Wood (1993*a*: 414).

subjectivity (Bauer and Stirner), its constitutional monarchism into democracy (Ruge), and its historical basis in the New Testament into mythology (Strauss and Bauer).[51] Hegelian philosophy was attacked on other fronts as well. In Denmark the broadside was led by Bishop Mynster and two of Kierkegaard's teachers, Frederik Christian Sibbern (1785–1872) and Poul Martin Møller (1794–1838), against Hegel, Martensen, and Johan Ludvig Heiberg (1791–1860), the foremost Danish exponent of Hegelian philosophy of the time.[52]

It was primarily right-wing Hegelian speculative theology and critiques thereof to which Kierkegaard was introduced in the lectures of Martensen and in his readings on the subject, which included works by Erdmann, Marheineke, Franz Xavier von Baader (1765–1841), and Immanuel Herman Fichte (1797–1879), as well as articles by Erdmann, Rosenkranz, Daub, and others in the German periodical *Zeitschrift für Spekulative Theologie* (Journal for Speculative Theology) (*SKS* xviii. *KK* 11. 19; NB 4. 3–12, 13–46; *SKP* i, C 25–7; xiii, II C 26–8, 61; *JP* v. 5066, 5222; *KJN* i, DD 1–2, 8, 10, 12–13).[53] Martensen had studied Hegelian speculative theology with Daub and Marheineke in Germany but professed to go beyond Hegel as well as orthodox supernaturalism and rationalism in the development of a theonomous theology that grounds human freedom and reason in divine power.[54] In this way he sought to reassert the primacy of faith and revelation over Hegelian autonomous reason while continuing to employ the Hegelian dialectical method. The concept of mediation or reconciliation, the central category of Hegel's dialectic and Martensen's speculative dogmatics, became the primary target of Kierkegaard's later critique of speculative philosophy and theology.[55]

Kierkegaard also became acquainted with the left-wing Hegelian school, especially critiques of Strauss's epoch-making book of 1835, *Das Leben Jesu kritisch bearbeitet* (The Life of Jesus Critically Examined), by Julius Schaller (1807–68), von Baader, and Marheineke (*SKS* xviii, KK 2; xix, NB 9. 1; *SKP* xiii, II C 54).[56] He also formed a friendship with Hans Brøchner (1820–75), a distant relative who translated Strauss's *Die christliche Glaubenslehre* (The Doctrines of the Christian Faith, 1842–3) into Danish, a copy of which Kierkegaard owned.[57] Later he acquired Feuerbach's revolutionary work,

[51] Brazill (1970); Welch (1972: 147–54, 170–7); Toews (1993: 378–413). See also Stewart (2007*a*, 2007*b*).

[52] Mynster (2004); Kirmmse (1990: 140–5); N. Thulstrup (1980*d*: 33–9, 150–4, 178); Widenmann (1982: 76).

[53] See also N. Thulstrup (1980*d*: 49–50, 115–49).

[54] Thompson and Kangas (1997: 6–9).

[55] Stewart (2004*b*: 583–7); Martensen (2004).

[56] See Pattison (2007); Hannay (2001: 210–11); Rohde (1967: nos. 407, 759).

[57] Kirmmse (1996: 225–52); Sorainen (1981: 198–203); Rohde (1967: nos. 803–4).

Das Wesen des Christenthums (The Essence of Christianity, 1841), and was even mentioned in company with Strauss and Feuerbach in a book by the Danish left-wing Hegelian Andreas Frederik Beck (1816–61).[58] As for the writings of Hegel himself, Kierkegaard apparently had little direct acquaintance with them during this period, and his attitude toward Hegel's philosophy was both appreciative and critical, depending on the topic being discussed.[59] One commentator claims that Kierkegaard underwent 'a phase of infatuation' with Hegel's philosophy, and Kierkegaard himself, looking back on these years in a late journal entry, declared: 'What a Hegelian fool I was!' (*JP* iv. 4281).[60]

Politics and Philosophy

In addition to studying theology at the university, Kierkegaard engaged in light-hearted political debates at the Student Association and in a series of newspaper articles (his first published writings) on the freedom of the press, which had been under strict censorship in Denmark since 1799, and the emancipation of women, a goal of the budding feminist movement in Europe at that time (*EPW* 1–52).[61] Although wittily critical of both the press and the Crown on the first issue and ironically opposed to the second through mock praise of 'woman's great abilities', Kierkegaard demonstrates at this young age an awareness of important political issues of the time even though politics was not a subject of serious interest to him (*EPW* 1–52). Academically, he gravitated more and more toward philosophy under the influence of Poul Martin Møller, his intellectual mentor and revered friend whom he credited with being 'the mighty trumpet of my awakening' (*SKP* s, B 46).[62] As a result of the deaths of both Møller and Kierkegaard's father in 1838, and perhaps also due to a personal religious experience of 'an *indescribable joy*' that same year, Søren finally settled down in earnest to prepare for his theological examination, which he took and passed in July 1840. He then entered the Pastoral Seminary for a year of homiletics and catechetical training to qualify him to become an ordained minister (*JP* v. 5324; *LD* 10–22). Although he often contemplated becoming a rural pastor or a teacher at the seminary in later years, he was never ordained and never actually applied for either position. Having inherited half of his father's large estate, he lived the rest of his life as an independent author.

[58] Rohde (1967: nos. 424, 488); Czak (2007: 31–2).

[59] N. Thulstrup (1980*d*: 46–212); Stewart (2003: 27–34).

[60] Stewart (2003: 17).

[61] See Perkins (1999*b*); Watkin (1999*a*); Kirmmse (1990: 45–52).

[62] Hannay (2001: 47–8, 58–87); Garff (2005: 86–95).

Denmark's Golden Age

During these years Kierkegaard was very interested in drama, music, and literary subjects, including romanticism, the poetry of the troubadours, the art of telling children's stories, mythology, the aesthetic categories of comedy, irony, and humour, and the figures of Faust, the Wandering Jew, and Don Juan as the representatives of doubt, despair, and sensuousness respectively—all of which provided a wealth of material for his early aesthetic writings (*KJN* i, BB 1–25, 27–37, 49; DD 3, 6, 18–19, 22, 38, 68–9, 75; *SKP* i, C 46–127). The first half of the nineteenth century was known as the Golden Age of Denmark inasmuch as it was a period of high culture that boasted a number of fine literary artists, including the noted romantic poet Adam Oehlenschläger (1779–1850) and J. L. Heiberg, a dramatist, poet, prose writer, translator, aesthetician, literary critic, and director of the Royal Danish Theatre as well as Hegelian philosopher. Heiberg's mother, Madame Thomasine Gyllembourg (1773–1856), was an accomplished novelist whose works Kierkegaard read and reviewed favourably (*EPW* 64–7; *TA*). Heiberg's wife, Johanne Luise Heiberg (1812–90), was a celebrated actress of the Danish Royal Theatre whom Kierkegaard also admired and later reviewed appreciatively (*C*). Hoping to become part of the Heibergian cultural circle, which was 'the leading Copenhagen salon of its time', Kierkegaard wrote a long critical review of a novel by the contemporary Danish writer, Hans Christian Andersen (1805–75), who at this point in his literary career had won more acclaim as a novelist than as a writer of fairy tales.[63] Issued in 1838 under the odd title, *From the Papers of One Still Living*, perhaps with the recent deaths of his father and Møller in mind, this was Kierkegaard's first published monograph.[64]

The Concept of Irony

In the fall of 1841 Kierkegaard petitioned the king for permission to submit a dissertation written in Danish, along with a statement of its theses in Latin, for conferral of the magister (doctoral) degree, the highest degree awarded by the faculty of philosophy at the University of Copenhagen (*LD* 23–5). This work, titled *The Concept of Irony with Continual Reference to Socrates*, marked the beginning in his published writings of a lifelong fascination with Socrates, who is credited therein with introducing the principle of subjectivity to the ancient world in the form of irony or an infinite absolute negativity toward the established order of his time. Kierkegaard

[63] Kirmmse (1990: 139).

[64] See also Cappelørn *et al.* (2006); Perkins (1999*a*); Walsh (1994: 23–41).

concludes that Socratic irony was historically justified but must be controlled in order to become a ministering spirit in the development of the personal life.[65] He also comes to terms with German romantic irony in this work, viewing it à la Hegel as an unwarranted expression of total irony or the negation of actuality as such in the exercise of an arbitrary and boundless freedom to create and to destroy at will.[66] Thus ended an early interest in and inclination toward romanticism, to which Kierkegaard was initially attracted by its passionate, imaginative, and infinite striving toward the ideal.

Kierkegaard's dissertation was successfully defended at a public forum conducted in Latin, the official academic language of the time, on 29 September 1841.[67] Soon thereafter he departed for Berlin to attend lectures by the famous German philosopher Friedrich Wilhelm Joseph Schelling (1775–1854), an erstwhile romantic and idealist thinker turned critic of Hegel who had been called out of retirement to counter 'the dragon-seed of [left-wing] Hegelian pantheism'.[68] He also attended lectures by Henrich Steffens (1773–1845), who is credited with introducing German romanticism to Golden Age Denmark, the right-wing Hegelian speculative theologian Marheineke, and the Hegelian logician Karl Friedrich Werder (1806–93). At first excited by, but soon disappointed in, Schelling's new 'positive philosophy' of revelation and finding Steffens's performance as a lecturer unappealing, Kierkegaard soon abandoned them and spent most of his time in Berlin attending and taking notes on Marheineke and Werder's lectures and working on the brilliant arabesque novel that would soon launch his literary career: *Either/Or* (*CI* 331–412; *LD* 55; *SKP* xiii, III C 26, 29; *SKS* xix, NB 8. 50; NB 9. 1, 2–9).[69]

LOVE, ENGAGEMENT, RUPTURE

'I Came, I Saw, *She* Conquered'

Before turning to Kierkegaard's career as a writer, however, we must take note of a momentous event in his life. On 8 May 1837 he met a young girl named Regine Olsen (1822–1904). She apparently made a strong impression on Kierkegaard, as soon afterward he recorded in his journal: 'good God, why should the inclination begin to stir just now?' (*JP* v. 5220). Other than a series of mostly undated love letters and notes which he sent to her,

[65] See also Perkins (2001); Söderquist (2003). [66] See further Walsh (1994: 43–62).

[67] See Kirmmse (2001). [68] Kosch (2006: 123); Toews (1993: 383).

[69] See also Schulz (2007*a*) and Stewart (2007). On the arabesque novel, see Walsh (1994: 63–4).

little information exists about their courtship (*LD* 61–88). These messages were typically romantic, quoting bits of poetry, expressing his deep longing for her, showering her with compliments, arranging meetings, referring to small gifts and pictures being exchanged between them, etc. Slightly revising Julius Caesar's famous boast, *veni, vidi, vici* (I came, I saw, I conquered), Kierkegaard quips in one letter, 'I came, I saw, *she* conquered', and years later he reveals that 'even before my father died my mind was made up about her' (*LD* 76; *JP* vi. 6472). On 8 September 1840 he proposed to Regine informally and two days later formally asked her father for her hand.

The next day Kierkegaard realized that he had made a terrible mistake—not because he did not love her or want to marry her but because he felt there were certain extenuating circumstances that made marriage inadvisable if not impossible for him. The reasons, as stated in a retrospective journal entry years later, were basically these: 'If I had not been a penitent, if I had not had my *via ante acta* [life prior to the act], if I had not had my depression—marriage to her would have made me happier than I had ever dreamed of becoming' (*JP* vi. 6472). What events in his prior life made him feel so guilty and penitent that marriage must be ruled out have been the subject of much speculation and remain obscure. Kierkegaard felt that his depression alone was sufficient to make marriage to him unbearable for her, and whatever his past was, so much would have to be kept from her that their marriage would be based upon a lie. In a page torn from his journal and crossed out, obviously not intended for public consumption, he states:

> But if I were to have explained myself, I would have had to initiate her into terrible things, my relationship to my father, his melancholy, the eternal night brooding within me, my going astray, my lusts and debauchery, which, however, in the eyes of God are perhaps not so glaring; for it was, after all, anxiety which brought me to go astray, and where was I to seek a safe stronghold when I knew or suspected that the only man I had admired for his strength was tottering. (*JP* v. 5664)

'If I had had Faith, I would have Stayed with Regine'

Kierkegaard nevertheless remained in the engagement for thirteen months. On 11 August 1841 he formally broke it by letter and returned the engagement ring Regine had given him.[70] Needless to say, this was a very trying time for both parties, and Regine did not let him go without a fight,

[70] Garff (2005: 186).

pleading to him again and again not to leave her and threatening to despair if he did. His action was also a matter of great concern to her family and damaged his reputation in the city, where it soon became the talk of the town. Hoping to make it easier for her to accept the broken engagement, Kierkegaard tried to make himself look like a scoundrel in her eyes, poetically portraying himself in one of his early works ('The Seducer's Diary', in *Either/Or*, part 1) as a calculating seducer in order to repulse her, while suffering internally all the more as he continued to agonize over his action and responsibility in the whole affair. Much of his side of the story would later be poetically transmuted and told in one of his works in a section with the telling title: 'Guilty?'/'Not Guilty?' (*SLW* 185–397). Here and elsewhere in earlier and later journal entries and works, the rationale for the break that gained prominence in his own mind was a religious one, namely that he was under 'a divine counter order' that required him to forgo marriage and live as a penitent, giving religious expression to his erotic love for her through a relationship to God or the ideality of the religious (261, 330, 381, 423; cf. *JP* vi. 6472; *FT*). As Kierkegaard understood it, his personal relationship to God was 'in a way' a reduplication of his relation to Regine inasmuch as it helped him to understand what faith is (*JP* vi. 6470). In a journal entry from 1843, he states: 'If I had had faith, I would have stayed with Regine' (*JP* v. 5664). Six years later, in a rare admission, he writes: 'The fact that I have gone through this experience has helped me in my own faith-relationship to God. Although my life goes against me and the world is sheer opposition, I nevertheless do have faith' (*JP* vi. 6470).

THE AUTHORSHIP AND ITS STRATEGY

The Early Pseudonymous and Upbuilding Writings

In a retrospective accounting of his authorship written in 1848, Kierkegaard maintained that it was 'religious from first to last', designed to cast the religious, more specifically the essentially Christian, into reflection for the sake of clarifying Christian categories, thus enabling his reader, whom he always addressed as 'that single individual', to become aware of what Christianity is and how to become a Christian (*PV* 6). Although this conception of the religious character and thrust of his writings was certainly not apparent to him or his readers from the outset, it became clearer to him as the authorship unfolded, which came at a furious pace. *Either/Or*, consisting of two large volumes, erupted on the public scene in 1843, followed by the publication of *Fear and Trembling* and *Repetition* on the same day later that year. Then three more works appeared in 1844: *Philosophical Fragments*, *The Concept of Anxiety*, and *Prefaces*. 1845 brought forth another huge tome, *Stages on Life's Way*, and 1846 an equally long volume, *Concluding Unscientific Postscript to 'Philosophical Fragments'*, his most important philosophical work. Of these works, Kierkegaard correctly predicted that '*Fear and Trembling* alone will be enough for an imperishable name as an author' (*JP* vi. 6491).

These works were published at Kierkegaard's own expense but not under his own name as author; instead, they were issued under the auspices of various pseudonyms, a literary strategy adopted in order to allow each work and its 'author' to express its own viewpoint and to indicate indirectly that his own life was lived in 'altogether different categories' (*PV* 86). In a statement appended to the *Postscript*, Kierkegaard explains:

> What has been written, then, is mine, but only insofar as I, by means of audible lines, have placed the life-view of the creat*ing*, poetically actual individuality in his [the pseudonym's] mouth . . . Thus in the pseudonymous books there is not a single word by me. I have no opinion about them except as a third party, no knowledge of their meaning except as a reader, not the remotest private relation to them . . . Therefore, if it should occur to anyone to want to quote a particular passage from the books, it is my wish, my prayer, that he will do me the kindness of citing the respective pseudonymous author's name, not mine . . .
>
> (*CUP* i. 625–7)

With the exception of the *Postscript*, which Kierkegaard regarded as *sui generis* (in a class by itself), these early works constituted what he called his 'aesthetic' writings (*PV* 7, 29 n. 31). Beginning with a portrayal of the aesthetic (from the Greek *aisthēsis*, meaning 'sense perception') stage of existence, which is a relatively non-reflective life in immediacy based on the satisfaction and enjoyment of one's sensate or natural inclinations and capacities, these works employ an indirect or maieutic (Socratic) method of communication through the use of a variety of literary genres, strategies, and poetic figures designed to 'deceive' people into the truth by helping them become aware of the need for a higher form of life in the ethical and religious stages of existence (*PV* 7, 53–4). Parallel to these indirect communications Kierkegaard published under his own name a series of direct communications in the form of upbuilding or ethical-religious discourses (*EUD*; *TDIO*).[71] These discourses, he later claimed, provided a clear testimony that he was a religious author from the beginning and betokened that the upbuilding was what should come to the fore: 'With my left hand I passed *Either/Or* out into the world, with my right hand *Two Upbuilding*

[71] See Pattison (2002*b*).

Discourses; but they all or almost all took the left hand with their right' (*PV* 36; cf. *EUD* 179).

The 'Second Literature'

With the publication of *Concluding Unscientific Postscript*, which posed the problem of the whole authorship, namely how to become a Christian, Kierkegaard thought that he had reached the end of his career as a writer. On the contrary, this work became 'the turning point' that initiated a new burst of writing, often referred to as his 'second literature' (*PV* 55).[72] Most of these works were explicitly religious and/or Christian in character and were published in his own name as author except for a few that presented Christianity in its strictest, most ideal sense, thus representing an existential position higher than he personally embodied. This flood of new writings, some of which were published posthumously or not at all, included: *Two Ages: A Literary Review* (1846), *The Book on Adler* (1846/7), *'The Single Individual': Two 'Notes' Concerning My Work as an Author* (1846–9), *Upbuilding Discourses in Various Spirits* (1847), *Works of Love* (1847), *Christian Discourses* (1848), *The Crisis and a Crisis in the Life of an Actress* (1848), *The Point of View for My Work as an Author* (1848), *Armed Neutrality* (1848–9), *The Lily in the Field and the Bird of the Air: Three Devotional Discourses* (1849), *Two Ethical-Religious Essays* (1849), *The Sickness unto Death* (1849), *Three Discourses at the Communion on Fridays* (1849), *Practice in Christianity* (1850), *An Upbuilding Discourse* (1850), *An Open Letter* (1851), *Two Discourses at the Communion on Fridays* (1851), *On My Work as an Author* (1851), *For Self-Examination* (1851), and *Judge for Yourself!* (1851/2). This phenomenal outpouring then ceased for three years until 1854, when Kierkegaard suddenly burst into print again with a series of polemical articles against the state church in a local newspaper and serial pamphlet called *The Moment* which he published himself. His authorship ended shortly before his death in 1855 with the publication of *What Christ Judges of Official Christianity* and *The Changelessness of God*.

TRANSFORMATIVE EVENTS

There were three events that precipitated and/or profoundly conditioned the emergence of these two new phases of Kierkegaard's authorship: (1) his encounter with a local tabloid called *The Corsair* in 1846; (2) the Danish political revolution of 1848; and (3) the death of Bishop Mynster in 1854.

[72] Elrod (1981: p. xi).

These events played an important role in the development of Kierkegaard's understanding of Christianity, the ecclesiastical-political establishment of the time, and his own personal life in relation to the common folk of Copenhagen, with whom he was accustomed to enjoy daily conversations on his habitual walks around town.[73]

The Corsair Affair

The first of these events was occasioned by one of Kierkegaard's pseudonyms being singled out for praise in a satirical weekly tabloid called *The Corsair* (from the French *corsaire*, meaning 'a pirate or pirate ship'), which in keeping with its name specialized in plundering and destroying the reputations of Copenhagen citizens of note. This scandal sheet, or 'pirate paper' as its editor Meir Goldschmidt (1819–87) called it, enjoyed the largest circulation of any newspaper in the city and appealed to the basest instincts of its readers, who apparently relished seeing their fellow citizens exposed, ridiculed, caricatured, and hung out to dry by all the rumours, gossip, and distorted facts anonymously reported in it.[74] Writing as his pseudonym, Kierkegaard published a response designed not only to protest this malicious practice but also to expose a person secretly involved in the whole enterprise, Peder Ludvig Møller (1814–65), a notorious aesthete and aspirant for a position as professor of aesthetics at the university who had published a vicious review of Kierkegaard's pseudonymous works (*COR* 38–46, 96–104). Expressing a desire to be treated like everyone else, Kierkegaard's pseudonym complains: 'It is really hard for a poor author to be so singled out in Danish literature that he (assuming that we pseudonyms are one) is the only one who is not abused there' (46).

Accommodating this request, *The Corsair* unleashed a barrage of pieces over the next six months that subjected Kierkegaard to unrelenting comic ridicule. It identified him with a local insane horse trader called 'Crazy Nathanson' and caricatured his personal appearance, especially his humped shoulders, spindly legs, and uneven pant legs, leading him to comment in his journals that 'my whole life will never be as important as my trousers have come to be' (*COR* 108–37; *JP* v. 5863). This attack on his person had the terrible consequence of making Kierkegaard the laughing-stock of Copenhagen, so that even schoolchildren mocked him when he went out to walk and the name Søren became a pejorative nickname and euphemism for Satan that was often used for ludicrous characters in new plays of the time

[73] See also Bukdahl (2001); Kirmmse (1990); Elrod (1981).

[74] Garff (2005: 377); see also Perkins (1990).

(*COR* 238 and nn. 443, 451, 480). But this cruel episode in Kierkegaard's life was also the occasion of 'an awakening of awareness' in him, requiring him, as he put it, to 'think about or think through the dialectic of contemptibleness' (*COR* 160). Not only did it teach him to know himself and the world better but also to discover 'a whole side of Christianity' not previously recognized or addressed in his writings, namely its outward dimension and external consequences, with the result that, as he lyrically expressed it in his journals, 'As author I have gotten a new string in my instrument, have been enabled to hit notes I never would have dreamed of otherwise' (*JP* vi. 6548; cf. 6594).

'In These Times Everything is Politics'

Looking back on his life a few years later, Kierkegaard remarked in his journal: 'Then came 1848. Here I was granted a perspective on my life that almost overwhelmed me' (*JP* vi. 6843). Besides being an extraordinarily productive year in terms of his authorship, it was during this year that the second major event occurred which profoundly affected Kierkegaard's life and the society in which he lived, namely the peaceful political transition from government by absolute monarchy to a constitutional, parliamentary monarchy in the state of Denmark. Absolute monarchy with the right of inheritance was established in Denmark in 1660, followed by a royal law in 1665 that granted ultimate authority over the church to the king and established the Evangelical Lutheran Church as the official state church.[75] This political-ecclesiastical arrangement remained in place and unchallenged until the nineteenth century, when a peasant awakening movement in the 1820s brought about a rural religious revival emphasizing individual piety and self-assertion as well as the enactment of agrarian reforms that allowed farmers to own their own land and to elect representatives to estate assemblies and town councils.[76] This was followed in the 1830s and 1840s by an urban liberal political movement espousing freedom of the press and, in alliance with the peasant movement, a host of broader economic and political reforms, including the establishment of a representative constitutional government.[77] Under threat of a popular uprising, on 21 March 1848 the king agreed to their demands, and the next year a constitution was adopted replacing the Danish absolute monarchy with a constitutional monarchy based on a representative government elected by universal male suffrage.[78]

[75] Lausten (2002: 132).

[76] Kirmmse (1990: 40–4); Lausten (2002: 226–7).

[77] Kirmmse (1990: 45–68).

[78] Ibid. 66–70.

Technically, according to the new constitution the state church was also abolished, inasmuch as the state no longer officially endorsed a state church as such and did not require members of parliament to belong to the Evangelical Lutheran Church.[79] However, the constitution did state that 'The evangelical-Lutheran church is the Danish people's church and, as such, is supported by the state.'[80] The Danish state church thus became the Danish People's Church (so-called because a majority of the people belonged to it), the only difference being that now one had to be baptized into the church instead of automatically becoming a member by virtue of being born a Dane, as was the case formerly. State support of the people's church consisted in granting it income from church property, tithes, and state budget appropriations, and church governance remained in the hands of the king and parliament, as the church did have not have an independent constitution.[81] *De facto*, then, the Danish People's Church remained a state church.

Kierkegaard's reaction to these political and ecclesiastical changes was somewhat ambivalent, as he was sympathetic towards the monarchy but also a strong supporter of the common folk and human equality.[82] As he saw it, the fundamental problem of his country lay not in its form of government, whether that be the old or the new governing body, but in the spiritual demoralization and disintegration of the age which these changes expressed (*JP* iv. 4149; vi. 6255). In Kierkegaard's view the country had simply replaced the old forms of tyranny with a new one, the tyranny of the fear of men, carried out by the mob rule of the crowd, the majority, the public, the people, which 'Of all tyrannies ... is the most excruciating, the most mindless, unconditionally the downfall of all greatness and elevation' (*JP* iv. 4144; cf. 4131, 4134; *PV* 19). What the times in the deepest sense needed, he believed, was not political equality, which in his view was not true or perfect human equality, as that is impossible to achieve in the temporal realm, which is characterized by dissimilarity (*PV* 103–4). Rather, it was the ethical and ethical-religious that should be advanced, since ultimately 'only the essentially religious can with the help of eternity effect human equality ... and this is also why ... the essentially religious is the true humanity' (*PV* 104).Thus, while everything appeared to be politics at the time, Kierkegaard regarded the 'catastrophe' of 1848 as indicative of a 'crucial age' in which 'history was about to take a turn' towards the religious (*JP* vi. 6255). Moreover, he perceived himself as having been singled out by God to be 'that single individual' or extraordinary agent by which an awareness of the religious could be brought about (*JP* vi. 6843).

[79] Lausten (2002: 229). [80] Ibid. 230.
[81] Ibid. 230, 283. [82] Bukdahl (2001).

'Now he is Dead'

The third and final phase of Kierkegaard's authorship was precipitated by the death in 1854 of Bishop Mynster, whom Kierkegaard had known and revered since childhood but over the years increasingly had come to criticize in his capacity as Primate Bishop and chief representative of the Danish People's Church. The problem, as Kierkegaard saw it, was that Mynster and the established church he represented promoted a toned-down version of Christianity that actually had compromised, changed, and abolished true Christianity, virtually identifying it with paganism, aestheticism, worldliness, and Danish nationalism. Prior to Mynster's death Kierkegaard had called for an honest admission on the part of the established church in this regard, and when it was not forthcoming, he bided his time, waiting for the old bishop to die before attacking him openly.

The occasion for that presented itself when Professor Martensen, who was appointed Mynster's successor as Primate Bishop, eulogized him as 'a witness to the truth'—a figure whom Kierkegaard understood to be 'a person who directly demonstrates the truth of the doctrine he proclaims' and who is associated with the imitation of Christ, suffering, and martyrdom. None of these characteristics, in Kierkegaard's estimation, applied to Bishop Mynster, who had enjoyed a life of comfort, pleasure, and public esteem in the bishop's palace (*JP* iv. 4967). Thus, after three years of silence, Kierkegaard unleashed the pent-up polemic that had been smouldering inside him and brewing in his journals, venting it in an uncompromising attack upon the state church in a series of newspaper articles and pamphlets.

This attack, however, was short-lived, as Kierkegaard fell ill and was hospitalized in the fall of 1855, dying on 11 November of unknown causes.[83] During the attack he ceased attending church services and on his deathbed was willing to take communion only from a layman because 'the pastors are civil servants of the Crown and have nothing to do with Christianity'.[84] Ironically, Kierkegaard's funeral was held in the cathedral church of official Christendom, Our Lady's Church, which was overflowing with people who came to pay their respects and to hear the 'eulogy' given by his brother Peter, whose words about Søren were scarcely laudatory.[85] At the burial site a nephew voiced a protest against the funeral proceedings, which in his view were inconsistent with the deceased's views and wishes.[86] What little remained of Kierkegaard's estate, which literally had been used up in publishing his writings and maintaining the comfortable lifestyle to which

[83] See Søgard (2007); Garff (2005: 793–4).
[84] Kirmmse (1996: 125–6).
[85] Ibid. 132.
[86] Ibid. 133–5.

he was accustomed, was left to Mrs Regine Schlegel, née Regine Olsen, who had married her former suitor, John Frederik (Fritz) Schlegel, in 1843. Kierkegaard stated in his will: 'What I wish to express is that for me an engagement was and is just as binding as a marriage; and that therefore my estate is to revert to her in exactly the same manner as if I had been married to her.'[87] Since Regine was the muse who made him a poet, he also declared: 'It is my unalterable will that my writings, after my death, be dedicated to her and to my late father. She must belong to history' (*LD*, no. 239, p. 337; *JP* vi. 6537).

[87] Ibid. 48.

2

Christianity is an Existence-Communication

Kierkegaard did not consider himself to be a theologian but only 'a singular kind of poet and thinker' who wrote '*without authority*' (*WA* 165). Like Luther, he did not claim to teach anything new but sought 'once again to read through, if possible in a more inward way, the original text of individual human existence-relationships, the old familiar text handed down from the fathers'(165; cf. *CUP* i. 629–30).[1] While basically affirming and reflecting orthodox Lutheran theology in his authorship, Kierkegaard placed his stamp of original interpretation on a number of Christian doctrines and concepts. In his many works, composed in the short span of little more than a decade, he also mounted a devastating theological critique of the prevailing philosophical, theological, ecclesiastical, cultural, and sociopolitical ideologies and structures of his time, which in his view had severely compromised, confused, changed, and virtually abolished true Christianity. Seeking to reintroduce Christianity into Christendom, a term that encompasses all of these aspects of the Christian religion as a historical phenomenon, Kierkegaard maintained that Christianity is not a doctrine but an 'existence-communication' (*JP* i. 187, 484, 517, 676, 1060; iii. 3748; vi. 6528). By this he meant that what Christianity seeks to communicate to individuals is not *knowledge* about Christianity, although some preliminary information must first be imparted, but an *inward capability* for existing authentically through a relation to God or the eternal in time in the form of an individual human being, Jesus Christ (*JP* i. 650–3, 657).

At first blush, this conception of Christianity would seem to throw the whole enterprise of theology into question, for if Christianity is essentially a matter of inwardness or subjectivity, how do we legitimately go about thinking Christianly, or thinking theologically in a Christian manner, without misunderstanding and misrepresenting Christianity? Kierkegaard's answer is: by becoming subjective thinkers rather than objective theologians; by thinking dialectically in the self-referential form of 'double reflection' or inward appropriation of one's thought; by engaging in theological reflection with an eye towards its meaning for one's own existence; by reflecting on the 'what' of Christianity in the interest of 'how' to become a

[1] Cf. Luther (1978: 21).

Christian. This is the way Kierkegaard himself went about thinking Christianly and sought to communicate the content of his theological reflection to others. If we are to engage his thought in an appropriate manner, then, we must likewise orient our thinking in the existential mode or subjective context within which Kierkegaard understood Christianity. This involves not only taking cognizance of the subjective nature of Christianity but also thinking theologically along with him in the inward, dialectical, self-referential manner indicated above. As Hegel, in a surprisingly Kierkegaardian manner, puts it, we must 'go into the water'.[2] To do otherwise is to miss the whole point of Kierkegaard's existential mode of thinking Christianly.

BECOMING A CHRISTIAN IN CHRISTENDOM

Although Kierkegaard's attack on Christendom came to a head and reached its highest pitch in the final writings of his authorship, it began much earlier, arguably even from the very beginning, in the implied or indirect critiques of modern culture, philosophy, theology, and society in his early aesthetic writings. The work that brought this attack to the fore, however, was *Concluding Unscientific Postscript*, which explicitly poses the fundamental issue of the whole authorship: how to become a Christian in the situation of modern Christendom, where everyone is presumably already a Christian by virtue of being born a Dane yet lives in entirely different categories (*PV* 41, 55, 63, 88). It is also in this work that Kierkegaard's fundamental thesis that Christianity is an existence-communication is introduced; in fact, apart from his journals it is the only work in his authorship in which this claim is explicitly made.[3] Published under the pseudonym Johannes Climacus (John the Climber),[4] with Kierkegaard's name as 'editor', the *Postscript* is a large sequel to a much smaller work, *Philosophical Fragments*, by the same 'author', who does not claim to be a Christian but is interested in how to become one. As the 'editor' rather than author of this work, Kierkegaard cannot be said to endorse everything in it, but on the whole the views set forth by Climacus are compatible with his own views as expressed in his journals and other works published in his own name. However, respecting Kierkegaard's request to attribute the views set forth by his pseudonyms only to them, I shall allow Johannes Climacus to speak for himself in the *Postscript* and refer to the editor's views only by way of comparison.

[2] Hodgson (2005: 69). [3] McKinnon (1971: 202).

[4] A Syrian monk (*c.*525–606) who wrote a book titled *Ladder of Paradise* outlining thirty steps on the ladder to perfection.

The theological issue of particular concern to Climacus is not the objective issue of the *truth* of Christianity but the subjective issue of the individual's *relation* to Christianity, that is, how one can come to share in the eternal happiness or blessedness promised by Christianity (*CUP* i. 17). Climacus had already addressed this issue in *Philosophical Fragments* in a poetic, hypothetical fashion without explicitly mentioning Christianity by name until the very end, where he promises a sequel that will 'clothe the issue in its historical costume' (*PF* 109). The intensely personal yet universally human significance of this issue for Climacus is apparent in his comment that it 'pertains to me alone, partly because, if properly presented, it will pertain to everyone in the same way' (*CUP* i. 17). Climacus also feels alone in raising this issue and even admits to 'a kind of lunacy' in bringing it up because presumably everyone in his age already has faith as 'something given' that is a mere 'trifle' of little or no value unless it can be objectively demonstrated (17). What interests them, then, is the objective issue of establishing the truth of Christianity as a rational support for faith, not their personal relations to Christianity.

THE OBJECTIVE ISSUE

In order to distinguish the subjective issue of the individual's relation to Christianity as clearly as possible from the objective issue of the truth of Christianity, Climacus begins with a brief characterization of how the latter is determined in the modern age. Reflecting Leibniz's famous distinction between contingent and necessary truths, or truths of fact and truths of reason, he points out that, objectively viewed, truth can be understood as being either *historical* or *philosophical* in nature (*CUP* i. 21).[5] Viewed as a historical truth, the truth of Christianity is determined in the same way as any other historical truth, namely through a critical examination of the historical documents, reports, etc. pertaining to it in order to verify its historicity. Viewed as a philosophical or metaphysical truth, the truth of Christianity is determined by a rational examination of the relation of its historically given and verified doctrines to eternal truth. As examples of these two ways of establishing the truth of Christianity in the modern age, Climacus cites the *historical* point of view of modern biblical scholarship, Grundtvigian church theory, and orthodoxy's 'proof of the centuries', and the *speculative* point of view of Hegelian philosophy and theology. It is primarily against the latter perspective that Climacus takes aim in this book, as he rather quickly dismisses the historical point of view because

[5] Leibniz (1965: 13, 25).

it provides only an *approximation* to truth, which in his view is not enough on which to base eternal happiness (23–49).

THE BIBLE AS THE SECURE STRONGHOLD OF FAITH

If the Bible is to be regarded as 'the secure stronghold' that is supposed to establish the truth of Christianity, then from a historical point of view it is important to acquire 'the greatest possible reliability' concerning the authenticity, trustworthiness, and inspiration of the Holy Scriptures by means of philology or historical-critical scholarship (*CUP* i. 24). While Climacus professes to have great respect for philology, which in his view is a 'wholly legitimate' form of scholarship, he nevertheless detects a certain dubiousness in its efforts inasmuch as it assumes that faith or eternal happiness can be built on the basis of its historical findings, which are never final and always subject to revision (25–6). Climacus thus maintains that historical-critical biblical scholarship does not bring us a single step closer to faith but results instead in the loss of that which is the very condition of faith, namely an 'infinite, personal, impassioned interestedness' in one's eternal happiness (26). In relying on biblical criticism, the enquiring subject gets stuck, as it were, in a parenthesis, held in suspense and led to postpone the passionate decision of faith until the final results are in, which are never forthcoming (26–9, 33–4). Modern biblical scholarship thus makes the mistake of confusing faith with knowledge or rational certainty, whereas for Climacus faith is rooted in uncertainty, for 'if passion is taken away, faith no longer exists, and certainty and passion do not hitch up as a team' (29).

THE APOSTLES' CREED AS THE FOUNDATION OF FAITH

Abandoning the written word of the Bible as the secure stronghold of faith and taking recourse in the 'Living Word' of the church, its creed, and sacraments, the Grundtvigian movement seeks to establish the historical originality and continuity of the Apostles' Creed as the objective foundation of faith (*CUP* i. 34–46). In Climacus's judgement, however, this historical expedition is just as approximate and subject to sceptical attack as biblical scholarship, 'for with regard to historical issues it is of course impossible to reach an objective decision of such a nature that no doubt would be able to insinuate itself' (42). Thus, while Climacus finds merit in the Grundtvigians' emphasis on the present rather than the past and in their zealous passion for eternal happiness, in his view they are nevertheless comic-tragic figures in that their passion is comically incongruous with their objectivity and tragically staked on an approximation rather than certainty (43).

THE PROOF OF THE CENTURIES

Paraphrasing a statement attributed to the German romantic philosopher Jean Paul (1763–1825) to the effect that 'if all demonstrations of the truth of Christianity were abandoned or disproved, one demonstration would nevertheless remain, namely, that it has survived for eighteen hundred years', Climacus also takes aim at the so-called 'proof of the centuries' advanced by orthodoxy (*CUP* i. 47 n.; cf. *BA* 36–50). In his estimation, attempts to demonstrate the truth of Christianity on the basis of its survival for 1,800 (now 2,000) years are likewise hypothetical and approximate, since no matter how much probability of truth may be gained through such evidence it would never amount to 'an eternal truth that can be decisive for a person's eternal happiness' (47). In making this claim Climacus relies upon a thesis put forth by the distinguished German dramatist, philosopher, and literary critic Gotthold Ephraim Lessing (1729–81). Building on Leibniz's distinction between truths of fact and truths of reason, Lessing claimed that 'contingent truths of history can never become the proof of necessary truths of reason'.[6] That is so, Lessing contends, because historical truths belong to a different class of truths than rational truths and do not provide the absolute certainty that is required for establishing necessary or eternal truths. 'We all believe that someone called Alexander lived who in a short time conquered almost the whole of Asia. But who, on the strength of this belief, would risk anything of great and lasting importance whose loss would be irreplaceable?' Lessing asks, for it is possible that the exploits of Alexander could turn out to be just as mythical as the siege of Troy in the poems of Homer.[7] Climacus wholeheartedly agrees that eternal happiness, which for him is equivalent to the 'anything of great and lasting importance whose loss would be irreplaceable' of which Lessing spoke, cannot be based on the contingency of historical truths, which are only probable and always subject to modification and refutation by further investigation. Lessing further held that the transition from historical truths to eternal truth takes place by way of a *leap*, which for Climacus means that there is no 'direct transition from historical reliability to a decision on an eternal happiness' (*CUP* i. 95–6).[8] For Lessing, the lack of a direct transition created a 'broad and ugly ditch' that he as an eighteenth-century

[6] Lessing (2005: 85). [7] Ibid. 86. [8] Ibid. 87.

rationalist could not get across. For Climacus, however, the leap constitutes the 'category of decision' that is 'decisive for what is Christian and for every dogmatic category', even though he, like Lessing, has not yet been able to make that jump (99, 105).[9]

THE SPECULATIVE POINT OF VIEW

The speculative point of view of Hegelian philosophy and theology also regards Christianity as a historical phenomenon but seeks to determine its truth through reason rather than by historical methods. As Climacus sees it, however, the question of the thinker's own eternal happiness does not even arise in this perspective, inasmuch as the speculative task requires one to move away from oneself in abstract thought, abandoning or losing oneself in objectivity, as in the natural sciences (*CUP* i. 50, 52, 56). The speculative thinker may or may not be a believer, but in Climacus's view it is a mistake to think that speculative thought has any significance for faith, as in its concern to comprehend the truth of Christianity objectively it is 'totally indifferent' to the individual's eternal happiness (55). Moreover, the speculative point of view assumes that everyone already is a Christian, with the result that anyone who has self-doubts on that score is frowned upon and regarded as eccentric (50). Climacus satirizes this situation in Danish society by putting into the mouth of the wife of such a person the following amusing reprimand:

> Hubby, darling, where did you ever pick up such a notion? How can you not be a Christian? You are Danish, aren't you? Doesn't the geography book say that the predominant religion in Denmark is Lutheran-Christian? You aren't a Jew, are you, or a Mohammedan? What else would you be, then? It is a thousand years since paganism was superseded; so I know you aren't a pagan. Don't you tend to your work in the office as a good civil servant; aren't you a good subject in a Christian nation, in a Lutheran-Christian state? So of course you are a Christian.
>
> (*CUP* i. 50–1)

This humorous satire on the presumed isomorphism between being a Christian and being a Dane suggests to Climacus that objectivity is so omnipresent in Danish society that 'even the wife of a civil servant argues from the whole, from the state, from the idea of society, from geographic scholarship to the single individual' (51, translation modified). In other words, there is an ideological isomorphism between speculative thought and Danish society as well as between being a Christian and being a Dane, making Climacus's critique of the speculative point of view applicable to

[9] Ibid. 87.

Danish society as a whole.[10] But speculative thought is not alone in identifying religion and nationalism in this manner. According to Climacus, the Bible (orthodox/rationalist) and Church (Grundtvigian) objective theories also presuppose that everyone is a Christian, resulting in the contradictory situation that those who already are Christians require rational certainty in order to become what they already are (608)!

At a later point in the text Climacus further charges that modern speculative thought has virtually identified itself with Christianity inasmuch as it claims to have 'completely understood Christianity and declares itself to be the highest development within Christianity' (*CUP* i. 361). In making this claim, modern speculative theology, in Climacus's estimation, has gone *beyond* Christianity and *back* to paganism in its view that human reason is capable of discerning eternal truth. In *Philosophical Fragments* he had advanced precisely the opposite claim, namely that Christianity went beyond paganism in positing revelation as the condition for coming to know eternal truth.[11] In claiming to comprehend the truth of Christianity through human reason, therefore, speculative theology has actually regressed to paganism. Moreover, as a result of the confiscation of Christian terminology and concepts that are explained speculatively, Climacus claims that Christianity itself has been 'set back one whole stage in life' by being confused with paganism in speculative thought (*CUP* i. 363). Consequently, a preliminary task of theology in the modern age, as Climacus sees it, is to clarify what Christianity is in distinction from paganism and speculative thought, with which it has been erroneously identified.

WHAT CHRISTIANITY IS

It is 'of utmost and decisive importance', Climacus declares, to establish a 'preliminary agreement' with speculative thought concerning what Christianity is (*CUP* i. 370). 'If Christianity is essentially something objective, it behooves the observer to be objective', he concedes, but if it is 'essentially subjectivity', then it is a mistake to be objective (*CUP* i. 53). In Climacus's view, however, theological reflection on this issue must not be carried out in a 'learned or partisan manner', as that would lead us back to a never-ending process of approximation; instead, it must be raised 'in terms of existence' or what Christianity is for someone interested in existing in it (370). In the present age, he observes, 'the matter has been turned in such

[10] See Westphal (1996: 55), for a comparison and contrast of Climacus's ideology critique to that of Marx.

[11] Going beyond faith to a rational comprehension of Christianity was a trademark of Martensen's speculative theology that Kierkegaard often alludes to derisively. See e.g. *FT* 3–6.

a way that one takes an interest in being a Christian in order to be able to decide what Christianity is, and not in what Christianity is in order to be a Christian' (612). For Climacus the latter motivation is clearly what should inform one's deliberation on what Christianity is (612).

Climacus further insists that 'the question about what Christianity is must not be confused with the objective question about the truth of Christianity' (*CUP* i. 371). This is an extremely important point, for he wants to argue that it is possible to ask objectively about what Christianity is quite apart from the question of whether it is true or not. One can also know what Christianity is without being a Christian, but 'whether one can know what it is to be a Christian without being one', Climacus contends, is quite another question that 'must be answered in the negative' (372). Nor does one become a Christian by merely knowing what Christianity is. But if one is interested in becoming a Christian, one does need to know what Christianity is, and if one is a Christian, there must have been a time when one was not a Christian, then came to find out what Christianity is, and can now say what it is by comparing one's earlier life with one's present life (372). In Christendom, however, Climacus observes that 'learned Christians argue about what Christianity actually is, but it never occurs to them to think otherwise than that they themselves are Christians, as if it were possible to know for sure that one is something without knowing definitely what it is' (374)!

What then is Christianity? Given the current state of affairs in Christendom, in which Christianity has been confused with paganism and everyone is considered to be a Christian as a matter of course, Climacus observes that 'it becomes more and more difficult to know what Christianity is' (*CUP* i. 368). But one thing is clear to him: 'If modern Christian speculative thought has categories essentially in common with paganism, then modern speculative thought cannot be Christianity' (368, cf. 375). As Climacus sees it, however, modern speculative thought does not even bother to raise the question of what Christianity is but immediately assumes an identity with it that actually makes mediation or reconciliation of conceptual contrasts between them impossible since Christianity has already been mediated in speculative thought by being changed into a philosophical theory or doctrine that has been rationally comprehended (375–9).

Over against the speculative understanding of Christianity as a doctrine, therefore, Climacus declares (in agreement with his Danish editor) that Christianity is not a doctrine but an existence-communication (*CUP* i. 379–80; cf. *JP* i. 484, 517, 676, 1060).[12] More precisely, Christianity is not a doctrine in the sense of being a philosophical theory, for if it were, Climacus

[12] See also Adams (2003).

observes, 'the relation to it would not be one of faith, since there is only an intellectual relation to a doctrine' (326). For Climacus 'the immediate identifying mark of every misunderstanding of Christianity is that it changes it into a doctrine and draws it into the range of intellectuality' (327). Insofar as Christianity has doctrines, such as the doctrines of the incarnation and atonement, and in that sense can be called a doctrine, it is a doctrine that is to be actualized in existence rather than speculatively comprehended (379 n.). With respect to a doctrine of this kind, Climacus claims, it is a misunderstanding to want to speculate about it and 'the ultimate of misunderstanding' to have understood it speculatively; rather, the task of the understanding in relation to Christianity is simply 'to understand that it is to be existed in' and 'to understand the difficulty of existing in it' (379 n.). In its claim to have understood Christianity through mediation, therefore, modern speculation constitutes 'the ultimate misunderstanding of Christianity' (380 n.). That being the case, in addition to the fact that 'the nineteenth century is so frightfully speculative' that the word 'doctrine' is 'immediately understood as a philosophical theory that is to be and ought to be comprehended', Climacus has decided to call Christianity an existence-communication 'in order to designate very definitely how it is different from speculative thought' (380 n.).

SUBJECTIVITY IS TRUTH AND TRUTH IS SUBJECTIVITY

If Christianity is an existence-communication rather than a doctrine, a truth to be appropriated in existence rather than comprehended by thought, then it must be regarded as being essentially subjective rather than objective in nature. Accordingly, Climacus defines Christianity in the following manner: 'Christianity is spirit; spirit is inwardness; inwardness is subjectivity; subjectivity is essentially passion, and at its maximum an infinite, personally interested passion for one's eternal happiness' (*CUP* i. 33). Objectively, he contends, Christianity 'does not exist at all' inasmuch as its being and truth exist only in the subjectivity of those individuals who are passionately concerned about their eternal happiness (130–1). This leads Climacus to posit the following dual theses: 'subjectivity is truth' and 'truth is subjectivity' (189, 203–4, 281). Beginning with the first claim, Climacus suggests that, in relation to all knowing that is essentially related to existence, namely ethical and ethical-religious knowledge, the individual is in the truth 'if only the how of this relation is in truth, even if he in this way were to relate himself to untruth' (199). In other words, even if Christianity is objectively untrue (which is an issue Climacus has bracketed in this work), individuals may still be regarded as being in the truth by virtue of the subjective passion with which they sustain a relation to it in existence. The same can be said with respect to subjective relations to other religious ideals and traditions. In fact, Climacus suggests that there is more truth in a person who prays passionately to an idol than in someone who has knowledge of the true God but prays in untruth to the deity (201).[13] This is so, he explains, because 'at its maximum the "how" is the passion of the infinite, and the passion of the infinite is the very truth. But the passion of the infinite is precisely subjectivity, and thus subjectivity is truth' (203).

In claiming that Christianity is subjectivity and subjectivity is truth, Climacus (or his Danish 'editor' at least) has often been accused of subjectivism, which is decidedly not the case.[14] Climacus is not saying that truth is subjective in the sense that there is no objective truth. On the contrary, he clearly recognizes that Christianity or any other religion for that matter may be objectively true or untrue. Nor does he deny the possibility of acquiring objective truth in other areas of investigation, such as mathematics and science. Rather, Climacus's point is that, with respect to ethical and ethical-religious truth, the 'how' or passion with which one is related to a truth claim constitutes the 'deciding factor' and qualitative content of one's being, and it is in this sense that 'the subjective "how" and subjectivity are the truth' (*CUP* i. 203).

If subjectivity is truth, the reverse claim that truth is subjectivity also obtains, for 'when subjectivity is truth, the definition of truth must also contain in itself an expression of the antithesis to objectivity' (*CUP* i. 203). Accordingly, Climacus offers the following definition of subjective truth: 'An objective uncertainty, held fast through appropriation with the most passionate inwardness, is the truth' (203). This definition also corresponds to the definition of faith in a formal or general sense as the passionate leap or risk by which one becomes related to an objective uncertainty as the basis of one's eternal happiness. According to Climacus, 'if I am able to apprehend God objectively, I do not have faith; but because I cannot do this, I must have faith', which he likens to being 'out on 70,000 fathoms of water'—Kierkegaard's favourite expression for the uncertainty of faith (204).

OBJECTIVITY IN SUBJECTIVITY

The fact that faith is related to an objective uncertainty does not mean, however, that it lacks intellectual content or an objective referent outside the inwardness of the individual. On the contrary, we have seen that

[13] On the implications of Climacus's view of subjective truth for multiculturalism and religious pluralism, see Perkins (2004*a*).

[14] See also Gouwens (1996: 19–21, 105–8, 150–1), and Evans (1983: 126–31).

Climacus clearly recognizes that Christianity possesses intellectual content in the form of doctrines and conceptual ideals that are to be actualized in existence rather than merely conceptually comprehended. More importantly, however, he maintains that Christianity is a historical phenomenon or *fact* that has transhistorical significance inasmuch as it proclaims that the eternal has come into existence at a particular moment in time in the form of an individual human being (Jesus Christ), thereby providing a historical point of departure for the eternal happiness of the single individual in every age (*PF* 87–8; *CUP* i. 369). Indeed, in *Philosophical Fragments* Climacus goes so far as to claim that 'Christianity is the only historical phenomenon that despite the historical—indeed, precisely by means of the historical—has wanted to be the single individual's point of departure for his eternal consciousness, has wanted to interest him otherwise than merely historically, has wanted to base his happiness on his relation to something historical' (*PF* 109).

Climacus further contends that no philosophy, no mythology, and no historical knowledge 'has ever had this idea', that 'it did not arise in any human heart' (*PF* 109).[15] Objectively viewed, in claiming that the eternal, which by definition is not temporal or finite, has entered into time, Christianity professes an absolute paradox that is not only *objectively uncertain* but also *objectively absurd* inasmuch as 'it contains the contradiction that something that can become historical only in direct opposition to all human understanding has become historical' (*CUP* i. 211; cf. *PF* 37–48). Far from being probable or reasonable and thus capable of being speculatively understood and comprehended, then, Christianity is the most improbable of historical facts. Therefore its truth—supposing it has any, which is a question Climacus leaves undecided—cannot be known through human reason but can only be believed through a leap of faith requiring the highest pitch of passion or subjectivity on the part of the believer.

That Kierkegaard agrees with Climacus on the subjective and objective status of Christianity is corroborated in a journal entry referring explicitly to the *Postscript* in which he states:

> In all the usual talk that Johannes Climacus is mere subjectivity etc., it has been completely overlooked that, in addition to all his other concretion, he points out in one of the last sections that the remarkable thing is that a How is given which has the characteristic that when it is scrupulously rendered the What is also given, that this is the How of 'faith'. Right here, at its very maximum, inwardness is shown again to be objectivity. And this is then a turning of the subjectivity-principle, which, as far as I know, has never before been carried through or accomplished in this way.
>
> (*JP* iv. 4550, translation modified)

[15] See further Rae (1997: 26–108).

The statement to which Kierkegaard refers is probably one in which Climacus makes the following claim: 'Being a Christian is defined not by the "what" of Christianity but by the "how" of the Christian', which 'can fit only one thing, the absolute paradox' (*CUP* i. 611). In being defined specifically by its relation to the objective, transhistorical event of the absolute paradox or eternal in time, the inwardness of the Christian believer thus incorporates objectivity as well as subjectivity in itself, which to Kierkegaard is what distinguishes his view of subjectivity from that of other thinkers, such as Kant and Schleiermacher, who were severely criticized by Martensen in his doctoral dissertation for presumably espousing an autonomous, pantheistic subjectivism.[16]

BECOMING SUBJECTIVE

If Christianity is inwardness or maintains itself within the individual in the form of subjectivity, the proper way to relate to it, then, is by becoming subjective through the cultivation of subjectivity in oneself. We thus arrive at the subjective issue of how subjectivity must be constituted in the individual in order for the decision of faith, which is 'the highest passion of subjectivity', to take place (*CUP* i. 132). As Climacus sees it, becoming subjective is equivalent to becoming ethical, which in his view is 'the highest task assigned to a human being' inasmuch as it is ethically incumbent upon every human being to develop him/herself inwardly to the utmost in order to become a 'whole human being' or 'self' who is a synthesis of the temporal and the eternal, the finite and the infinite (129, 346). Since we already are temporal and finite beings in our immediate existence, becoming ethical or subjective consists principally in relating ourselves to the eternal and infinite in such a way as to actualize these constituents in our lives. Inasmuch as existence is a lifelong process of becoming, however, this task is not something that is achieved as a matter of course but involves the cultivation of passion or subjectivity within ourselves in a continual process of striving.

THE SUBJECTIVE THINKER

According to Climacus, the way to cultivate subjectivity in oneself is to become a subjective thinker, whose task is to achieve self-understanding in existence (*CUP* i. 73–80, 349–60). Whereas objective thinking is indifferent to the thinker's own existence, requiring the abandonment of oneself in

[16] Martensen (1997: 100–44).

objectivity, subjective thinking does not forget the fact that the thinker is an existing person and includes that thought in reflection in the interest of existing in what is thought. Due to the 'copiousness of knowledge' in the modern age, however, Climacus contends that 'people have entirely forgotten what it means to *exist* and what *inwardness* is' (249, 242). Consequently, the mode of reflection needed in the modern age is not objective reflection but subjective reflection on such fundamental existential issues as *what it means to die, what it means to be immortal, what it means to marry, what it means to thank God for the good one has been given*, etc. (165–81). While it is possible to reflect on these and other existential matters in an objective manner, treating them as detached, abstract questions concerning human existence in general, Climacus maintains that these are not intellectual issues but belong instead to the realm of inwardness as the sort of private and personal questions each one of us must ask with reference to our own lives (165–81). In thinking about death and immortality, for example, as a subjective thinker I do not reflect on death and immortality in general but on what it means for *me* to die and become immortal. Moreover, the question of my own death and immortality is not something that can be answered or comprehended once and for all but involves continual personal reflection and inward preparation for these eventualities.

Just as, according to an old proverb, 'prayer, trial, meditation make a theologian', Climacus maintains that 'imagination, feeling, and dialectics in impassioned existence-inwardness' are required for becoming a subjective thinker, and among these capacities, 'first and last, passion, because for an existing person it is impossible to think about existence without becoming passionate' (*CUP* i. 350). Unlike an objective thinker, who excludes passion in the process of thinking, the subjective thinker is a dialectician who combines passion and reflection in an 'intellectual passion' that holds the contradiction or 'qualitative disjunction' between thought and existence together by remaining conscious of oneself as an existing person in the process of thinking rather than abstracting from existence as in objective thought (350). Whereas an objective thinker seeks to understand the concrete abstractly, the subjective thinker moves in the opposite direction by striving to understand the abstract concretely. For example, an objective thinker abstracts from concrete human beings in order to form a general concept of humanity, whereas the subjective thinker seeks to understand the abstract concept of humanity in terms of a concrete human being, namely 'this individual existing human being' (352).

DOUBLE REFLECTION

Subjective thinkers also differ from objective or abstract thinkers by the fact that they engage in a process of *double reflection* (*CUP* i. 73–6). Like objective thinkers, subjective thinkers first think the universal or form a general concept of some actuality, such as a human being. While objective thinkers are content with obtaining a proper general concept of reality as a basis for knowledge, subjective thinkers engage in a second form of reflection in which the content of thought is related to the thinker's own existence for the purpose of appropriating or existing in what has been thought (73, 75–6). For example, in thinking about what Christianity is, subjective thinkers first engage in reflection on the 'what' of Christianity, just like objective thinkers, but they further reflect on how to appropriate this 'what' in their lives. In order truly to know and understand what it means to be a Christian, however, one must move beyond even subjective reflection, in which one passionately contemplates becoming a Christian as a 'thought-actuality' or possibility for one's own life, to the reduplication of this possibility in actuality (320–1, 340). Just as there is a difference between a thought-action and an actual action, Climacus points out that thinking about something, even thinking about something subjectively by considering its significance for one's own life, is not the same as actually existing in it (339–40). Unlike Hegel and his followers, Climacus steadfastly maintains the separation of thought and being (329–30, 335). As he sees it, however, actuality and action are not to be equated with external action but with 'an interiority in which the individual annuls possibility and identifies himself with what is thought in order to exist in it' (339). For example, Luther may be said to have acted the very moment he willed 'with all the passionate decision of subjectivity' to appear at the Diet of Worms to defend himself against the papal charges lodged against him (341).

Climacus further maintains contra Hegel and his followers that existence cannot be thought, for thought always transposes existence or actuality into possibility, thereby annulling it (*CUP* i. 314–16). The only actuality that does not become a possibility by being thought is the existing thinker's own ethical actuality:

> The ethical can be carried out only by the individual subject, who then is able to know what lives within him—the only actuality that does not become a possibility by being known and cannot be known only by being thought, since it is his own actuality, which he knew as thought-actuality, that is, as possibility, before it became actuality. (320)

'With regard to every actuality outside myself', Climacus observes, 'it holds true that I can grasp it only in thinking', that is, as a possibility, since otherwise one would have to become that actuality in order to know it as an actuality, which is impossible (321). Moreover, 'to ask ethically about another person's actuality is a misunderstanding, since one ought to ask only about one's own' (323).

THE ART OF INDIRECT COMMUNICATION

Double reflection is thus necessary in the communication of all knowledge pertaining to existence, or what Climacus calls 'essential knowing', namely ethical and ethical-religious knowledge or truth, which requires an indirect rather than a direct mode of communication to others (*CUP* i. 74, 197–8, 274).[17] Direct communication, or the communication of objective knowledge or information to others, is appropriate for conveying the results of certain kinds of objective truth, such as mathematical, historical, and scientific truths. This sort of knowledge can be passed on directly from one person to another in a typical teacher–student relationship. Ethical and ethical-religious truth, however, is not the sort of knowledge or truth that can be communicated directly, for what is being communicated in this instance is not information that can be learnt and repeated by rote but an inward capability for ethical and ethical-religious existence. This capability cannot be passed directly to another person but must be communicated in such a way as to elicit the recipient's own ethical and ethical-religious capability, which every individual must be assumed to possess as an inward potentiality. With respect to specifically Christian communication, however, Kierkegaard concedes that some preliminary knowledge about Christianity must first be communicated, since 'a human being as such does not know about the religious in the Christian sense' (*JP* i. 650, 651, 653, 657). In *Philosophical Fragments*, for example, Climacus suggests: 'Even if the contemporary generation had not left anything behind except these words, "We have believed that in such and such a year the god appeared in the humble form of a servant, lived and taught among us, and then died"—this is more than enough' (*PF* 194). Even so, Kierkegaard maintains that Christian communication is still essentially indirect communication, or more precisely, 'direct-indirect' communication, inasmuch as, like ethical and ethical-religious communication, it has the communication of human capability as its goal (*CUP* i. 653, 657).

Indirect communication of ethical, ethical-religious, and Christian capability to others is also made dialectically difficult by the fact that the recipient is an existing person, which is the essential factor in this form of communication (*CUP* i. 277). Indirect communication is thus likened by Climacus to 'having to say something to a passerby in passing, without standing still oneself or delaying the other, without wanting to induce him to go the same way, but just urging him to go his own way—and such is the relation between an existing person and an existing person when the communication pertains to the truth as existence-inwardness' (277). The

[17] See also Houe and Marino (2003); Walsh (1994: 206–9); Pattison (1992: 63–94).

purpose and desired effect of indirect communication is to set the recipients free so they can enter into their own subjective relations to existential truth and appropriate it as their own (74). For this to happen, however, self-control and the practice of an 'inexhaustible artistry' are required on the part of the communicator, who must pay close attention to the *form* of the communication, being careful to cast it in such a way as not to interfere with the recipient's God-relationship by becoming a meddling third party or by making oneself an object of admiration as an ethical or religious prototype for the recipient to emulate (80, 358–9). There is, then, a certain secrecy in indirect communication inasmuch as the content of the communication is private and personal to both the communicator and the recipient, and one can never be certain whether the recipient has been helped or not (74, 78–80). The model of indirect communication for Climacus is Lessing, to whom he ascribes, potentially if not actually, the thesis that 'The subjective existing thinker is aware of the dialectic of communication' (72). Another exemplar is Socrates, who 'artistically, maieutically', that is, in the role of a midwife, helped others 'give birth' to themselves and achieve self-knowledge on the assumption that everyone has to acquire truth by oneself (80, 277–8).

SOCRATES AND THE CHRISTIAN BELIEVER

According to Climacus, to become a subjective thinker who seeks self-understanding in existence was the Greek principle, exemplified in the Socratic exhortation to 'know yourself' (*CUP* i. 352). Socrates serves as the paradigm of the subjective thinker for Climacus because he expresses the thesis that subjectivity is truth in his philosophizing by paying attention to 'the essential meaning of existing' and to the fact that the thinker is an existing person whose task as a thinker is first and foremost to understand oneself as an existing person (204).[18] For Climacus the infinite merit of Socrates consists in the fact that he was 'an *existing* thinker, not a speculative thinker who forgets what it means to exist' (205; cf. 207). As a subjective thinker, Socrates sought to relate himself to eternal truth as an objective uncertainty *negatively* through ignorance. For example, he did not know whether there is an immortality of the soul but he was willing to stake his life on it, ordering his life 'with the passion of the infinite' so that upon death it might be acceptable if there is (201–2).

As Climacus sees it, to understand oneself in existence is also the Christian principle, except that in Christianity the self 'has received much richer

[18] On the role of Socrates in the Climacan writings, see also Howland (2006).

and much more profound qualifications that are even more difficult to understand together with existing' (*CUP* i. 353). These qualifications consist in the development of a *sharpened pathos* or deeper expression of subjectivity by undergoing an inward development and transformation in relation to eternal happiness and by confronting certain *dialectical factors* that contradict one's essential understanding of oneself and the eternal, thereby requiring subjective passion and reflection to the utmost. Existential pathos first comes to expression in the development of ethical-religious subjectivity in immanent religiosity or what Climacus calls Religiousness A, in which, according to the inverse dialectic that informs this type of religious inwardness, a positive relation to the eternal is expressed in and through negative forms of existential pathos. That is, one sustains a positive relation to the eternal indirectly or inversely by progressively becoming aware of one's inability to bring one's existence into conformity with the eternal through the expression of existential pathos in the negative forms of resignation, suffering, and guilt.[19] Resignation constitutes the *initial* expression of ethical-religious pathos wherein an absolute relation to the eternal is established through the adoption of eternal happiness as one's absolute *telos* or goal and the process of inward transformation is begun by dying away from immediacy or one's egocentric attachment to finite, worldly, relative ends in order to attain that goal (387–431). Suffering becomes the *essential* expression of ethical-religious pathos in this attempt due to the continual failure to bring one's life into conformity with one's absolute *telos* or to find any satisfactory external expression for one's relation to the eternal (431–525). The consciousness of guilt constitutes the *decisive* expression of religious pathos in the anguished consciousness of being totally guilty, be it in just one respect or ever so slight, in failing to conform to one's absolute *telos* (525–55). When existential pathos has reached this degree of intensity, the possibility of the still deeper pathos of Christian subjectivity can then arise through the introduction of two dialectical factors or problems requiring subjective reflection.

SUBJECTIVITY AS UNTRUTH

The first dialectical problem that confronts the subjective thinker in Christianity concerns the condition of the thinker's own subjectivity. Seeking to show how Christianity makes an advance upon the Socratic position that subjectivity is truth, Climacus claims that in Christianity one must begin by positing the opposite thesis, namely that 'subjectivity is untruth'

19 On the inverse dialectic of Religiousness A, see Walsh (2005: 8, 83–5, 114–16). See also Law (1997); Westphal (1996: 150–79); Evans (1983: 161–84).

(*CUP* i. 207).[20] This does not mean the negation of subjectivity in favour of objectivity as in speculative thought. Rather, subjectivity is still affirmed as the truth, but Christianity begins with the revelation that one exists in a state of untruth or *sin* inasmuch as a radical alteration has taken place in one's being, resulting in a break in one's relation to the eternal and a loss of one's essential self-identity as an eternal being (584). In the Socratic or immanent ethical-religious relation to the truth, the individual anticipates the eternal conformity of being and truth and is prevented from the realization of that *telos* only by the fact that existence is continually unfinished and one is always in the situation of only approximating the truth. In Christianity, by contrast, the revelation of one's condition as a sinner radically alters one's self-understanding and relation to the eternal. Existing in a state of untruth or complete discontinuity with the eternal, one cannot begin the task of inward self-transformation assuming, as could Socrates or a person in immanent religiosity, that one is 'essentially *integer*', that is, uncorrupted or innocent in relation to the truth (205).

According to Plato, Socrates advanced the thesis that all knowledge is recollection.[21] This thesis assumes that truth resides eternally within human beings; thus they already know the truth and need only to be reminded of it or become conscious of what they have forgotten. From the Socratic viewpoint, therefore, human beings exist essentially in conformity with truth. According to Climacus, however, Socrates constantly departed from this proposition in order to emphasize existence (*CUP* i. 205–7). While the possibility of affirming the unity of thought and being by way of recollection was always open to him, Socrates preferred to bring it to expression by accentuating existing rather than speculative thought. He perceived that a human being is first of all an existing individual and that existence makes a claim upon all human beings by presenting the task of existing as their essential task in life. The task of existing is to become concrete, not abstract, to accentuate existence rather than to negate it. Thus Socrates moved forward in existence rather than backward in recollection, transforming his existence in inwardness in the wisdom that subjectivity is truth.

In Climacus's estimation, then, Socrates went beyond speculative philosophy in affirming existence rather than recollection as the way to truth. The theory of recollection thus belonged more to Plato and his idealist followers than to Socrates (*CUP* i. 206). But because Socrates retained the possibility of taking himself back into eternity through recollection, existence in time did not hold for him the decisiveness or extent of alteration that it does for Christian subjective thinkers, who begin by discovering that they exist in a state of untruth or sin. For the Christian, then, there

20 See also Barrett (1997).

21 Plato, *Meno* 870–97.

is no eleventh hour escape from existence through recollection, and the task of becoming the truth in Christianity is a far more difficult and crucial matter when one is not already in the truth than it is for someone who is essentially in conformity with the truth and needs only to demonstrate it in existence through a concrete reduplication or actualization of the truth in one's personal life. The individual in sin is faced not only with the task of reduplication but also with an inward contradiction that makes reduplication impossible. This has the effect of intensifying passion to the utmost, for 'it cannot be expressed more inwardly that subjectivity is truth than when subjectivity is at first untruth, and yet subjectivity is truth' (213).

THE ABSOLUTE PARADOX AS THE ABSURD

The second dialectical problem confronting the subjective thinker in Christianity has to do with the qualification of eternal, essential truth itself as the absolute paradox and the absurd as a result of having entered into the temporal realm at a specific moment in time. Climacus warns first of all against conceiving this coming into existence speculatively as an *eternal-historical* event in which 'the coming into existence of the eternal in time is supposed to be an eternal coming into existence', for in that case Christianity is changed into 'an ingenious metaphysical doctrine' and, à la Feuerbach, 'all theology is anthropology' (*CUP* i. 579).[22] 'Speculatively to transform Christianity into an eternal history, the god-in-time into an eternal becoming-of-the-deity, etc., is nothing but evasion and playing with words', Climacus contends (578). The difficulty lies in basing one's eternal happiness on a relation to something historical, which is incongruous in itself, and especially so when it is based on something historical that can become historical only against its own nature. By coming into existence the eternal essential truth now stands outside the individual, who must lay hold of it in time via a relation to the eternal in time. The absurdity of the paradox, or the fact of eternal truth's having come into existence, thus introduces an element of *objective certainty*, namely that objectively it is absurd, and a *heightened repulsiveness* that qualify both the definition and the intensity of Christian faith as 'this absurdity, held fast in the passion of inwardness' (210). For Climacus, then, Christian faith has essentially two tasks: 'to watch for and at every moment to make the discovery of improbability, the paradox, in order then to hold it fast with the passion of inwardness' (233). Passion and paradox thus form a perfect fit wherein

[22] See Feuerbach (1989: p. xvii).

the strongest expression of inwardness or subjectivity occurs. An objective uncertainty as such is not outside the range of the probable, but the absurd or improbable excites the highest pitch of passion by refusing to be understood, permitting the understanding (*Forstand*) to understand only that it cannot be understood.[23] For to base one's eternal happiness on something historical that has the added peculiarity of being absurd by virtue of the fact that it contains a contradiction and to hold fast that it is essentially incomprehensible requires a breach with all our customary thinking. The absolute paradox, then, can only be believed, not known or understood. But in order to believe against the understanding, one must use one's understanding, first of all, to understand what it means to break with the understanding (to understand that one cannot understand), and second, to distinguish the Christian paradox, which one believes, from nonsense, which one cannot believe against the understanding precisely because the understanding 'will penetratingly perceive that it is nonsense and hinder him in believing it' (568).[24]

THE GOAL OF CHRISTIAN REFLECTION

The existence of the Christian subjective thinker in relation to the Christian paradox is thus placed both ethically and cognitively in contradiction. These dialectical contradictions must be deeply reflected upon in an existential manner by the Christian subjective thinker. One must exercise the 'passion of thought' to grasp the dialectical difficulties, but also 'concentrated passion' for the task of existing in what one has understood (*CUP* i. 386). For Climacus, then, the goal of Christian reflection or theology is not to acquire a higher intellectual understanding of the Christian paradox but to understand that one cannot understand it. This every person can do, whether one has little or much intellectual ability. There is no advantage on the side of intellect; in fact, in his view greater difficulty exists for those who are clever than for those who are not, for the temptation to rely on the understanding and to be reluctant to give it up is stronger in the intellectually gifted (181–2). The primary difficulty for every individual consists not in possessing or acquiring the intellectual ability to engage in dialectical thought but in gaining and exercising concentrated passion for

23 See Burgess (1994), who points out that Kierkegaard does not distinguish between understanding and reason like Kant and Hegel but generally uses them synonymously to refer to what David Swenson has described as 'the reflectively organized common sense of mankind' (117).

24 On the relation of the absolute paradox to nonsense see Lippitt (2000) and Rudd (2000) versus Weston (1999); Conant (1993); Mulhall (1994: 37–52).

existing as a Christian. For the dialectical difficulties posed by Christianity are not abstract-intellectual in character but existential contradictions that cut across the grain of ordinary reason or common sense. Moreover, it is not *by* reflection but only *after* reflection that one becomes a Christian. There is no direct transition to faith or Christian subjectivity either pathetically or reflectively. If the transition occurs, it transpires by way of a leap, through a resolution or decision of the will that brings reflection to an end. Climacus thus perceives the development of Christian subjectivity to be both pathos-filled and dialectical, requiring passion and reflection. At the conclusion of the *Postscript* he states: 'Since the highest is to become and to continue to be a Christian, the task cannot be to reflect on Christianity but can only be to intensify by means of reflection the pathos with which one continues to be a Christian. That is what this whole book has been about' (*CUP* i. 607).

THE NEED FOR EDUCATION IN CHRISTIAN CONCEPTS

Shortly after the publication of *Concluding Unscientific Postscript* Kierkegaard drafted *The Book on Adler*, a work occasioned by the deposing of the Danish parson and theologian Adolph Peter Adler (1817–69) by the state church on grounds of mental confusion concerning his claim to have received a new revelation from Christ. Kierkegaard was interested in the case of Adler partly because he knew the man personally but mainly because Adler provided a timely, concrete example of just the sort of conceptual confusions about Christianity and Christian subjectivity pointed out by Climacus in the *Postscript*. On the one hand, Adler constituted a 'bitter epigram' or satire on the modern age inasmuch as he was representative of a general theological confusion and volatilization of Christian concepts that was characteristic of the time, especially in Hegelian speculative theology and philosophy, of which Adler was a faithful adherent and expositor prior to receiving his so-called revelation (*BA* 23, 93–4, 121–3). On the other hand, Adler stood out as a 'phenomenon' or special individual over against the universal or established order of the time by virtue of his claim to have received a revelation and by the fact that, unlike most people in Christendom, where 'all are Christians of sorts', he apparently had undergone a genuine religious awakening (25, 28–31, 49, 103–4, 133). In Kierkegaard's estimation, it was highly doubtful that Adler had received a revelation, especially since he did not stand firm in asserting that claim and eventually acquiesced to the judgement of the church authorities, but it was also highly doubtful that he had experienced a *Christian* religious awakening (88, 112–16). Adler thus constituted an actual contemporary subject, not a poetic or imaginary figure such as Kierkegaard was accustomed to concoct in his pseudonymous writings, through whom he could illustrate and emphasize the need for 'proficiency and schooling in the Christian conceptual definitions' that constitute the 'qualitative, unshakable criterion' by which both a revelation and a Christian religious awakening can be distinguished from a more universal ethical-religious enthusiasm (89, 114–15).

ADLER'S QUALITATIVE LEAP INTO RELIGIOUS INWARDNESS

Like Kierkegaard, Adler was baptized and confirmed in the Christian faith and was a theological graduate of Copenhagen University. Upon receiving his degree, he immersed himself in Hegelian philosophy, delivering lectures at the university and publishing a popular account of Hegel's logic. He then became a pastor in a remote rural community, where he was brought into contact with simple, ordinary people who lacked acquaintance with Hegel. The humorous incongruity of this situation gave Kierkegaard an opportunity, first of all, to highlight class differences in Danish society between the common people of the countryside, who in his view earnestly represented the essentially Christian even though they had received little formal Christian education, and the cultured elite of the city, among whom Hegelian philosophy was popular and regarded as the highest development of Christianity (*BA* 96–8).[25] As a dyed-in-the-wool, sophisticated Hegelian urbanite, Adler was 'a wild, alien bird in the country', having essentially nothing in common with simple people, with the result that his situation was one not only of loneliness but also self-contradiction, since it was his duty to preach what he was by education presumably already far beyond (97–8). Then an event occurred that changed Adler's life, transporting him via a qualitative leap from 'the fantastic medium of Hegelian philosophy . . . into the sphere of religious inwardness', from the objectivity of abstract thinking to the subjectivity of religious self-concern, whereby, as Kierkegaard characterizes it, his life 'acquired a rhythm very different from the cab-horse trot in which most people, in the religious sense, dawdle through life' (98–100, 103).

[25] On the contrast between city and country in Kierkegaard's writings, see Pattison (1999). See also Kirmmse (1990) on the cultural and political differences between the peasant and bourgeois classes in 19th-cent. Denmark.

RELIGIOUSNESS-AT-A-DISTANCE

In agreement with Climacus, Kierkegaard maintains that 'all religiousness lies in subjectivity, in inwardness, in emotion, in being jolted, in the qualitative pressure on the spring of subjectivity' (*BA* 104, translation modified). In his view, however, 'most people, in the religious sense, go through life in a kind of absentmindedness and preoccupation' in which 'they never in self-concern sense each his own *I* and the pulse beat and heart beat of his own self' (103). In other words, they live too objectively, at a distance from themselves, 'as if they were continually out, never at home' (103–4). At most, they become present to themselves only in the past or the future, not in the present, or at least not totally so in self-concern, which for Kierkegaard is the highest task for the personal life and constitutes the highest form of religiousness, since 'only in this way is it absolutely comprehended that a human being absolutely needs God at every moment' (106). To the extent that people have some religiousness and think about it, they have it in the form of a *wish*, *intention*, or *idea* about which they are undecided, not knowing what it is or how and when it is to be used (105, 107). Most importantly, they do not grasp that 'the religious is the *one thing needful*' in life but consider it to be, among other things, *also needful*, 'especially for difficult times' (105).

UNIVERSAL RELIGIOUS AWAKENINGS VERSUS A CHRISTIAN AWAKENING

Unlike most people, then, Adler had been 'deeply moved' and 'shaken in his inmost being' by being 'fetched home by a higher power' and 'tossed out into extreme mortal danger' over '70,000 fathoms of water' (*BA* 104, 108, 112). As Kierkegaard sees it, however, to be deeply moved in this manner is not equivalent to having a Christian awakening, as pagans and Jews, for example, are also capable of being deeply moved by something higher or abstract such as the eternal or an idea. Thus 'not every outpouring of religious emotion is a Christian outpouring' nor does one 'become a Christian by being religiously moved by something higher' (113). In contrast to an immanent or more universal religious awakening, in which one's self-identity remains intact and one is shaken in such a way as merely to wake up and become oneself, a Christian awakening lies in the sphere of transcendence; that is, it takes place via a relation to the eternal in time outside oneself through which one becomes a qualitatively different person (114). In order for a Christian awakening to occur, therefore, a specifically

Christian emotion (*Grebethed*),[26] in which one is 'in the stricter sense deeply moved by the essentially Christian', as well as a firm and definite conceptual language within which to express it are required, both of which, in Kierkegaard's judgement, were in short supply in the present age (114–15).

According to Kierkegaard, the fundamental defect in Adler was that he did not take time to understand himself in what had happened to him and was not adequately schooled in the basic Christian conceptual language in order to be able to determine whether he had had a revelation, a Christian awakening, or a more universal religious awakening (*BA* 111, 115, 117–18). Adler thus confused his more universal religious awakening with a Christian awakening and erroneously expressed it in terms of the Christian concept of revelation. As Kierkegaard puts it, '*he confuses the subjective with the objective, his altered subjective state with an external event*, the dawning of light upon him with the coming into existence of something new outside him, *the falling of the veil from his eyes with his having had a revelation*' (117). As Kierkegaard understands it, a revelation is an objective qualification that is not identical to or an element in subjectivity itself but constitutes a new, transcendent, paradoxical point of departure that cannot be mediated or explained away by reflection (117–18, 120). While Adler bore a personal responsibility for not acquiring a rigorous, fundamental education in Christian concepts in order to be able to express his religious emotion in the appropriate language, Kierkegaard faults theological training in Christendom in general and Hegelian philosophy in particular for initiating him into 'the total confusion of the essentially Christian' (114, 116). Not only does Hegelian philosophy espouse 'the immediate identity of subject-object', whereby the Christian concept of revelation is explained away and volatilized in the subjectivity of the human race, it also lacks an ethics inasmuch as it is oriented toward explaining the world-historical movement of the past rather than occupying itself with the future, which is the medium of ethics (120, 129). 'Only ethics can place a living person in the proper position', Kierkegaard declares, for 'it says: the main thing is to strive, to work, to act, and if one has taken a wrong direction of reflection, then above all to come back from it' (131).

[26] 'Emotion' as used here connotes the deep inward enthusiasm or feeling 'of a specific qualitative kind' within which Christian subjectivity comes into existence, while passion (*Lidenskab*) and pathos (*Pathos*), the terms associated with subjectivity in the *Postscript*, give expression respectively to one's underlying subjective concern for eternal happiness and the heightened negative forms of subjectivity (resignation, suffering, guilt, sin consciousness) through which one is related to and transformed by the eternal (*BA* 112–14; *CUP* i. 387–94). On religious emotion in Kierkegaard, see also Kangas (2008), Roberts (1997), and Gouwens (1996: 76–80).

Like Johannes Climacus, then, Kierkegaard calls individuals of the modern age back to ethical self-concern and underscores the need for the appropriate subjective passion and emotion as well as conceptual clarity concerning the essentially Christian qualifications for thinking and expressing oneself Christianly in an existential mode. Keeping that in mind, let us turn now to some basic Christian concepts which Kierkegaard sought to clarify for the sake of enabling a Christian awakening and upbuilding of the single individual to occur.

3

Venturing a Relation to God

For Kierkegaard, theology or discourse about God is rooted in and arises out of the single individual's God-relationship, which is a possibility for every human being and the only way one really comes to know the divine. The proper context for thinking Christianly about God, therefore, is within a personal relation to God, not by engaging in abstract speculation on the nature of the deity.[1] As Kierkegaard sees it, a relation to God is 'a voyage of discovery' in which one comes to know God through an 'inland journey' into oneself (*JP* ii. 1451). It is a venture fraught with uncertainty, fear and trembling, lifelong striving, self-denial, and suffering on the part of the single individual, but not to venture such a relation is in his view 'to lead a religious still-life' that avoids all risk and danger (*JP* ii. 1383; *TDIO* 24–7). One cannot become involved with God 'without bearing the marks of being wounded' or 'suffering heterogeneity in this life' (*JP* ii. 1405). In fact, Kierkegaard claims that 'to become involved with God in any way other than being wounded is impossible, for God himself is this: *how* one involves oneself with Him . . . In respect to God, the *how* is *what*' (1405). The way to discover what God is, then, is by becoming involved with him in the only way possible, namely by an absolute devotion to God that is 'instantaneously recognizable' by the 'limp' or wound of suffering one bears as a result of venturing a relation to the divine.

The God-relation is thus a 'daring venture' in which one must be willing 'absolutely to venture everything, absolutely to stake everything, absolutely to desire the highest *τέλος*' of human existence, which is eternal happiness (*CUP* i. 404, 423). Like the inscription on the pagan temple at Delphi, *ne quid nimis* (nothing too much), which according to Climacus/Kierkegaard is the motto of all 'finite worldly wisdom' or sagacity, one may be willing to venture a relation to God 'to a certain degree' (404; *JP* ii. 1405). And if one could be sure that there is such a thing as eternal happiness, one might even be willing to venture all for it, but like passion and certainty, venturing and certainty do not hitch up as a team. As Climacus expresses it: 'To venture is the correlative of uncertainty; as soon as there is certainty, venturing stops' (*CUP* i. 424). Over against the secular mentality,

[1] See also Law (1993: 163–5).

which wants to be exempt from all danger and effort as well as immediately certain of success, Christian venturing—indeed, in Kierkegaard's view, all truly religious venturing—requires that one *relinquish probability* in reliance upon God, which means that one is just as likely to fail as to succeed in the world (*JFY* 98–104). In fact, from a merely human standpoint, the most probable outcome in religious venturing is that one will be defeated rather than victorious in the world. But according to the inverse dialectic that informs Christianity, which is always the opposite of the secular mentality, what the world understands as failure is inversely a sign that one has truly ventured all in reliance upon God and that victory is assured eternally even if one loses temporally (96).[2] The probability of failure in the world thus prevents the true venturer from taking God in vain by presuming that temporal victory will occur as a result of relying on God. But it also prompts the worldly, sagacious mentality in Christendom to renounce true Christianity in favor of a lenient, comfortable religiosity that does not dare to venture beyond the bounds of probability, thereby slipping out of all personal effort and slipping in credit 'dirt cheap' for presumably being a 'God-fearing pious Christian' (102). Such 'deification of sagacity in our day', Kierkegaard contends, 'is precisely the idolatry of our age' which he seeks to expose in his critique of Christendom (102–3; cf. *JP* ii. 1354).

GOD AS SPIRIT, SUBJECT, AND PURE SUBJECTIVITY

For Kierkegaard, the first thing to be said about God from a Christian standpoint is that God is Spirit (cf. John 4: 24), in relation to whom a human being is also defined as spirit (*JP* iii. 2446, 3098, 3099; *EUD* 88; *SUD* 13). But what does it mean to be spirit? In the Christian tradition the concept of spirit is associated primarily with the third person of the Trinity, but it has also been understood as constituting the very core of the divine essence, especially in nineteenth-century speculative theology.[3] Hegel identified the concept of spirit (*Geist*) as 'the distinctive ontological quality of God' that constitutes 'the Trinity as such and as a whole' rather than as 'an aspect or person of the divine Trinity'.[4] He understood divine spirit in a dynamic and cognitive sense as the creative power and mind or thought (*Idee*) that comes to know itself and to be known concretely through a historical process of mediation or reconciliation of itself as *substance* and *subject* in nature and human consciousness. As substance or the essential, underlying ground of everything that is, spirit has being *in itself* in the

[2] On the inverse dialectic of Christianity, see Walsh (2005).
[3] Schmid (1961: 111–17); Schelling (2006: 32–3).
[4] Hodgson (2005: 16–17).

form of immediate consciousness. As subject or actual, determinate being, it relates itself to itself or knows itself in relation to an object other than itself and thus has being *for itself* in the form of human self-consciousness. In being outside itself, however, it remains within itself and thus has being *in and for itself* in the form of a spiritual substance that includes subject and object, self and other, thought and being, inner and outer, identity and difference.[5]

Hegel identified three stages in the unfolding and mediation of divine spirit in human history: subjective spirit (in the soul, consciousness, and mind as such), objective spirit (in the social and political order), and absolute spirit (in art, religion, and philosophy).[6] Theologically, he understood divine spirit as an *immanent Trinity* that exists eternally in and for itself prior to and apart from creation and as an *economic Trinity* at work temporally in a drama of creation, fall, redemption, and reconciliation that re-enacts the immanent trinitarian dialectic in the necessary movement of world history towards the consummation of all things in God as Absolute Spirit.[7] Defining spirit in this context as 'the living process by which the *implicit* unity of divine and human nature becomes *explicit*, or is brought forth', Hegel envisioned the Father as the idea of spirit in abstract, universal form, the Son as the historical appearance of the idea of divine–human unity in a single individual (Jesus Christ), and the Holy Spirit as the cultus or religious community.[8]

Kierkegaard was introduced to the Hegelian concept of spirit in Martensen's lectures on speculative dogmatics (*SKP* xiii, II C 28, §§ 71–2). Like Hegel, he made the New Testament identification of God as spirit central to his theology, but while he affirms the doctrine of the Trinity, it is not an organizing principle of his theology as in Hegel's and Martensen's, nor is it understood as a process of actualization of the one universal spirit through a historical objectification and mediation of itself in and through nature and culture.[9] Rather, for Kierkegaard, the individual's God-relationship is the lens through which the Trinity is encountered and known in human existence. This relationship begins with an unmediated relation to God the Father, whose fatherliness is not just a metaphor but 'the truest and most literal expression' of his being (*EUD* 98–9). The Father then directs us to the Son as our personal mediator

[5] Hodgson (2005: 18–20); Hegel (1977: 1–21).

[6] Hegel (2007).

[7] Hodgson (2005: 127–40).

[8] Hegel (1984–7: iii. 21–2, 66–7, 77–8, 83, 109–10, 149–51, 189–98, 230–2, 328, 360–74).

[9] Cf. Martensen (2004: 593): 'If the Trinity is really to have meaning for thought, as the absolute truth, then it must become the key to the entire system of the world. All actuality in heaven and earth must be taken up into its circle, and it must be known as the Concept which conceives everything and itself.'

and prototype, and the Son in turn directs us to the Holy Spirit for help in striving to become like the prototype (*JP* ii. 1432). There is mediation in Kierkegaard's concept of spirit, then, but the reconciliation that occurs is not within the Godhead itself or between divine and human nature as such but between the individual and God through the atonement of Christ and the revitalizing inspiration of the Holy Spirit, which work hand in hand for the redemption and sanctification of the single individual in faith.[10]

Kierkegaard likewise does not understand the divine spirit as the identity of subject and object. In his view, God is not an object or something external that can be perceived or known objectively, although this does not mean that God lacks independent reality.[11] Rather, God is a transcendent subject who is accessible to human beings only through a personal relationship in inwardness or subjectivity (*CUP* i. 162, 200; cf. *JP* ii. 1347; *SUD* 80; *TDIO* 64).[12] In several late journal entries Kierkegaard even goes so far as to claim that 'God is pure subjectivity, sheer unmitigated subjectivity', by which he means that 'intrinsically the divine has no trace at all of the objective' in itself and relates objectively only to its own subjectivity through self-reflection, in which the divine subjectivity redoubles itself in an unconditioned, perfect objectivity (*JP* iii. 2570, 2576; iv. 4571).[13] As an 'infinitely faint analogy' to what he sees as the deity's objective relation to itself, Kierkegaard cites Socrates' ability to relate to himself objectively as if he were an 'entirely separate third party' or another 'I' at the moment he was condemned to death (*JP* iv. 4571). Kierkegaard observes that most people are subjective towards themselves and objective towards others, whereas 'the task is precisely to be objective towards oneself and subjective toward all others' (*JP* iv. 4542). In other words, like God, we should relate to ourselves objectively in self-reflection, and to others, including God, subjectively as subjects or persons. This does not mean, of course, that we should forgo becoming subjective; on the contrary, it is precisely through subjectivity that one becomes self-reflective or objective toward oneself in passionate self-concern. God's self-reflection in infinite subjectivity thus provides a model for human self-reflection and self-knowledge as well as for interpersonal relations, which should be construed as subject-to-subject rather than subject-to-object in character.

10 On the Holy Spirit in Kierkegaard's thought see Frawley (2003) and Martens (2002).

11 On realism and antirealism in Kierkegaard's view of God, see Evans (2006: 29–46, 54–9) versus Cupitt (1988: 153–5; 1997: 83–7).

12 On God's relational transcendence, see also Sponheim (2004).

13 See also Come (1997: 75–7).

DEMONSTRATING THE EXISTENCE OF GOD

If God is a subject to whom one is related in a subjective rather than objective manner, it goes without saying that God's existence cannot be objectively or rationally proved. In fact, as Kierkegaard sees it:

> The idea of proving the existence of God is of all things the most ridiculous. Either he exists, and then one cannot prove it (no more than I can prove that a certain human being exists; the most I can do is to let something testify to it, but then I presuppose existence)—or he does not exist, and then it cannot be proved at all.
>
> (*JP* ii. 1334)

There has been a long tradition of attempts to prove the existence of God through the ontological, cosmological, and teleological arguments of Anselm, Aquinas, Descartes, Spinoza, Leibniz, Paley, and others. There have also been numerous critics of those attempts, most notably Hume and Kant in the modern age. Kierkegaard belongs to the latter group but faults attempts to demonstrate God's existence on somewhat different grounds than his modern predecessors. The only sustained critique of proofs for the existence of God in his writings comes in *Philosophical Fragments*, where Johannes Climacus takes up the matter in the context of a discussion of the passionate attempt of human understanding to discover what thought cannot think, namely the unknown or the god (*Guden*).[14] In agreement with Kierkegaard, Climacus states:

> It hardly occurs to the understanding to want to demonstrate that this unknown (the god) exists. If, namely, the god does not exist, then of course it is impossible to demonstrate it. But if he does exist, then it is foolishness to want to demonstrate it, since I, in the very moment the demonstration commences, would presuppose it not as doubtful—which a presupposition cannot be, inasmuch as it is a presupposition—but as decided, because otherwise I would not begin, easily perceiving that the whole thing would be impossible if he did not exist. (*PF* 39)

According to Kierkegaard and Climacus, then, proofs for the existence of God generally beg the question by presupposing what they set out to prove. Pointing out that 'it is generally a difficult matter to want to demonstrate that something exists', Climacus prefers the opposite approach:

> Therefore, whether I am moving in the world of sensate palpability or in the world of thought, I always draw conclusions from existence, not to existence. For example, I do not demonstrate that a stone exists but that something which exists

[14] The Danish word for god in this text generally contains the definite article as in the German translation of Plato's works by Schleiermacher which Kierkegaard owned and read. On Climacus's critique of proofs for the existence of God, see also Law (1993: 167–73); Evans (1992: 63–71); Roberts (1986: 70–8).

is a stone. The court of law does not demonstrate that a criminal exists but that the accused, who does indeed exist, is a criminal. (*PF* 40, translation modified)

Alluding to Kant and Schelling, Climacus thus concludes: 'Whether one wants to call existence an *accessorium* [addition] or the eternal *prius* [presupposition], it can never be demonstrated' (*PF* 40).[15] In a passage deleted from the final text, however, he notes that 'the connection [between the concept of God and existence] is somewhat different from what Kant meant—that existence is an *accessorium*' (190; cf. *JP* i. 1057). Kant rejects the ontological proof for the existence of God on the grounds that existence is not a property or attribute contained in the concept of God or anything else for that matter, but is simply the positing of the subject together with its predicates.[16] Climacus argues simply that existence is something one already knows or presupposes about a thing, so that 'I would be mad to want to draw a conclusion to what I know' (190, translation modified; cf. *CUP* i. 545). In the *Postscript* he further reduces the ontological argument to an absurdity, maintaining that if God is not presupposed, it will run like this:

A supreme being who, please note, does not exist, must be in possession of all perfections, among them also that of existing; ergo, a supreme being who does not exist does exist. This would be a strange conclusion. The highest being must either not be in the beginning of the discourse in order to come into existence in the conclusion, and in that case it cannot come into existence; or the highest being was, and thus, of course, it cannot come into existence, in which case the conclusion is a fraudulent form of developing a predicate, a fraudulent paraphrase of a presupposition. (*CUP* i. 334)

Standing in the background and undoubtedly influencing Climacus's viewpoint is the Leibnizian distinction, later embraced by Lessing and Hume, between truths of fact and truths of reason, according to which factual or contingent truths are ascertained empirically through experience, since they cannot be known by human beings a priori (on the basis of reason alone) and with certainty as are truths of reason.[17] According to Leibniz, only necessary truths can be rationally demonstrated. Since God is a necessary being whose essence necessarily involves existence, God's existence can be demonstrated a priori on the basis of the concept of God's essence or being (the ontological proof). However, in an extended note on Spinoza's ontological proof, in which being is regarded as a perfection of God, Climacus points out that the kind of being involved in the concept

15 According to the translators, Kant does not actually use this term. On God as the eternal *prius* or ground of existence, see Schelling (2006: 27–8), and Kangas (2007).

16 Kant (1956: 500–7).

17 Leibniz (1965: 13, 154–5); Hume (1988: 71–3); see also Evans (1992: 65–6).

of God in this proof is *ideal being*, which pertains to God's essence (*what* God is), not *factual being*, which pertains to existence (*that* something is) (*PF* 41 n.; cf. *JP* i. 1057). Spinoza's proof lacks this distinction, thus confusing the issue and confounding it even more by introducing the notion of degrees of being, according to which the more perfect a thing is, the more being it has and vice versa. As Climacus sees it: 'With regard to factual being, to speak of more or less being is meaningless. A fly, when it is, has just as much being as the god' (*PF* 41 n.). Strictly speaking, 'God does not exist (*existere*), he is eternal', as existence belongs to the finite or temporal realm, not to the eternal, which simply is and does not come into existence (*CUP* i. 332). That is why, on Climacus's view, the entry of the eternal into time as claimed by Christianity constitutes an absolute paradox to the human understanding. This difficulty, however, is completely circumvented by Spinoza's proof inasmuch as the necessary being of God 'cannot become dialectical in the determinants of factual being, because it is; and neither can it be said to have more or less being in relation to something else' (*PF* 42 n.).

The teleological argument for the existence of God, or the argument from design based on God's works, is also subjected to criticism in *Philosophical Fragments* (*PF* 40–2). Noting how curious it would be if someone wanted to demonstrate Napoleon's existence from his works, since one must presuppose Napoleon's existence in order to see them as *his* works, Climacus applies this analogy, with one qualification, to the relation of the god to his works. Just as proofs for the existence of God in general presuppose the existence of the deity, the argument from design relies on the same presupposition. However, there is an absolute relation between God and his works that does not obtain in the case of human beings, inasmuch as God's works belong only to God, whereas the most one can demonstrate with reference to Napoleon's works is that they are the works of a great general, not necessarily Napoleon. Nevertheless, in order to see God's works as God's works, one must presuppose them as God's works, since it is not immediately apparent from the works themselves that they are works of God. Ergo, one does not demonstrate the existence of God from his works but simply presupposes God's existence in relation to the works that are ideally presupposed to belong to him.

Using the example of a Cartesian doll (a misnomer for the so-called Cartesian devil) that is weighted so as to stand on its head as soon as one lets go of it, Climacus suggests that as long as we try to demonstrate the existence of the deity, God's existence does not emerge (*PF* 42; cf. 291 n. 28). Only when we let go of the demonstration does God's existence become present to us. This moment of letting go thus corresponds to the leap or break with rational thought that is required for faith (*PF* 42). With an ironic tip of the hat to 'the rare wise man' who wants to demonstrate the existence of God, Climacus concludes:

Therefore, anyone who wants to demonstrate the existence of God (in any other sense than elucidating the God-concept and without the *reservatio finalis* [ultimate reservation] that we have pointed out—that the existence itself emerges from the demonstration by a leap) proves something else instead, at times something that perhaps did not even need demonstrating, and in any case never anything better. For the fool says in his heart that there is no God, but he who says in his heart or to others: Just wait a little and I shall demonstrate it—ah, what a rare wise man he is! If, at the moment he is supposed to begin the demonstration, it is not totally undecided whether the god exists or not, then, of course, he does not demonstrate it, and if that is the situation at the beginning, then he never does make a beginning—partly for fear that he will not succeed because the god may not exist, and partly because he has nothing with which to begin. (*PF* 43–4)

But Climacus does not entirely deny the usefulness of proofs, inasmuch as he refers approvingly to the physico-teleological proof for the existence of God advanced by Socrates, who sought 'to infuse nature with the idea of fitness and purposiveness' by constantly presupposing that the god exists (*PF* 44). On the whole, however, neither Climacus nor his alter ego Kierkegaard finds the preoccupation with demonstrating the existence of God to be efficacious. Not only do the arguments fail, they distract us from focusing on our own personal relationships to God, which is where the existence of God truly becomes present to and is known by us.

GOD'S OMNIPRESENCE

If God is infinite subjectivity, a divine spirit or subject encountered and known only in and through the deepening of one's own subjectivity, this means that the deity is not directly present or seen in nature, as believed in paganism, nor is the divine spirit to be conceived and comprehended as the moving spirit of the world-historical process, as claimed in Hegelian speculative thought. Here we reach the heart of Kierkegaard's bone of contention with the speculative theology and philosophy of the ancient and modern world concerning God. As he sees it, God is *omnipresent* in the world but not *immanent* in it. What is the difference between these two attributes of the divine and how is God's omnipresence to be perceived? Let us look first at the difference between Christianity and paganism on this issue as presented in the *Postscript* (*CUP* i. 243, 245–6). Climacus contends that God is everywhere present (omnipresent) in the creation, but the divine is not there directly (immanently), as the only thing that is directly present is nature, which is the work of God, not the divine itself (243). He thus explicitly rejects the identification of God with nature as found in ancient paganism and its modern forms such as the immanent or pantheistic philosophy of Spinoza, Schelling, Hegel, Martensen, Strauss, and Feuerbach, among others.[18] The only way one can have a true God-relationship and see the divine everywhere, Climacus claims, is by turning inward, where the possibility of being awakened to a spiritual relationship to God in inwardness can take place, thereby breaking with the direct relation to God of ancient and modern paganism. Indeed, Climacus contends that God is so elusive, so invisible, so unremarkably present in the world that one might easily go through life without ever discovering the divine in nature, since the divine has chosen not to reveal itself directly in some striking form, such as a 'rare, enormously large green bird, with a red beak' or a twelve foot tall man, which would immediately call attention to itself and amaze everyone (245–6). In fact, such a direct revelation would annul the omnipresence of the divine by its very visibility and would be untrue and deceptive. Since God is not a deceiver, Climacus concludes that 'the spiritual relation in truth specifically requires that there be nothing at all remarkable about his form' (246). The relation between omnipresence and invisibility thus mirrors the relation between revelation and mystery, inasmuch as the latter is 'the one and only mark' by which the former can be known (245; cf. also *PC* 155).[19] This is not to say that God cannot be known or made manifest in nature, as nature itself is a sign of God's greatness for Kierkegaard if not for Climacus also, but the Christian comes to know God 'in a different way, more intimately', Kierkegaard claims, through an inward or spiritual relationship with the divine (*UDVS* 192–3; *CD* 291).

For Climacus, however, the immanence of ancient and modern paganism runs deeper than a direct identification of God and nature, for he sees it as underlying the relation to eternal truth in both ancient and

[18] See Spinoza (1951: ii. 68–9). On the pantheism controversy in the 18th and 19th centuries, see Beiser (1987: 44–126); Williamson (1984: 231–49); Jaeschke (1990: 361–5); Breckman (1999: 23–7, 101–7, 177–220). Both Schelling and Hegel were accused of pantheism but denied the charge. See Schelling (2006: 11–28, 70–2), and Hegel (1988: 122–8). See also Hodgson (2005: 248–59), who argues that Hegel was a panentheist rather than a pantheist. Martensen recognized pantheism as a 'necessary moment' in the Godhead's historical process, and like Hegel he viewed God's absolute personality as being composed of both substance (in the creation) and subject (in the incarnation). See *SKP* xiii, II C 26–7, § 5; Martensen (1997: 97–8, 115–16, 129–31). Schleiermacher was also accused of pantheism, especially in *On Religion*, but he somewhat ambiguously denies the charge in *The Christian Faith* (1956: 38–9, 173–5, 192).

[19] On the apophatic, unknown, or hidden nature of God as transcendent, abysmal ground (*Afgrund*) in Kierkegaard's theology, see Kangas (2007: 6–11, 126); Law (1993: 162–81).

modern philosophy as expressed in the Platonic doctrine of recollection. To recap this doctrine briefly, all knowledge is recollection, which means that, by virtue of the pre-existence and immortality of the soul, human beings already possess all theoretical and moral knowledge and need only to recollect what has been temporarily forgotten at birth in order to regain a consciousness of the eternal truth within them. In *Philosophical Fragments* Climacus explicitly associates this doctrine with both ancient and modern speculation:

> ...this Greek idea is repeated in ancient and modern speculation: an eternal creating, an eternal emanating from the Father, an eternal becoming of the deity, an eternal self-sacrifice, a past resurrection, a judgment over and done with. All these ideas are that Greek idea of recollection, although this is not always noticed, because they have been arrived at by going further. (*PF* 10 n.)

And in the *Postscript* he explicitly identifies recollection with immanence and pantheism:

> The thesis that all knowing is recollecting belongs to speculative thought, and recollecting is immanence ... (*CUP* i. 206 n.; cf. also 148–9 and 205)

> ...the only consistency outside Christianity is that of pantheism, the taking of oneself out of existence back into the eternal through recollection, whereby all existence-decisions become only shadow play compared with what is eternally decided from behind.... The pantheist is eternally reassured backward; the moment that is the moment of existence in time, the seventy years, is something vanishing. (*CUP* i. 226–7)

While modern speculation purports to have gone further than Greek thought and thus does not explicitly subscribe to the doctrine of recollection in its Platonic formulation, the parallel Climacus sees between ancient and modern speculation is nevertheless apparent in the world-historical viewpoint of Hegelian speculation, which in Climacus's view is 'rooted precisely in immanence' (*CUP* i. 157; see also 148). In Climacus's view, the Hegelian world-historical perspective is an objective, backward-looking orientation in which the speculative thinker purports to know and comprehend eternal truth by becoming a systematic observer and interpreter of the past. Since world history is unfinished, however, Climacus contends that this perspective, like every historical perspective, is only an approximation that is incomplete and arbitrary in its judgements (149–50). Moreover, by focusing on world history so much, one may be tempted to seek world-historical importance for oneself rather than strive to become ethically developed to the utmost in inwardness (133–7). As Climacus sees it, in Hegelian philosophy the ethical is realized in the world-historical order rather than the individual, and God is seen as the moving spirit of the world-historical process rather than Lord over it (144, 156). In his judgement, therefore, the Hegelian world-historical viewpoint may be faulted on two grounds. (1) It completely skips the ethical in the individual and advances 'something world-historical' as the ethical task for individuals, thereby confusing the ethical with the world-historical. (2) In the Hegelian schema of world history God becomes 'metaphysically laced in a half-metaphysical, half-aesthetic-dramatic, conventional corset, which is immanence', leading Climacus to exclaim: 'What a devil of a thing to be God in that way' (144, 151, 156)! Not only is God's freedom constrained and done away with in immanence, God cannot be seen at all in the world-historical process, since the only way the deity can be seen there is in the role of Lord, which it does not play in immanence. In contrast to the Hegelian world-historical perspective, therefore, Climacus contends that, properly understood, 'God's freedom . . . will not in all eternity, neither before nor afterward, become immanence' (156–7).

With regard to the ethical, however, Climacus does not deny that it is present in world history, since it is present wherever God is, but he does deny that it *can be seen* there by a finite individual. 'Wanting to see it there,' he says, 'is a presumptuous and risky undertaking that can easily end with the observer's losing the ethical in himself', which is an original element in every human being and not something abstracted from world-historical experience (*CUP* i. 141). Only God, who is omniscient as well as omnipresent in world history, possesses eternal knowledge of the commensurability of the outer and the inner of the ethical in world history, for only God knows 'the innermost secret in the conscience of the greatest and of the lowest human being' (141). The human mind 'cannot see world history in this way', Climacus claims, and anyone who wants to try 'is a fool' (141).

To illustrate the difference between the ethical relation of the individual to God and the relation of the world-historical to God, Climacus employs the metaphor of a royal theatre in which God plays the role of a royal spectator of the drama played out in 'the little private theatre' of the individual's ethical development as well as the 'royal drama' performed on the stage of world history (*CUP* i. 157–8). Individuals are essentially actors and occasionally spectators like God in the private dramas of their own ethical development, but only God is a spectator in the drama of world history since 'admission to this theatre is not open to any existing spirit' (158). In other words, no human being can see and comprehend world history *sub specie aeterni* (under the aspect of the eternal). Climacus unmercifully ridicules 'the speculating, honorable Herr Professor', presumably Hegel, who wants to explain all of existence in a system that promises in the final paragraph to discover the ethical in the present generation of world history while absentmindedly forgetting that he is a human being whose ethical task is to understand himself in existence (145).[20]

Climacus's ridicule of the preoccupation with world history and its confusion with the ethical extends beyond Hegel and his speculative followers to include Grundtvig, who wrote several chronicles of world history before and after making 'the matchless discovery' that launched his long career as a religious leader in Denmark. What Climacus finds particularly ludicrous in Grundtvig's world-historical perspective is the idea that discovery of the ethical in world history requires 'a prophet with a world-historical eye on world history', which Climacus regards as 'a rare, ingeniously comic invention' that is doubly ludicrous inasmuch as it not only confuses the ethical with the world-historical but also requires a *seer* to discover the ethical, whereas in his view 'the ethical is an ancient discovery' that all human beings are capable of making and comprehending within themselves through a personal relation to God (*CUP* i. 144–5, 155).

THE INFINITE QUALITATIVE DIFFERENCE BETWEEN GOD AND HUMAN BEINGS

One reason Kierkegaard, via the persona of Johannes Climacus, so adamantly opposes the immanence or pantheism of ancient and modern speculation is that it does away with the infinite qualitative difference between God and human beings. As Kierkegaard sees it, the law governing the relation between God and human beings is that 'there is an infinite, radical, qualitative difference' between them (*JP* ii. 1383; translation modified; cf. *CD* 63). Consequently, when a human being wants to speak about God, it cannot be done on a comparative scale with the human because

> God and the human being resemble each other only inversely. You do not reach the possibility of comparison by the ladder of direct likeness: great, greater, greatest; it is possible only inversely. Neither does a human being come closer and closer to God by lifting up his head higher and higher, but inversely by casting himself down ever more deeply in worship. (*CD* 292)

In Kierkegaard's view, the obliteration of this difference in an attempt to affirm an essential continuity and unity of the human with the divine constitutes the 'fundamental derangement at the root of modern times' in all areas, including 'logic, metaphysics, dogmatics, and the whole of modern life', resulting in a 'depth of blasphemy' in theology unknown in ancient

[20] Cf. Hegel (1955: iii. 552–3).

paganism, the demise of ethics altogether, and a general insubordination and effrontery toward the divine (*JP* v. 6075).

Two explanations are given in Kierkegaard's authorship as to why this difference exists and must be acknowledged. The first has to do with our human finitude and its inherent limitations in the realm of existence *vis-à-vis* the infinity and eternity of God:

> But the absolute difference between God and a human being is simply this, that a human being is an individual existing being (and this holds for the best brain just as fully as for the most obtuse), whose essential task therefore cannot be to think *sub specie aeterni* (under the aspect of the eternal), because as long as he exists, he himself, although eternal, is essentially an existing person and the essential for him must therefore be inwardness in existence; God, however, is the infinite one, who is eternal. (*CUP* i. 217; cf. 412)

Here temporal existence itself is seen as the differentiating and limiting factor of a human being in relation to God. But Kierkegaard makes it clear in *The Book on Adler* that the difference between them is not merely temporal but eternal in nature:

> *But between God and a human being there is an eternal essential qualitative difference*, which only presumptuous thinking can make disappear in the blasphemy that in the transitory moment of finitude God and a human being are certainly differentiated, so that here in this life a human being ought to obey and worship God, but in eternity the difference will vanish in the essential likeness, so that God and human beings become peers in eternity, just as the king and the valet. (*BA* 181)

This difference is given expression even in paganism by Socrates, who in *The Sickness unto Death* is seen as guarding 'the frontier between God and a human being, keeping watch so that the deep gulf of qualitative difference between them was maintained, ... so that God and a human being did not merge in some way ... into one' (*SUD* 99, translation modified).

The second explanation confirms the first even more radically by predicating sin of a human being. As Kierkegaard's Christian pseudonym, Anti-Climacus, states it:

> The [Christian] teaching about sin—that you and I are sinners—a teaching that unconditionally splits up 'the crowd,' confirms the qualitative difference between God and a human being more radically than ever before ... In no way is a human being so different from God as in this, that he, and that means every human being, is a sinner, and is that 'before God' ... Sin is the one and only predication about a human being that in no way, either *via negationis* [by denial] or *via eminentiæ* [by affirmation], can be stated of God. (*SUD* 121–2, translation modified)

In Anti-Climacus's view, the Christian teaching on sin is also what most decisively distinguishes Christianity from paganism:

It is specifically the concept of sin, the teaching about sin, that most decisively differentiates Christianity qualitatively from paganism ... The qualitative distinction between paganism and Christianity is not, as a superficial consideration assumes, the doctrine of the Atonement. No, the beginning must start far deeper, with sin, with the doctrine of sin—as Christianity in fact does. (*SUD* 89)

In the next chapter I shall examine the Christian doctrine of original or hereditary sin and its psychological precondition and manifestation in anxiety and despair. Here sin will be considered only in terms of its role in positing an absolute difference between God and human beings. In *Philosophical Fragments* and the *Postscript* sin is seen as constituting a radical breach with the eternal in which the essential condition or potentiality for actualizing the eternal is lost in a human being as a result of the individual's own act (*PF* 14–15; *CUP* 1: 571, 583). Sin thus constitutes a 'new existence-medium' in which one becomes a different person or undergoes a qualitative change in one's essential self-identity in coming into existence:

'To exist' generally signifies only that by having come into existence the individual does exist and is becoming; now it signifies that by having come into existence he has become a sinner. ... By coming into existence the individual becomes another person, or in the instant he is to come into existence he becomes another person by coming into existence, because otherwise the category of sin is placed within immanence. (*CUP* i. 583)

Sin thus constitutes a break with immanence and the possibility of knowing the divine via thought or recollection. The eternal is no longer present *ubique et nusquam* (everywhere and nowhere) as believed in immanent religiosity but can only be encountered and regained via a relation in time to the eternal in time (Jesus Christ) as claimed in Christianity. Moreover, if God is absolutely different from a human being as a result of sin, there is 'no distinguishing mark' by which one can know this difference or the divine (*PF* 45). The human understanding cannot think what is absolutely different from itself: 'It cannot absolutely transcend itself and therefore thinks as above itself only the sublimity that it thinks by itself' (45). Consequently the understanding arbitrarily confuses the absolute difference with itself and the deity becomes a product of the individual's own imagination. As Climacus sees it, therefore, neither the god nor the absolute difference between the god and a human being, which is sin, can be thought or known by the human understanding by itself but must be revealed by the deity. For 'if a human being is to come truly to know something about the unknown (the god), he must first come to know that it is different from him, absolutely different from him', which the understanding is incapable of knowing and can only come to know from the god (46). Even if this difference is revealed by the god, however, the understanding still cannot understand or know the god as absolutely different from itself since it cannot understand the absolutely different. The understanding thus finds itself in the quandary of a paradox: 'Just to come to know that the god is the different, a human being needs the god and then comes to know that the god is absolutely different from him' (46, translation modified).

Sin thus introduces an epistemological gulf between the god and a human being that seemingly cannot be overcome. This gulf is not due to the metaphysical difference between the god and a human being noted earlier but is caused by human beings themselves (46–7). Thus the only way it can be overcome, Climacus proposes, is by *annulling the absolute difference in absolute equality* through the entry of the god in time in the form of an individual human being (47). As Climacus sees it, this event is motivated by God's love, not out of any divine need, and is the result of God's eternal resolve to bring about a relation of love and understanding between them:

> Out of love, therefore, the god must be eternally resolved in this way, but just as his love is the basis, so also must love be the goal, for it would indeed be a contradiction for the god to have a basis of movement and a goal that do not correspond to this. The love, then, must be for the learner, and the goal must be to win him, for only in love is the different made equal, and only in equality or in unity is there understanding. (*PF* 25)

GOD IS LOVE

With the theme of God's love we arrive at what for Kierkegaard is the main 'thesis of Christianity', namely that God is love (*JP* ii. 1446). As he sees it, love is not a predicate or attribute of God such as omnipresence or omnipotence but constitutes 'the only substantive' qualification or very essence of God (*JP* ii. 1319, 1446).[21] What does it mean, then, to say that God's essence is love? Perhaps the best explanation is given in a late journal entry in which Kierkegaard states: 'The law of loving is quite simple and familiar: to love is to be transformed into likeness to the beloved' (*JP* iii. 2450, 2438). This definition squares nicely with the thought experiment of *Philosophical Fragments*, where the eternal resolve of the god to establish an absolute likeness to human beings out of love is illustrated by a parable about a king who loved a maiden of lowly station (*PF* 26–35). The king decides that the only way truly to establish equality, unity, and understanding between them in a happy love relation is not by an *ascent*, that is, by drawing her up in adoration and glorification of himself, but by a *descent* of the king into likeness with her in the lowly form of a servant. Climacus

[21] Cf. Schleiermacher (1956: 730).

emphasizes, however, that with respect to the god 'this form of a servant is not something put on like the king's plebeian cloak' but is 'his true form', expressing 'the boundlessness of love' in willing to be the equal of the beloved (31–2). Climacus declares:

> For love, any other revelation would be a deception, because either it would first have had to accomplish a change in the learner (love, however, does not change the beloved but changes itself) and conceal from him that this was needed, or in superficiality it would have had to remain ignorant that the whole understanding between them was a delusion (this is the untruth of paganism). (*PF* 33)

But there is a twofoldness in the thesis that God is love inasmuch as God not only loves human beings but wants to be loved by them in return (*JP* ii. 1446; iii. 2448, 2452, 2453). Thus, in Kierkegaard's estimation it is 'pure nonsense' to suggest, as is commonly done in Christendom, that God is 'pure love' in the sense that the deity is transformed into likeness to humans without also seeking to transform them into likeness to him (*JP* iii. 2450). 'No, that God is love means, of course, that he will do everything to help you to love him, that is, to be transformed into likeness to him', he explains (2450). The inducement for this reciprocity of love is the forgiveness of sins, which is the starting point for Christianity and the transition to loving God and being remade into likeness to the divine. For Kierkegaard, then, 'To love God is to be a Christian' (*JP* iii. 2453). But learning to love God is not as simple or as easy as one might think, for according to Kierkegaard 'God must make you unhappy, humanly speaking, if he is to love you and you are to love him' (*JP* iii. 2450; cf. 2443, 2449). This is so, he suggests, because one cannot love God in addition to the world, for 'it is the greatest possible high treason to want to love God *also*, to enjoy life, be attached to the world, and *also* love God' (*JP* iii. 2437). On the contrary, 'to love God is possible only by clashing with all human existence (hating father and mother, hating oneself, suffering because one is a Christian, etc.)' (*JP* iii. 2453).

These statements, drawn from Kierkegaard's late journals, anticipate the terrible and inevitable clash between Christianity and culture that awaits the person who ventures to love God Christianly in contrast to the accommodation of Christendom to the worldliness and aestheticism that Kierkegaard sees all around him and protests so vehemently in his writings. The opposition of Christianity to worldliness and the inevitability of Christian suffering are constant themes in the second literature or later religious writings of Kierkegaard. But the other side of the coin is dialectically presented in these writings as well, namely that 'all things must serve us for good—when we love God' (*CD* 188–201). To get a balanced picture of what it means to say that God is love and to love God, therefore, we need to look at the positive side as well. Kierkegaard contends that the only way a person can truly love God is out of a *need* for God. Although it may seem high-minded to say that one loves the deity because 'God is the highest, the holiest, the most perfect being', and selfish to love God because one needs him, it is the latter condition of need that constitutes 'the fundamental and primary basis for a person's love of God' (188). Indeed, Kierkegaard says it would be presumptuous and fanatical to love God without needing him, for even in human love relations one does not normally love another person 'solely for the beloved's perfection' (188). Thus one must first humbly acknowledge one's need of God and then ask oneself whether one believes that God is love, for if one believes that God is love, then one also loves God and all things serve one for good (193).

The appropriate way to settle the question of whether God is love, then, is not by trying to demonstrate it in an impersonal, objective manner but by asking out of self-concern and with fear and trembling whether one personally believes that God is love, which in Kierkegaard's view is the main and decisive question as well as the 'best means' of allaying 'all doubt about the truth of the doctrine' (*CD* 189). If I believe that God is love, 'then everything else follows without any demonstration—from the demonstration nothing follows *for me*; from faith everything follows *for me*' (191; cf. *JP* iii. 3453). One may successfully demonstrate that God is love, but it does not follow from God's being love that one believes that God is love or that one loves him. This is so, Kierkegaard explains, because 'knowledge that God is love is still not a consciousness of it. Consciousness, personal consciousness, requires that in my knowledge I also have knowledge of myself and my relation to my knowledge. This is to believe, here to believe that God is love, and to believe that God is love is to love him' (194). When one is personally conscious that God is love and feels the need of him, then and only then does everything that normally counts as good fortune, such as riches, good health, mental gifts, honour, prestige, spouse, and children, serve one for good.

According to the inverse dialectic that governs Christian thought, in which everything is understood as the inverse or opposite of the natural, merely human, secular or worldly mentality, even if one meets what is generally regarded as bad fortune in life, it is still good fortune and can serve one for good—when one loves God. To illustrate this situation, Kierkegaard asks us to imagine an extraordinarily gifted thinker who has pondered the nature of God as love and written a scholarly book on the subject that is used by pastors to demonstrate this Christian truth (*CD* 197–8). Then some terrible misfortune happens that plunges the thinker into wretchedness and he begins to doubt that God is love. Finally, at his wit's end he goes to visit a pastor who does not know him personally in order to open himself and seek comfort. The pastor makes several unsuccessful attempts to convince the stranger that his misfortune is good fortune and for the best because God is love. Unknowingly and ironically, the pastor then recommends the thinker's own book as the only resource that may be of help to him. From this experience the thinker learns that even though his thoughts about God were undoubtedly true, 'until now he had lived under the delusion that when it had been demonstrated that God is love it followed as a matter of course that you and I believe it', and he learns to take a somewhat dimmer view of thought, especially 'pure thought', as the basis of faith (198). More importantly, his 'train of thought' becomes inverted, so that he no longer says, 'God is love; ergo all things serve for one's good', but says instead: '*When* I believe that God is love, then all things serve *me* for good' (199). Kierkegaard claims that when we come to love God, an eternal change takes place within us, but no one can tell whether or when that will happen. The voice of conscience, or what he calls 'the preacher of repentance' within us, can help to make us aware of God and keep us awake in incertitude in order to seek the certitude of faith, which only God can grant (194).

In another discourse Kierkegaard asserts: 'We are not, after all, required to be able to understand the rule of God's love, but we certainly are required to be able to believe and, believing, to understand that he is love' (*UDVS* 268). Thus, 'if the slightest thing happened that could demonstrate or could even merely appear to demonstrate that God was not love—well, then all would be lost, then God would be lost, for if God is not love, and if he is not love in everything, then God does not exist at all' (267). In the twentieth century, for many Jews and Christians the Holocaust was just the sort of event that called God's love into question. But to Kierkegaard this possibility is unbearable, 'inasmuch as no human being would be able to endure this horror' (270). Although he recognizes that many people live in such a way as to lose faith if something dreadful were to happen to them, in his view this way of living is 'indefensible' because it vitiates 'the highest passion in a semi-drowsiness between doubt and trust' and 'loses everything, loses that without which life really is nothing' (269). Not only do they suffer 'the shipwreck of eternity's joy of living', they suffer damage 'in the innermost joint in a human being' (269). Further connecting these two images, Kierkegaard states:

> Whether there are any spikes that in particular can be said to hold the ship's structure together, I do not know, but this I do know—that this faith is the divine joint in a human being and that if it holds it makes him the proudest sailing ship, but if it is loosened it makes a wreck of him and thereby makes the content of his whole life futility and miserable vanity. (*UDVS* 269)

Kierkegaard is confident and finds joy in the fact that 'it is eternally true that nothing has happened or ever can happen . . . that can rock the faith that God is love' (*UDVS* 268). We may be reassured of this fact by the consciousness of guilt, namely that 'in relation to God a person always suffers as guilty', for unless one can claim to be innocent before God, *which no human being can possibly do*, doubt has no basis on which to accuse God (265, 273–4). Before God we are not merely guilty in this or that but 'essentially and unconditionally guilty' as a result of sin (285).[22] Kierkegaard further points out:

> If in relation to God a sufferer could be in the right, if it were possible that the fault is with God, well, then there would be hopelessness and the horror of hopelessness, then there would be no task. The tasks of faith and hope and love and patience and humility and obedience—in short, all the human tasks, are based on the eternal certainty in which they have a place of resort and support, the certainty that God is love. If it had ever happened to a human being in relation to God that the fault lay with God, there would be no task; if this ever had happened to a single human being, there would be no tasks for the entire human race. It would not be only in this particular case that there is no task; no, if God just one single time had demonstrated that he was not love in the smallest or the greatest, had left the sufferer without a task—then for all humankind there is no longer any task, then it is foolishness and futility and soul-deadening pernicious laboriousness to believe, a self-contradiction to work, and an agony to live. Life issues from the heart, and if a person's heart suffers damage, then by his own fault there is no longer any task for him except the sedulous toil of sin and emptiness; but from the heart of God issues the life in everything, the life in the tasks. If it is so that the creature must die if God withdraws his breath, then it is also true that if God for one single moment has denied his love, then all tasks are dead and reduced to nothing, and hopelessness is the only thing there is. (*UDVS* 277)

This is a powerful statement on existential grounds, not rational ones, for believing that God is love. But the consciousness of guilt also makes it 'eternally certain that God is love', because the consciousness of guilt makes it 'impossible to begin to doubt that God is love' (*UDVS* 279–80, 282–3). This does not mean that Jews and others who were slaughtered in the Holocaust, for example, deserved death or were being punished because they were guilty before God. Kierkegaard's conviction that God is love utterly rules out that possibility. Moreover, he makes a clear distinction between *being in the wrong* and *suffering as guilty* and between innocent and guilty suffering *in relation to other people* and *in relation to God* (283). When a person is guilty, that person suffers as guilty in relation to both God and other people, but when a person is in the right, humanly speaking, and

[22] On essential guilt, see also Kangas (2005) and Law (2005).

suffers innocently at the hands of other people, as in the case of the Jews *vis-à-vis* the Nazis, that person still stands in the wrong before God—not for something in particular he/she has done but because 'in relation to God a human being always suffers as guilty' (283). Kierkegaard clearly rejects the notion that God is 'a cruel tyrant' who punishes people for particular sins (286–7). From his perspective, therefore, the genocide of the Holocaust could only be attributed to the unmitigated evil perpetrated by the Nazis, not to God, who out of love grants human freedom and thus the possibility of evil as well as good in the world.

By presupposing that a person is essentially guilty before God, Kierkegaard also subverts all attempts to construct a theodicy or rational justification to vindicate God for what appears to be innocent suffering in the world, thereby overcoming doubt through thought.[23] The way to overcome doubt, as he sees it, is not by presumptuously 'thinking through doubt' to a higher understanding but 'to believe without being able to understand' (*UDVS* 273–4; cf. 279). In taking this approach to the problem of doubt, Kierkegaard rejects the guiding principle of medieval theology, *credo ut intelligam* (I believe in order to understand), as well as the starting point of modern philosophy and speculative theology, inasmuch as modern philosophy begins with doubt in order to get beyond it to knowledge, and speculative theology, particularly that of Martensen, seeks to 'go further' to a higher understanding of the divine through mediation.

GOD'S CREATIVE OMNIPOTENCE, GOODNESS, AND MAJESTY

Just as God is the Omnipresent One for Kierkegaard, he is also the Omnipotent One whose omnipotence is identical to his goodness and whose absolute majesty is infinite and sublime and therefore incomprehensible as well as qualitatively different from the human. But as Kierkegaard sees them, God's omnipotence, goodness, and majesty are inseparable from God's essence as love and his work as creator (*EUD* 32–48, 141–58, 233–51).[24] In a journal entry from 1851 Kierkegaard writes: 'God's majesty seems to be forgotten; therefore, instead of the customary expositions on God's qualities, I could be tempted to concentrate on God's majesty, in order that there might be proper appreciation of—love' (*JP* iii. 2557; cf. ii. 1432, 1449; iii. 2558, 2559). Similarly, with respect to the omnipotence of God, he observes: 'Everyone who assumes that there is a God of course

[23] On Kierkegaard's critique of theodicy see also Kangas (2005: 306–12), and Law (2005: 345–8).

[24] See also Lindström (1982).

considers him the strongest, as he indeed eternally is—he, the Omnipotent One, who creates out of nothing, and to whom all creation is as nothing—but presumably he scarcely thinks of the possibility of a reciprocal relationship' (*CD* 127). Affirming the traditional Christian doctrine of creation *ex nihilo*, Kierkegaard sees God's omnipotence as being manifested first of all in the creation of the world out of nothing. But that which is 'as nothing' to the Omnipotent One is lovingly called to become 'something' in a reciprocal relation to God through the power (*Magt*) or omnipotence (*Almagt*) of divine love, which for Kierkegaard is even more incomprehensible than the omnipotence that creates out of nothing (128). The omnipotence of God is thus understood as operating in concert with God's love, which through its own omnipotent power makes possible a purpose and reciprocal relation to the divine which a human being otherwise would not have: 'omnipotence made him come into existence, but love made him come into existence *for* God' (128). But unlike God's primal omnipotence, which requires nothing of a human being because a human being is nothing before it, God's omnipotent love also requires something of a human being; otherwise there would be no reciprocity between them. This is the inverse of the common understanding of the relation of omnipotence and love to requirements, as omnipotence is generally associated with imposing rigorous requirements and love with being lenient. But as Kierkegaard sees it, the existence of God's infinite love must be presupposed 'in order for a person to exist in such a way for God that there can be any question of requiring anything of him' (128).

What God in his infinite love, omnipotence, goodness, and divine majesty as creator requires of a human being is obedience—unconditional obedience (*JP* ii. 1345, 1436; *EUD* 98–9; *WA* 23–35; *UDVS* 256–63). Humorously and ironically, the 'divinely appointed teachers' and models of unconditional obedience for human beings, according to Kierkegaard, are none other than the lilies of the field and the birds of the air (cf. Matthew 6: 24–34), which like everything in nature are totally subject to God's will and entirely dependent on his sustaining care (*WA* 25–31; *UDVS* 155–212; *CD* 3–91). But obedience, if it is to be true obedience rather than submission to a blind necessity, must be grounded in freedom (*UDVS* 205). The greatest good that can be done for a being, Kierkegaard contends, is to make it free (*JP* ii. 1251; cf. *WL* 276–8). For that to happen, however, omnipotence is required. This seems strange and contrary to the common conception of omnipotence, which seeks to make the other dependent rather than independent through the exercise of power. But as Kierkegaard sees it, 'Only a wretched and mundane conception of the dialectic of power holds that it is greater and greater in proportion to its ability to compel and to make dependent' (*JP* ii. 1251). Unlike all finite power, God's omnipotence has 'the unique qualification of being able to withdraw itself', thereby allowing a human being to be independent. This no finite power can do, because it remains 'ensconced in a relationship to an other' that keeps the other from being wholly free (1251). Kierkegaard further points out that there is an element of 'finite self-love in all finite power', whereas God's omnipotence gives itself away completely (1251). In this instance, however, God's self-giving is identified not with God's love, as one might expect, but with God's goodness, which Kierkegaard defines as 'to give oneself away completely, but in such a way that by omnipotently taking oneself back one makes the recipient independent' (1251). God's omnipotence, then, is the same as God's goodness, which is the same as God's love.

Kierkegaard's theology of creation is thus intimately bound up with his understanding of the omnipotence, goodness, and love of God, from whom every good and perfect gift comes (cf. James 1:17–22; *EUD* 32–48, 133–9, 141–58). Besides being favoured with the gift of independence, human beings have the added distinction of being created in the image of God, thus sharing in the invisible glory of God as spirit (*UDVS* 181–2, 192–3). Unlike nature, which lives entirely in the moment and lacks the eternal, human beings possess a consciousness of the eternal and have the task of becoming the lofty creatures they are intended to be, namely single individuals or separate and distinct entities rather than generic animals or mere numbers in a crowd (*UDVS* 189–90; *EUD* 88). As Kierkegaard sees it, the meaning of creation is not completed until individuality is given, which is 'the true period' or end of creation (*JP* ii. 1981). As 'creation's wonderwork', human beings are divinely destined to be God's co-workers by ruling over nature, which in its beauty and ingenious formation honours, bears witness to, and reminds us of God but does not resemble him (*EUD* 84, 86–7, 333; *UDVS* 165, 189, 192, 199). But human beings are rulers over nature and resemble God only insofar as they are obedient to God and submit to being his humble servant, prostrating themselves in adoration and worship (*EUD* 84–7; *UDVS* 193). For Kierkegaard, to worship God is precisely what it means to resemble God, inasmuch as 'to be able truly to worship is the excellence of the invisible glory above all creation' (*UDVS* 193). In his estimation,

> The human being and God do not resemble each other directly but inversely; only when God has infinitely become the eternal and omnipotent object of worship and the human being always a worshipper, only then do they resemble each other. If human beings want to resemble God by ruling, they have forgotten God; then God has departed and they are playing the rulers in God's absence. (*UDVS* 193)

Another aspect of God's love, goodness, and infinite majesty that confounds the human understanding is the belief that suffering comes from God (*JP* ii. 1443, 1447; iii. 2558, 2560). In Kierkegaard's view, the idea that suffering is incompatible with the Christian belief that God is love and that only the good comes from God has led many Christians, especially in Protestantism and Luther in particular, to attribute suffering to the devil (*JP* ii. 1447, 1449). As Kierkegaard sees it, however, this idea is not truly Christian because it posits a majesty over against God and degrades the divine majesty by making it unable to avert suffering caused by a foreign power (1447). God's way of punishing the ungodly in the world is not by bringing sufferings upon them but by *ignoring* them as if they were non-existent, which in Kierkegaard's view is precisely God's 'truly majestic punishment upon Christendom' (*JP* ii. 1440; iii. 2560, 2563, 3644, 3648). God brings sufferings only upon those he loves and who love him in return so that they may be called through sufferings to become heterogeneous to the world, which is 'immersed in evil' (*JP* iii. 2560). Suffering, then, is a sign that one is being educated for eternity by being 'weaned' from the world:

> Alas, it is certainly true that through sufferings a person comes to know a great deal about the world, how deceitful and treacherous it is, and much else like that, but all this knowledge is not the schooling of sufferings. No, just as we speak of a child's having to be weaned when it no longer is allowed to be as one with the mother, so also in the most profound sense a person must be weaned by sufferings, weaned from the world and the things of this world, from loving it and from being embittered by it, in order to learn for eternity. (*UDVS* 257)

As *human beings* we are created in the image of God but as *Christians* we have God for our prototype in Christ, who is the fulfilment of creation (CD 41–2; *UDVS* 231; *JP* ii. 1391). Just as Christ learnt obedience from his sufferings, what we learn for eternity in the school of sufferings is obedience, 'to let God be master, to let God rule', which for Kierkegaard constitutes the sum and substance of all eternal truth and knowledge of God: 'Everything that a human being knows about the eternal is contained primarily in this: it is God who rules, because whatever more a person comes to know pertains to *how* God has ruled or rules or will rule' (*UDVS* 250–8, 263). As finite beings created with independence, human beings are therefore faced with a choice, an either/or: either to love God or to hate him, for they cannot serve two masters, both God and the world, good and evil (*UDVS* 201–12; *WA* 21–35; *JP* i. 952). In actuality, however, there is really only one choice, which is God, since to choose the other is perdition.

To Kierkegaard it is clear what the choice is, *en masse*, in Christendom (*JP* iv. 4911). His late journals abound with charges that God's majesty has been belittled, degraded, and obliterated, that it has been 'fantastically infinitized' in such a way as to get God 'smuggled out of everything to some point infinitely distant from actuality' and thus to get rid of him (*JP* iii. 2561; cf. *JP* ii. 1436, 1449; iii. 2562, 2570, 2571, 2576; iv. 4917). Perhaps the most damning charge of all is that, by downgrading God's majesty to being merely the superlative of human majesty, 'as if God were some human Majesty who aspires to extend himself and become the mightiest', Christendom has served Christianity as if it were *politics* (*JP* iii. 2571). As Kierkegaard sees it, God's majesty is 'anything but domineering or aristocratic' in a human sense (*JP* ii. 1432; cf. iii. 2574). God has no cause in the sense of 'aspiring to expand his power', which is already infinite and thus cannot be expanded; rather, God desires to be worshipped, which is not done by building beautiful churches and filling them with thousands of so-called Christians who seek to avoid suffering, but by adoring God in such a way as to 'look only to him and find it blessed to suffer' (*JP* iii. 2571, 2562). Kierkegaard's indictment of Christendom on this score is directed especially against the clergy, for whom, in his view, God has 'no use at all' because they are self-serving (*JP* iii. 2571). We shall have occasion to return to the relation of Christianity to politics in a later chapter, where Kierkegaard's indictment of Christendom will be spelt out more fully. Suffice it to point out here that, in Kierkegaard's estimation, 'all the confusion in Christendom centers in our having lost a conception of God's majesty, what majesty of spirit is' (*JP* iii. 2570).

'GOD IS THAT EVERYTHING IS POSSIBLE'

For Kierkegaard the majesty of God is perhaps best expressed in the biblical claim that for God everything is possible. In answer to the question in Matthew 19: 26 concerning who can be saved, Jesus responds: 'For men this is impossible; but everything is possible for God.' The belief that everything is possible for God is a central theological tenet for Kierkegaard and 'in the deepest sense' the watchword of his life and thought (*JP* v. 6535). It underlies his view of the incarnation, which is impossible from a human standpoint, and constitutes the very substance of his concept of faith. In line with the New Testament, Kierkegaard's Christian pseudonym Anti-Climacus declares that 'possibility is the only salvation' and explicitly equates believing in possibility with faith or the belief that for God everything is possible (*SUD* 38–9). But Anti-Climacus goes beyond the biblical assertion that all things are possible for God to define the deity itself as identical to possibility: 'since everything is possible for God, then God is this—that everything is possible' (*som nemlig for Gud Alt er muligt, saa er Gud det, at Alt er muligt*) (40; *SV1* xi. 153).[25] An older English translation by Walter Lowrie construes this statement in the following manner: 'Inasmuch as for God all things

[25] See also Theunissen (2005: 81–6); Come (1997: 227, 256–7).

are possible, it may be said that this is what God is, viz. one for whom all things are possible.'[26] The latter translation is less literal and wordier than the Hong version but may be closer to the meaning intended by the pseudonym. Yet Anti-Climacus goes on to reiterate: 'the being of God means that everything is possible, or that everything is possible means the being of God' (*thi Gud er det at Alt er muligt, eller at Alt er muligt, er Gud*) (40). This time the statement in question is rendered more literally by Lowrie as 'for God is that all things are possible, and that all things are possible is God'.[27] This could be taken to mean that God is ontologically equivalent to infinite possibility itself and not simply a being for whom everything is possible, which opens up the possibility of an intriguingly different way of understanding the divine in Kierkegaard's authorship. Since this is the only place in his writings that such a claim is made, however, there is no way to resolve the matter by comparison to other statements. But for that reason as well, one should perhaps not make too much of the claim in a metaphysical sense. In his journals Kierkegaard refers to God as having '100,000 possibilities at every moment' and 'possibilities to burn', which does not suggest an equation of God with possibility but only that God is the source or ground of possibility in the world (*JP* ii. 1382, iii. 3344). As the infinite ground of possibility, God transcends all human conceptions of what is possible based on experience, reason, and imagination. Kierkegaard thus suggests that instead of saying 'there is no possibility', one should say '*I* see no possibility' (*JP* iii. 3344). Similarly, in another journal passage he states: 'Just because I see no way out, I must never have the audacity to say that therefore there is none for God. For it is despair and blasphemy to confuse one's own little crumb of imagination and the like with the possibilities God has at his disposal' (*JP* v. 6135).

The fact that everything is possible *for God*, however, does not mean that everything is possible *for us* in the sense that we can be or do anything we wish. There is much that is not possible for human beings, and the recognition of one's given nature, social context, and limitations as a finite human being is requisite, along with possibility, for becoming oneself in likeness to God. Kierkegaard was highly critical of the German romantic poets in particular for promulgating the notion that everything is possible for a human being by virtue of the absolute freedom of the creative imagination, through which one is able not only to experiment poetically with a multiplicity of possibilities in the production of works of art but also 'to live poetically' by creating or making oneself a work of art (*CI* 272–323).[28] From a Christian standpoint, as Kierkegaard sees it, the human task is not to create oneself but to develop one's God-given potentialities in cooperation

[26] Kierkegaard (1968: 173). [27] Ibid. 173–4. [28] See Walsh (1994: 43–62).

with the divine so as to be 'poetically composed' by God rather than 'to compose oneself poetically' (280). God may also be likened to a poet in that 'poetically he permits everything possible to come forth' and puts up with all manner of evil, nonsense, wretchedness, mediocrity, etc. in the world (*JP* ii. 1445). But just as a poet should not be confused with the thoughts and actions of the characters in his or her poetic productions, one should not assume 'that God consents to all that happens and how' (1445). As a poet, then, God is the source of all possibility in the world, but not everything that happens accords with the divine will.

GOD'S PROVIDENCE, GOVERNANCE, AND CHANGELESSNESS

In associating God with possibility, Kierkegaard rejects determinism or fatalism, which according to Anti-Climacus either has no God or else identifies God with necessity (*SUD* 40). But Kierkegaard does believe in God's providence (*Forsyn*) and governance (*Styrelse*), which are synonymous terms for the special care (*providentia specialissima*) and guidance given to those individuals who are willing to venture a relation to God and are led further and further into suffering as a result (*PC* 190–1; *JP* iii. 3631, 3632). Kierkegaard was especially conscious of divine guidance or 'Governance' in his own life, viewing it as continually playing a major role in his work as an author and personal upbringing (*PV* 71–90). Oddly enough, however, while there are many references to these concepts, especially governance, in his journals, one finds little mention and even less sustained discussion of them in his published works. In *Practice in Christianity* governance is identified with God's love, which 'however tight it will turn the screws' on a person is never cruel and 'never tries a person beyond his ability' (*PC* 190).

Governance helps one to understand that suffering cannot be avoided in this life, that it will even increase as one goes forward, and that this is precisely what it means to exist as a human being in the world: 'to live under or to endure life under this pressure is what we call with emphasis to exist as a human being' (191). Suffering is further intensified in Christianity as a result of 'the Christian's having to live in this world and having to express in the environment of this world what it is to be a Christian' (196). Thus governance not only helps one to understand the unavoidability of suffering as a human being and Christian in the world but also to persevere in it by trusting in God's love.

Like every concept associated with the divine, however, God's providence and governance are frequently misunderstood and inverted in

Christendom, which typically associates them with rewarding good and punishing evil in the world. Piety is thus seen as being rewarded with good fortune, and the fortunate are given an excuse for ignoring those who suffer by advising them to 'turn to providence', which has the 'tranquilizing effect' of letting the fortunate off the hook and enabling them 'to enjoy life lavishly' (*JP* iii. 3632). Further justification for not helping those who suffer is provided by the explanation that suffering is self-inflicted and a punishment from God, whose 'purposes of providence for every individual' are not to be disturbed (3632). Of this self-serving affirmation of God's providence, Kierkegaard observes: 'But here as everywhere we treat Christianity as arbitrarily as possible. We human beings select what seems able to suit our self-indulgence and throw away what does not please us—and thus we cook up a rascally religiosity which is supposed to be Christianity' (3632, translation modified).

As early as 1834 it seemed to Kierkegaard that the equivalent of a 'Copernican Revolution' occurred when dogmatic theology discovered that 'God is not the one who changes . . . but that a human being changes his position in relationship to God' (*JP* ii. 1303, translation modified). The changelessness or immutability of God was 'a central thesis' of the rationalist theologians of Kierkegaard's time (*JP* ii. 1304). While wholeheartedly agreeing with this thesis, Kierkegaard was unhappy with the way it was understood by the rationalists, as it seemed to him that in their view the appearance of Christ was only a declaration of God's eternal changelessness, which made it possible to grasp the idea of God's changelessness philosophically without naming Christ. In a journal entry from 1846 he further objects to the abstract manner in which the changelessness of God is reflected upon by thinkers in his day, charging that 'by thinking abstractly about God's abstract unchangeableness a person wants to transform himself', that is, 'to make himself just as *unchanged* as God is unchangeable' (*JP* ii. 1348). As Kierkegaard sees it, this is contrary to the doctrine of the atonement, which 'teaches that God has remained unchanged while human beings changed, or it *proclaims* to human beings-altered-in-sin that God has remained unchanged' (1348, translation modified). Moreover, by focusing abstractly on God's changelessness, the whole deliberation is transformed into 'a phantom-battle about the predicates of God' instead of enquiring whether a change 'from what he eternally must be assumed to be' has occurred in the thinker's own being (1348). If such a change has occurred, then in Kierkegaard's view 'the proclamation of God's changelessness' is urgently needed in order for reconciliation to occur (1348). But if God's changelessness is 'an abstract something', reconciliation is impossible, as that requires a personal relation between two parties, whereas one has only an impersonal relation to an abstract being (1348).

This personal or subjective approach to God's changelessness is already apparent in Kierkegaard's early upbuilding discourses, where he states that 'this changelessness is not that chilling indifference, that devastating loftiness, that ambiguous distance, which the callous understanding lauded. No, on the contrary, this changelessness is intimate and warm and everywhere present; it is a changelessness in being concerned for a person' (*EUD* 393). This warm and intimate understanding of God's changelessness is especially evident in the only work penned by Kierkegaard that is specifically devoted to this topic, *The Changelessness of God*, a discourse delivered at the Citadel Church in 1851 and published in 1855 shortly before his death (*TM* 263–81). The biblical text on which this discourse is based is James 1: 17–21, described by Kierkegaard as 'my first, my favorite, text' inasmuch as it was the text for several upbuilding discourses published in 1843 (*JP* vi. 6769; *EUD* 32–48, 125–58). The first sentence of this text provides the biblical basis for the Christian claim of God's changelessness: 'Every good gift and every perfect gift is from above and comes down from the Father of lights, with whom there is no change or shadow of variation.' In the opening prayer of the discourse Kierkegaard subtly contrasts the changelessness of God in love, who is moved by everything but changed by nothing, to the unmoved mover of Aristotle which causes motion in the universe by being the object of desire or love but is not itself love or loving.[29] Like Aristotle, Kierkegaard associates the temporal realm with changeableness, and he particularly contrasts the changeableness of human beings to the changelessness of God. Because we lack the pure clarity or transparency of the divine, which has no darkness in it, we are changeable or variable, as things are sometimes clearer, other times darker to us, with the result that we are changed within ourselves as we respond to changes taking place in the world around us (*TM* 272).

The thought of God's changelessness is thus cause not only for 'sheer fear and trembling' as to whether we are in conflict with his changeless will but also for 'sheer consolation' in that rest from our weary changeableness is to be found in it (*TM* 272, 276, 278). When falsehood, violence, and wrong are victorious in the world, it may seem that God is not noticing or has changed, but Kierkegaard sees this divine inaction in a different light as further certainty of God's eternal changelessness in that God takes his time in order to give us time to turn around and reform, since in the accounting of eternity nothing is forgotten (273–4). Kierkegaard thus reminds the reader: 'If, then, your will is not in accord with his, consider this: you will

[29] Cf. Aristotle (1984: ii. 1694–5, 12. 7). See also Tornøe (2006), who contrasts Kierkegaard and Schleiermacher to Plato's view of the immutability of God and to the German idealists, especially Hegel, who ascribed change or becoming to God.

never escape him' (276). But the reader is also reminded that: 'When you allow yourself to be brought up by his changelessness so that you renounce instability and changefulness and caprice and willfulness—then you rest ever more blessedly in this changelessness of God' (278). Likening God's unchanging love to the delicious coolness of a desert spring, Kierkegaard ends the discourse and his authorship with a prayer to God that offers the following words of consolation: 'And whenever a person comes to you, at whatever age, at whatever time of day, in whatever condition—if he comes honestly, he will always find (like the spring's unchanged coolness) your love just as warm, you Changeless One! Amen' (280–1).

4

Our Human Condition: Anxiety, Sin, Despair, and Becoming a Self before God

In his journals of 1842 Kierkegaard writes: 'The nature of original sin has often been explained, and still a primary category has been lacking—it is anxiety (*Angst*); this is the essential determinant' (*JP* i. 94). The analysis of anxiety as the psychological precondition of original or hereditary sin (*Arvesynd*)[1] in *The Concept of Anxiety* (1844) is one of Kierkegaard's most original and most notable contributions to Christian thought.[2] It has also played a groundbreaking role in the development of existentialist philosophy, literature, and psychology.[3] Equally as profound, if not more so, in its psychological insight into the nature of sin is his analysis of despair in *The Sickness unto Death* (1849) as constituting a universal sickness of the human self in relation to itself and to God. In this chapter I shall focus on the twin psychological concepts of anxiety and despair and the ways these phenomena are probed by their pseudonymous 'authors' to illumine the psychological depths of the Christian doctrine of sin and the notion of authentic human selfhood in Kierkegaard's theological anthropology.[4]

THINKING PSYCHOLOGICALLY ABOUT HEREDITARY SIN

The subtitle of *The Concept of Anxiety*, a work attributed to the pseudonym Vigilius Haufniensis (the Watchman of Copenhagen), describes this book

[1] Usually translated as 'original sin', this term literally means 'hereditary sin', which is the translation used in the current English edn. of *The Concept of Anxiety*, following Luther's *The Smalcald Articles*, where 'hereditary sin' (*peccatum haereditarium*) is used. See Luther (1989: 516).

[2] See e.g. Tillich (1951–63: ii. 19–59); Niebuhr (1951: 178–264); Brunner (1939: 140–67).

[3] Existentialists influenced by Kierkegaard include theistic thinkers such as Gabriel Marcel, Miguel Unamuno, Karl Jaspers, and Lev Shestov, and non-theists such as Franz Kafka, Jean-Paul Sartre, Simone de Beauvoir, and Martin Heidegger. On Heidegger's indebtedness to Kierkegaard, see Magurshak (1985, 1987). On Kierkegaard and Unamuno, see J. Evans (2005). On Kierkegaard's contribution to existential psychology, see May (1977).

[4] See also Cappelørn *et al.* (2001); Marino (1998); Beabout (1996); Perkins (1985); Nordentoft (1978).

as 'a simple psychologically orienting deliberation on the dogmatic issue of hereditary sin' (*CA* p. iii). The reader is thus immediately alerted to the fact that this is not a theological treatise but a psychological treatment of the concept of anxiety which 'constantly keeps *in mente* [in mind] and before its eye the dogma of hereditary sin' (14). As Vigilius sees it, sin is not a subject that falls under the domain of any 'science' (broadly understood in the nineteenth century as including all scholarly disciplines), whose aim is to provide a rational explanation of its subject matter. Rather, sin is properly a subject for the sermon or 'art' of preaching, which has as its aim individual appropriation in an existential overcoming of sin (16). In other words, sin is an actuality that should be dealt with in a personal or existential manner, not in a scholarly context, which alters the true concept of sin by subjecting it to 'the nonessential refraction of reflection', thereby transforming it into a state that is annulled *(ophævet)* by thought rather than overcome (*overvundet*) in actuality in the life of the individual (15; *SV1* iv. 287).

It might seem that ethics is an appropriate scholarly discipline for the treatment of sin since it is oriented towards actuality in seeking to bring ideality into existence and assumes that human beings possess the requisite condition for actualizing the moral ideal, in other words, that 'ought implies can'.[5] But as Vigilius sees it, ethics becomes 'shipwrecked' on the actuality of sin, which shows itself to be not merely accidental to human existence but deeply embedded as 'a presupposition that goes beyond the individual' to include the whole human race (*CA* 17, 19). Thus ethics cannot explain sin, least of all original or hereditary sin, which lies entirely beyond its reach. In arriving at this conclusion, Vigilius thus agrees with Kant, who was forced to admit that the propensity to evil in human beings 'remains inexplicable' even though he strove mightily to account for it in his treatment of evil and original sin.[6]

Like ethics, dogmatics or systematic theology is also oriented towards actuality, but in the opposite direction, inasmuch as it 'begins with the actual in order to raise it up into ideality' (*CA* 19). Dogmatics thus presupposes the actuality of sin and explains it indirectly by presupposing hereditary sin as the ideal or conceptual possibility of sin (19, 23). Vigilius expressly praises Schleiermacher's 'immortal service' to dogmatics in this regard, describing him as 'a thinker in the beautiful Greek sense, a thinker who spoke only of what he knew', in contrast to Hegel, who 'must explain all things' (20). Over against classical metaphysics or 'first philosophy' (Aristotle), whose essence, like Hegelian philosophy and theology, is immanence or the recollection of eternal truth through reason,

[5] Kant (1998: 66). [6] Ibid. 64.

dogmatics represents the beginning of a 'new science' or 'second philosophy' (Christian theology) whose essence is transcendence or repetition, the recovery of existential truth through a relation to the eternal in time, which according to another Kierkegaardian pseudonym, Constantin Constantius, is the '*conditio sine qua non* [the indispensable condition] for every issue of dogmatics' (*R* 149). Along with dogmatics a 'new ethics' (Christian ethics) also comes into existence, an ethics that does not ignore sin or make ideal demands like the 'first ethics' but explains sin indirectly through hereditary sin while projecting the ethical ideal as a task to be achieved through a 'penetrating consciousness' of the actuality of sin in the single individual (*CA* 20). Although dogmatics and second ethics have the merit of presupposing the actuality of sin and taking it seriously, Vigilius nevertheless continues to claim that 'the concept of sin does not properly belong in any science', including second ethics, which deals only with the manifestation of sin, not with the coming into existence of sin, which remains inexplicable (21).

As a scholarly discipline, psychology is no more capable of explaining *why* sin comes into existence than any other science, but as a discipline whose subject is the human psyche, it has an interest in explaining the *possibility of sin* or the question of *how* sin comes into existence (*CA* 21–2). The kind of psychology Vigilius has in mind, however, is not *empirical psychology* as that discipline is generally understood and practised today but *rational psychology*, which in his view 'has nothing to do with the detail of the empirically actual', especially the actuality of sin, which is not an object for thought (22–3). Vigilius thus conceives psychology as it was understood and classified in Hegel's philosophy of mind, namely as a science of subjective spirit (together with anthropology and phenomenology) whose aim is to give a rational explanation of the theoretical and practical, mental and physical aspects of the human psyche.[7] As Vigilius sees it, psychology works in concert with dogmatics, explaining the real or actual possibility of sin so that dogmatics can begin its job of explaining the ideal or conceptual possibility of sin through the concept of hereditary sin (23). Towards that end, he begins with a discussion of some 'historical intimations' or implications of the doctrine of hereditary sin that developed in the Christian tradition, a brief overview of which will help to situate his remarks in historical context (25).

[7] See Hegel (2007: §§387–482, pp. 25–215). See also Schulz (2007*b*), Poole (2001), and Nordentoft (1978: 21), on similarities between Vigilius's book and a Hegelian psychology textbook by Karl Rosenkranz.

The Christian Doctrine of Hereditary Sin

The Christian doctrine of original or hereditary sin is based on the biblical story of the Fall of Adam and Eve in Genesis 3 and on the testimony of the Apostle Paul in Romans 5: 12: 'Therefore, just as sin came into the world through one man, and death came through sin, and so death spread to all because all have sinned'.[8] The term 'original sin' does not occur in the Bible, but in the second century of the Christian era the Greek church father Irenaeus (*c.*130–200) worked out a theory of original sin for the Eastern Church emphasizing the solidarity of the human race with Adam.[9] The Latin church father Tertullian (*c.*160–225) introduced the concept of inherited sin in the Western Church with the notion of a 'vice of origin' (*vitium originis*) or corruption of nature transmitted from generation to generation by procreation.[10] Tertullian's concept of hereditary sin was refined by later fathers of the Western Church and given consummate expression by St Augustine (354–430), whose formulation was strongly opposed by the British monk Pelagius (*c.*354–418). In contrast to the Augustinian view of Adam's original or first sin (*peccatum originans*) in the Fall as the cause of inherited sin (*peccatum originatum*) in later generations, Pelagius emphasized the natural ability and freedom of individuals to choose the good and denied the Augustinian doctrine of sin, for which he and his followers were condemned as heretics by the church councils of the time.[11] The Augustinian doctrine of original sin was modified in the Middle Ages by Anselm, Aquinas, and other scholastic theologians in such a way as to make original sin consist in the loss of an original righteousness granted to humans by supernatural grace (*donum supernaturalis*), leaving a human being's natural spiritual capacities weakened but still operative after the Fall.[12] In contrast to this interpretation, Reformation theologians such as Luther and Calvin advocated an intensified version of the Augustinian formulation affirming the deep corruption of all faculties in a person, including reason and the will, as a result of original sin.[13] Luther's views were adopted in the Augsburg Confession of 1530 and Smalcald Articles of 1537 as part of the official doctrine of the Evangelical-Lutheran Church. Theological differences between the Lutheran and Reformed (Calvinistic)

8 *The New Oxford Annotated Bible* (2001).
9 Thulstrup (1980*a*: 136); Tennant (1946: 288–91); Kelly (1968: 170–4).
10 Tennant (1946: 328, 333–5); Kelly (1968: 174–7).
11 Harrison (2000: 101–14).
12 N. Thulstrup (1980*a*: 140).
13 Ibid. 141–2. See also Barrett (1985).

churches and within Lutheranism itself were later addressed in the Formula of Concord of 1577.[14]

While Vigilius does not reject the orthodox doctrine of hereditary sin in the wholesale fashion some commentators have attributed to him,[15] he does regard the interpretations that evolved in the Catholic and Protestant traditions as being confused and problematic in certain respects. The first problem has to do with the relation of Adam's first sin to hereditary sin, namely whether the two are identical or not. Vigilius poses the question this way: 'Does the concept of hereditary sin differ from the concept of the first sin in such a way that the particular individual participates in inherited sin only through his relation to Adam and not through his primitive relation to sin' (*CA* 26)? If Adam's first sin is fundamentally different from the sinfulness inherited by later generations, then Adam stands fantastically outside of history as the only person in whom hereditary sin is not found, since it came into being through him and thus is not the same as his first sin. In that case hereditary sin would be explained as a consequence of Adam's sin, but Adam's sin itself would not be explained. The unsatisfactory implications of this view are made even more evident in light of the Lutheran doctrine of the atonement, which teaches that Christ has made satisfaction for hereditary sin.[16] If Adam's first sin is different from hereditary sin, then Adam would be the only person excluded from the atonement (28). Vigilius thus concludes:

> No matter how the problem is raised, as soon as Adam is placed fantastically on the outside, everything is confused. To explain Adam's sin is therefore to explain hereditary sin. And no explanation that explains Adam but not hereditary sin, or explains hereditary sin but not Adam, is of any help . . . The problem is always that of getting Adam included as a member of the race, and precisely in the same sense in which every other individual is included. This is something to which dogmatics should pay attention, especially for the sake of the Atonement. (*CA* 28, 33 n.)

Vigilius proceeds to resolve this dogmatic problem with the help of two guiding principles or propositions: (1) the individual is simultaneously him/herself and the whole race in such a way that each participates in the other; and (2) the transition from one quality to another occurs suddenly by way of a leap, not through a gradual, quantitative progression.

[14] See *The Book of Concord* (2000: 481–660).

[15] Cf. Poole (2001: 211–13); Beabout (1996: 39); Davenport (2000: 132).

[16] Cf. Schmid (1961: 342–70).

Unum Noris Omnes

The first proposition has its basis in a Latin expression by the Roman comic dramatist Terence (*c.*190–159 BCE). In a passage excised from the final draft of *The Concept of Anxiety* Vigilius states: 'It is important to maintain with profound psychological decisiveness: *unum noris omnes* [if you know one, you know all]. When the possibility of sin appears in one human being, it has appeared in all' (*CA* 183, translation modified; cf. *CA* 79; *CUP* i. 353, 571; *JP* iii. 2952, 2958, 3327). The reason for this solidarity, as Vigilius sees it, is that 'a human being is an *individuum* [individual] and as such simultaneously himself and the whole race, and in such a way that the whole race participates in the individual and the individual in the whole race' (*CA* 28; cf. *JP* ii. 2024). This definition of the individual profoundly qualifies the isolated, atomistic notion of the individual that is popularly attributed to Kierkegaard and his pseudonyms. It also provides the basis for a more communal social theory than is generally recognized in Kierkegaard's thought. The mutual participation of the individual and the race in one another is a contradiction that constitutes both a present reality and the ideal perfection of human beings, inasmuch as at every moment individuals are both themselves and the race and have the perfection of themselves as participants in the race as their ethical task. In this way both the individual and the race acquire a history through each other, and every individual acquires an essential, not merely accidental, interest in the history of all other individuals, who as a whole constitute the human race. In Vigilius's view, this contradiction applies to Adam just as much as it does to every other individual in the race. Thus Adam 'is not essentially different from the race, for in that case there is no race at all'; but neither is he simply identical to the race, 'for in that case also there would be no race' (29). Like every other individual, Adam is both 'himself and the race'; consequently, 'that which explains Adam also explains the race and vice versa' (29).

This notion of the solidarity of Adam and the race is not a novel idea, as it was prefigured in the Pauline–Irenaean view of Adam as a representative figure whose fall signifies 'the collective deed of the race' through a mystical identification of Adam and humankind.[17] But Vigilius's understanding of this solidarity differs somewhat in that the Pauline–Irenaean view simply identifies Adam with the race, whereas for Vigilius Adam is an individual who is both himself and the race, thereby preserving his particularity or distinctiveness over against the race. The solidarity of the race with Adam was also affirmed by the early Western Church fathers, particularly

[17] Tennant (1946: 288–90); cf. Kelly (1968: 172).

Ambrose and Augustine, but they interpreted it so as to implicate the race in Adam's sin *en masse*, 'as in a lump' (*quasi in massa*), rather than as individuals (Ambrose), or to exert an involuntary corrupting influence on later generations through procreation (Augustine).[18] Closer to Vigilius's view is that of Kant, who quotes Horace's saying, *Mutato nomine de te fabula narratur* (Change but the name, of you the tale is told), as indicative of our daily individual sinfulness and the biblical claim that 'in Adam we have all sinned'.[19] Echoing Kant, Vigilius states in a sentence excised from the final draft: 'If the explanation of Adam and his fall does not concern me as a *fabula, quae de me narratur* [story that speaks to me], one might as well forget both Adam and the explanation' (*CA* 186).

Kierkegaard also encountered the view of Adam as 'the human being in general' in Marheineke's lectures on dogmatic theology which he attended in Berlin in 1841–2 (*SKP* xiii. III C 26, pp. 213–14).[20] Theologically, however, the most likely influence upon him on this issue was Schleiermacher, whose treatment of original sin emphasizes both individual responsibility and corporate guilt for original sin: '*Original sin . . . is at the same time so really the personal guilt of every individual who shares in it that it is best represented as the corporate act and the corporate guilt of the human race. . . .*'[21] Schleiermacher also states:

> Whether, in fact, we regard it [sin] as guilt and deed or rather as a spirit and a state, it is in either case common to all; not something that pertains severally to each individual and exists in relation to him by himself, but *in each the work of all, and in all the work of each*; and only in this corporate character, indeed, can it be properly and fully understood.[22]

Like Schleiermacher, Vigilius thinks it is important to maintain the corporate character of original sin, for 'if this is not held fast, one will fall either into the Pelagian . . . singular or into the fantastic', that is, either into an individualistic viewpoint 'which permits every individual to play his little history in his own private theater unconcerned about the race' or into one in which Adam is seen as being more than the race or as standing outside it (*CA* 28, 34). In working out his own view of original or hereditary sin, therefore, Vigilius tries to steer a middle course between Augustine and Pelagius. With Augustine he wants to affirm the solidarity of

[18] Kelly (1968: 354, 364). [19] Kant (1998: 64).

[20] See also Hegel (1984–7: iii. 301): 'From the point of view of thought, the expression "the first human being" signifies "humanity in itself" or "humanity as such"—not some single, contingent individual, not one among many, but the absolutely first one, humanity according to its concept.'

[21] Schleiermacher (1956: 285). See also Wyman (2005); Boyd (1970).

[22] Schleiermacher (1956: 288, emphasis added).

Adam and the race without making hereditary sin involuntary in the race, while preserving individual responsibility for original sin without falling into the isolated individualism of Pelagius. The way Vigilius goes about doing this is by positing a second principle of interpretation in the notion of the qualitative leap.

The Qualitative Leap into Sin

If sinfulness in later generations is a consequence of Adam's first sin as traditionally believed, then the first sin of subsequent individuals would presuppose sinfulness as a state or given condition and Adam would stand outside the human race in such a way that the race would not have its beginning with him but through something outside itself, which according to Vigilius is 'contrary to every concept' (*CA* 30). This untenable conclusion leads him to re-examine the concept of 'the *first* sin', which in his view is not '*a* sin' like others or '*one* sin' in a numerical sequence but '*the* sin'; that is, it constitutes a *new quality* which is posited or comes into existence suddenly by a leap or sudden change (30, emphasis added). In proposing that sin comes into the world through a leap rather than through a gradual quantitative or numerical progression, Vigilius expressly sets himself against the view of Hegel, who also affirms the notion of a qualitative leap in the logical, natural, and moral spheres but maintains that it comes about through a quantitative progression.[23] Vigilius brands the Hegelian notion of a qualitative change through quantification a 'superstition' and a 'myth' of the understanding, inasmuch as it does not accord with actuality nor with the Genesis story, which in his view is not a myth but 'presents the only dialectically consistent view' in its claim that 'Sin came into the world by a sin' (30, 32).[24] Just as sin came into the world through Adam's first sin, it comes into the world in subsequent individuals *in precisely the same way*, by their own first sins through a qualitative leap. The first sin of later individuals is not caused by Adam's sin or by the quantitative build-up of sinfulness in the world after the Fall, as this would mean that sinfulness precedes sin, which is a contradiction. Rather, sin presupposes itself, which means that sinfulness comes into the world by sin rather than vice versa, and this is true for subsequent individuals just as much as it was for Adam (32–4). Vigilius observes: 'What often misleads and brings people to all kinds of fantastic imaginings is the problem of the relation of generations,

[23] Hegel (1969: 368–71); cf. *SKP* iv, C 80, where Kierkegaard contends that 'Hegel has never gotten the category of transition right.'

[24] Cf. also James and Moggach (2007) on the left-wing Hegelian Bruno Bauer, who also regarded the Genesis account of the prehistory of humankind as a myth.

as though the subsequent human being were essentially different from the first by virtue of descent' (34, translation modified). In his view, the notion of descent is 'only the expression for the continuity in the history of the race, which always moves by quantitative determinations and therefore is incapable of bringing forth an individual' (34). Consequently, if the second human being were not descended from Adam, there would be no race and no individual, since all human beings would be merely 'an empty repetition' of the first or simply themselves, not themselves and the race, as in Vigilius's concept of the individual (34).

It is on this issue of derivation and the notion of a prior sinfulness associated with it that Vigilius parts company with Schleiermacher, with whom, as we saw earlier, he is in basic agreement concerning the solidarity of Adam and humankind. While affirming that the first or actual sin of Adam's offspring is not derived from his first sin but is identical to it, Schleiermacher nevertheless maintains that sinfulness precedes sin—not only in Adam's progeny but in Adam himself. He suggests that the seduction of Adam and Eve 'could not have taken effect unless there was something already present in the soul which implied a certain readiness to pass into sensuous appetite; and any such inclination toward sin must therefore have been present in the first pair before their first sin, else they would not have been liable to temptation'.[25] Schleiermacher thus concludes that 'Adam must have been sundered from God before his first sin' and that 'whatever idea we may have of the first sin, we must always assume the priority of some sinful element'.[26] He further asserts that 'the universal sinfulness that precedes every actual sin in the offspring is to be regarded not so much as derived from the first sin of our first parents, but rather as identical with what in them likewise preceded the first sin, so that in committing their first sin they were simply the first-born of sinfulness'.[27] Schleiermacher thus denies that a qualitative change in human nature took place as a result of the first sin and affirms instead a universal incapacity for good in human beings (including Adam and Eve) that is innate in them.[28] In place of an original righteousness that is lost in time he substitutes a 'timeless original sinfulness always and everywhere inhering in human nature and co-existing with the original perfection given along with it'.[29]

25 Schleiermacher (1956: 293–4). 26 Ibid. 295–6.

27 Ibid. 299. 28 Ibid. 296, 301.

29 Ibid. 303. See also Kant, who affirms an innate or natural propensity to evil in human beings which has its origin in a rational free choice that is atemporal (1998: 52–5, 61–5), and Müller (1852–3: ii. 427), who agrees with Schleiermacher's notion of a timeless original sinfulness. Kierkegaard explicitly criticizes Müller's notion of a timeless fall as 'a basic dislocation of Christianity' (*JP* iii. 3093). See also Axt-Piscalar (2007: 155–7), who erroneously suggests that Müller's idea of an extratemporal self-determination to evil is unique. For a comparison of Kant, Schleiermacher, and Kierkegaard on original sin see Quinn (1990). On freedom and

In denying the notion of a qualitative leap and presupposing a timeless original sinfulness, therefore, Schleiermacher both exemplifies and further confounds the dogmatic confusions surrounding original or hereditary sin that Vigilius seeks to point out and to rectify.

The Concept of Innocence

In contrast to Schleiermacher's notion of an innate sinfulness in Adam and humankind prior to the first sin and in direct opposition to Hegel, Vigilius reaffirms the traditional notion of Adam's innocence before the Fall, which in his view has been confused with the concept of immediacy in Hegel's logic (*CA* 35).[30] As conceived by Hegel, immediacy is a pure state of being in innocence or ignorance that should be annulled by mediation or reflection in an immanent, necessary movement to a higher state of being in knowledge. Contra Hegel, Vigilius maintains that innocence is an ethical concept, not a logical one, and therefore should not be annulled, or more accurately, it is annulled by guilt, not by reflection. He thus contends: 'Just as Adam lost innocence by guilt, so every person loses it in the same way. If it was not by guilt that he lost it, then it was not innocence that he lost; and if he was not innocent before becoming guilty, he never became guilty' (35, translation modified). Moreover, in Vigilius's view, 'Every person loses innocence essentially in the same way that Adam lost it'—by a qualitative leap (36, translation modified). Innocence is therefore a crucial concept in the doctrine of original sin, for without it human beings could not be held responsible for having brought sin into the world. As Vigilius sees it, however, innocence is not a state of perfection that should be regained after having been lost, nor is it a state of imperfection that should be transcended, as in Hegel's view.[31] Rather, innocence is a quality or state 'that may very well endure', although Vigilius regards it as a waste of time, foolish, and sinful to speculate on what might have happened if Adam had not sinned (36–7, 50).[32] He does not subscribe, therefore, to the notion of a 'fortunate fall' (*felix culpa*) as suggested or implied by some commentators.[33] Vigilius agrees with Hegel that innocence is ignorance,

original sin in Kant and Kierkegaard see Rumble (1992); Green (1985; 1992: 156–67). On Schleiermacher and Kierkegaard see also Frawley (2006).

[30] Cf. Hegel (1991*b*: § 24, pp. 61–3). [31] Ibid.

[32] Cf. *EUD* 125–7, where Kierkegaard nevertheless engages in a bit of speculation in this regard.

[33] See Davenport (2000: 139); Tanner (1992: 73); McCarthy (1978: 39–40). See also Mahn (2006), who suggests that Vigilius's view reflects a *felix fallibilitas* (fortunate fallibility) rather than a *felix culpa*.

but to boast of becoming perfect through the gaining of knowledge 'at the expense of innocence' is not in his view something that would ever occur to anyone who has lost it by becoming guilty, which is the only way it can be lost (37).

Anxiety as the Precondition of Hereditary Sin

Of primary interest to Vigilius is the question of how innocence is lost, which brings him at last to the psychological explanation of the Fall promised at the beginning of his deliberation. Reminding the reader that no science can explain sin, which comes into existence suddenly and inexplicably through a qualitative leap, Vigilius aims to stay within the boundary of what psychology *can* explain, namely the psychological preconditions that lead up to but do not cause or explain sin itself. He briefly notes the failure of other attempts to provide an adequate psychological explanation of the Fall through the notions of prohibition, temptation, and concupiscence, which in his view lack the moral ambiguity required of a psychological explanation (*CA* 39–41).[34] The factor Vigilius regards as providing the only satisfactory psychological explanation of the possibility of sin and guilt is anxiety (*Angest* or *Angst*), which is a qualification of the unconscious or 'dreaming spirit' in the human psyche and thus is an appropriate subject for psychological treatment (42, 48).[35] Vigilius correctly observes that this concept 'is almost never treated in psychology' (42). But it is a concept that was at least mentioned in a number of psychological studies and philosophical anthropologies by authors with whom his alter ego Kierkegaard was familiar, including Kant, Hamann, Hegel, Michelet, Erdmann, Rosenkranz, Daub, Sibbern, and Schelling, among others (*SKS K* iv. 408–10; *CA* 59; *JP* i. 96). Of these, Kant and Schelling stand out as the thinkers who most likely stimulated Kierkegaard's association of the concept of anxiety with original sin and human freedom, although his own deep-seated melancholy undoubtedly also attuned him to discern the spiritual significance of this phenomenon in human existence. In an essay on the 'Conjectural Beginning of Human History', Kant makes the following observation:

> He [man] discovered in himself a power of choosing for himself a way of life, of not being bound without alternative to a single way, like the animals. Perhaps the discovery of this advantage created a moment of delight. But of necessity, anxiety and alarm as to how he was to deal with this newly discovered power quickly

[34] On Kierkegaard's critique of Franz von Baader's theory of temptation, see Koslowski (2007).

[35] On Kierkegaard's anticipation of Freud's psychology of the unconscious, see Evans (2006*b*: 277–98); Nordentoft (1978: 142–65, 176–80); Cole (1971).

followed; for man was a being who did not yet know either the secret properties or the remote effects of anything. He stood, as it were, at the brink of an abyss. Until that moment, instinct had directed him toward specific objects of desire. But from these there now opened up an infinity of such objects, and he did not yet know how to choose between them. On the other hand, it was impossible for him to return to the state of servitude (i.e., subjection to instinct) from the state of freedom, once he had tasted the latter.[36]

Like Kant (and Schelling), Vigilius associates the phenomenon of anxiety with the possibility of freedom in human beings, but he makes much more of it than Kant does. To begin with, he conceives anxiety as being 'altogether different from fear', which is generally how Kant and other thinkers of Kierkegaard's time understood it (*CA* 42).[37] In a journal entry from 1844 Kierkegaard observes: 'The word *anxiety* (*Angst*) has until now been territory open for the taking; we shall attempt to prescribe to it a definite meaning or, better, to affirm it in its definite meaning' (*JP* i. 98). More precisely defined, then, anxiety is '*a sympathetic antipathy* and *an antipathetic sympathy*' that is ambiguously related to fear in that one both desires what one fears and fears what one desires (*CA* 42; cf. *JP* i. 94).[38] This simultaneous feeling of attraction and repulsion toward the possibility of freedom is a common experience in human life.[39] According to Vigilius, anxiety is first posited in the state of innocence as a 'foreign power' that lays hold of a person in relation to the possibility of being able to do something, although at this stage one has no conception of what one is able to do and thus is anxious about nothing rather than something definite (*CA* 42–4). In the grip of this ambiguous power the human spirit looks down 'into the yawning abyss' (shades of Kant here) of its own possibility as freedom, of being able to choose itself as a synthesis of the physical (body) and the psychical (soul/mind) (43, 61). Then, as if in a spell of dizziness, 'freedom faints' and succumbs to sin by making the qualitative leap from innocence to guilt in the failure to posit itself as the spiritual synthesis it essentially is. In associating anxiety with dizziness, Vigilius echoes Kant's remark that 'the person who looks into an abyss is overcome by dizziness' and Schelling's statement that 'the will . . . awakes in freedom the appetite for what is creaturely just as he who is seized by dizziness on a high and steep summit seems to be beckoned to plunge downward by a hidden

[36] Kant (1963: 56); see also Green (1992: 27–8).

[37] Kant (1978: 161); see also Hoberman (1987: 186–9), and *SKS K* iv. 408–11.

[38] See *SKS K* iv. 409–10 and Poole (2001: 206–7), on Kierkegaard's indebtedness to his psychology teacher F. C. Sibbern for this definition, although Sibbern, like Kant, viewed anxiety as an intensified form of fear.

[39] See Pattison (2005: 55–61), on anxiety in adolescence.

voice'.[40] Further than this, Vigilius contends, psychology cannot go in explaining how innocence is lost and sin comes into the world. Anxiety is the psychological presupposition or precondition of hereditary sin but does not explain the qualitative leap into sin. In becoming guilty through anxiety, however, the human spirit becomes ambiguously guilty, that is, both innocent and guilty, inasmuch as 'the fall into sin always takes place in weakness' as a result of freedom becoming entangled in itself in anxiety and thus not really free (61, 49).

Vigilius also maintains that sin does not come into the world through the exercise of an abstract *liberum arbitrium* or equal and unfettered ability to choose either good or evil, since the distinction between good and evil itself only comes into existence through freedom or the capacity to choose (*CA* 49; cf. *JP* ii. 1249). Nor does sin happen by necessity, as claimed by Hegel, who finds the schism between nature and spirit in humankind's natural state, which he regards as evil, to be 'part of the concept of spirit' and cannot be otherwise.[41] But if sin happens by necessity, which in Vigilius's view is a contradiction, 'there can be no anxiety' (49). Hegel associates anxiety or anguish (*Schmerz*) with the awareness of the contradiction between what one ought to be and what one is as a natural being.[42] He thus presupposes knowledge of good and evil as the basis of anxiety rather than vice versa as in Vigilius's view.

The Consequences of Hereditary Sin

Having established that original or hereditary sin enters the world in every individual in the same way as it did in Adam, through the individual's own first sin in a qualitative leap from innocence to guilt as a result of becoming anxious about the possibility of freedom, Vigilius may appear to have dismissed the traditional notion of hereditary sin as having a corrupting effect upon later generations through generation. But he explicitly rejects such a conclusion, claiming that 'the view presented in this work does not deny the propagation of sinfulness through generation, or, in other words, that sinfulness has its history through generation', although not in an Augustinian fashion (*CA* 47). Moreover, he claims that 'Christianity has never assented to giving each particular individual the privilege of starting from the beginning in an external sense. Each individual begins in an historical nexus, and the consequences of nature still hold true' (73).

[40] Kant (1978: 68); Schelling (2006: 47); see also Hoberman (1987: 190); Kosch (2006: 87–104, 124–5), and McCarthy (1985).

[41] Hegel (1991*b*: 63).

[42] Hegel (1984–7: iii. 304–8).

What Vigilius is concerned to point out in this regard is that sinfulness, or the possibility of committing new sin after the Fall, increases *quantitatively* in the individual and the race through propagation. A predisposition to sin is propagated in individuals, but without actually making them guilty, inasmuch as actual sin and guilt continue to occur only through a qualitative leap. Since the human being is a synthesis of mind and body and not merely a physical, instinctive being like animals, one of the consequences of the Fall is that sexuality in the form of a conscious sensuous drive is posited in human beings at the same time sin is posited (*CA* 48–9). This means that sensuousness, which is present in the state of innocence but does not yet exist as a conscious drive, is not sinful as such but becomes so through the Fall.[43] In a passage excised from the final text, Vigilius explains that 'the sexual is the sinful only to the extent that the drive at some moment manifests itself simply as drive in all its nakedness, for this can occur only through an arbitrary abstraction from spirit' (195; cf. *JP* iv. 3964). When one first posits sin, then, one also posits the sexual as sinful. Yet Vigilius is careful to point out: 'The individual for whose arrival I am responsible does not become sinful through me but becomes that by positing sin himself and then himself positing the sexual as sinfulness' (195). In this way the possibility of the continuation of sin in sinfulness is introduced and multiplied through propagation or sexuality without compromising individual responsibility for sin or actually causing an individual's progeny to sin, as in the Augustinian view.

Another consequence of hereditary sin is that a second form of anxiety enters the world with sin and continues to enter it quantitatively every time sin is qualitatively posited by the individual. As Vigilius puts it: 'Sin entered in anxiety, but sin in turn brought anxiety along with it' (*CA* 53). In contrast to the *anxiety of innocence*, which precedes the Fall as the precondition of first sin in Adam and every subsequent individual, one could call this the *anxiety of sinfulness* or anxiety after the Fall, which appears in two forms: *objective anxiety* (the effect of anxiety on nature) and *subjective anxiety* (anxiety in the individual over the possibility of sinning again in the future) (56–60). It might seem strange to talk about nature being anxious, but what Vigilius has in mind is the anxiety that results from the corrupting effect of human sinfulness upon the whole creation, described in Romans 8: 19–23 as 'groaning' with 'eager longing' (anxiety) for redemption (58). An example of objective anxiety in our time would be the global warming caused by human destruction of the environment that

[43] Kierkegaard specifically credits von Baader for this view (*CA* 59). See also Koslowski (2007: 8–9), and Nordentoft (1978: 53–72).

is increasing quantitatively to the point of irreversibility as a result of the misuse of human freedom.

Subjective anxiety likewise reflects the 'more' or quantitative increase of anxiety that accrues as a consequence of generation. Whereas the anxiety of innocence is prefigured in Adam, the anxiety of sinfulness or subjective anxiety is prefigured in Eve. Having been created out of Adam, Eve is a derived being—a status shared in common with all subsequent individuals (*CA* 47, 63–4). Thus, what applies in the relation of Eve to Adam also applies to every subsequent individual. Sharing the imperfection of Eve resulting from derivation, which in Vigilius's view 'is never as perfect as the original', subjective anxiety becomes more reflective in later individuals in that the 'nothing' about which they were anxious in the state of innocence now becomes more and more a 'something' in the form of 'a complex of presentiments' that predispose (but do not cause) them to sin again (61–3). Both sensuousness and anxiety are also quantitatively greater in later individuals as a result of their being derived or procreated. The factor of sexual difference also comes into play here in that, according to Vigilius, sensuousness and anxiety are greater in woman than in man (64). That woman is more sensuous than man, he observes, is apparent in her physical structure, which is associated aesthetically with beauty and ethically with procreation, the latter constituting the culmination of her being (64–5). Although both man and woman are essentially qualified as spirit, which is their common task to become in existence, Vigilius contends that 'spirit is furthest away' at conception and childbirth, the latter constituting 'the furthest point of one extreme of the synthesis', that is, the physical or sensuous element in it (72). Both sensuousness and anxiety are therefore greatest at this time. In a passage excised from the final text Vigilius further claims that woman is not only more sensuous than man but also less spiritual than him because her being culminates in another being outside herself, whereas spirit is 'the true independent' (189; *JP* iv. 4989). Despite this difference, which is only quantitative, not qualitative in nature, Vigilius maintains that, religiously viewed, woman is still 'essentially identical with man' (189).[44]

A further qualification of the human spirit also comes into existence as a result of hereditary sin, namely the determination of the human being as a synthesis of the temporal and the eternal, which is composed differently from the first synthesis. Whereas the first synthesis consists of the physical and the psychical united in the third term of spirit, the second synthesis contains only two terms, the temporal and the eternal (*CA* 85). Yet Vigilius

[44] For feminist critiques of the view of woman in Kierkegaard's writings, see Léon and Walsh (1997).

maintains that the latter 'is not another synthesis but is the expression for the first synthesis' inasmuch as spirit is the eternal, which means that the first synthesis is posited only in and through the introduction of the eternal in the second synthesis (88, 90). The concept of temporality, or the division of time into past, present, and future, also comes into existence with the introduction of the eternal, which appears as possibility or the future in the context of temporality. Because human beings succumb to sin by positing an unwarranted actuality instead of the eternal in the exercise of freedom, temporality, like sensuousness, comes into being as sinfulness, signifying that the person who sins 'lives only in the moment as abstracted from the eternal' (91, 93). As Vigilius expresses it: 'The moment sin is posited, temporality is sinfulness' (92).

Within the temporal realm Vigilius maintains that 'the whole of paganism and its repetition within Christianity lie in a merely quantitative determination' of sinfulness (*CA* 93). Even though paganism lacked a consciousness of sin, which was first posited by Christianity, Vigilius nevertheless agrees with Christian orthodoxy that paganism lies in sin because it 'never arrives at sin in the deepest sense', which 'is precisely sin' (93). The sinfulness of paganism, therefore, may be characterized as *the absence of spirit*, qualified as moving *towards* spirit, whereas paganism within Christendom is simply *spiritlessness* or the 'stagnation of spirit', qualified as moving *away* from spirit (95). Of the two, Vigilius thinks paganism 'is much to be preferred', as 'the human being qualified as spiritless has become a talking machine' that merely repeats philosophical, religious, and political slogans by rote and understands nothing spiritually or as a task (95, translation modified).

Although anxiety, like spirit, is excluded in spiritlessness, Vigilius nevertheless claims that it is present in a hidden or disguised form, which is even more terrifying than when anxiety appears directly as what it is (*CA* 96). Anxiety was also present in paganism; in fact, Vigilius suggests that it might be more correct to say that paganism lies in anxiety rather than sin since 'on the whole' it is characterized by sensuousness (96). In paganism, however, the 'nothing' that constitutes the object of anxiety is fate or a blind necessity that stands in an external relation to spirit and thus is cancelled as soon as spirit is posited. In Christendom, the anxiety of sinfulness manifests itself either as an *anxiety about evil*, the possibility of committing new sin and thereby sinking deeper into sin, or as *anxiety about the good*, in which one becomes demonically enclosed or shut up within oneself, unable to relate positively to others and to the good. Vigilius suggests that the latter form of anxiety 'probably has never been as widespread as in our times, except that nowadays it manifests itself especially in the spiritual spheres' (136). He also identifies a 'lofty inclosing reserve' that is not demonic but synonymous with inwardness, subjectivity, or earnestness, whose object is to actualize the possibility of the eternal within oneself (126, 148, 151). Whoever becomes anxious in this manner is educated by anxiety in such a way as to anticipate faith, which for Vigilius is the only thing that is truly capable of disarming 'the sophistry of sin' and extricating the self from anxiety (117). Paraphrasing Hegel's definition of faith as an inner feeling of the certainty that God exists,[45] Vigilius describes faith as 'the inner certainty that anticipates infinity' or possibility (157). 'Whoever is educated by anxiety is educated by possibility, and only he who is educated by possibility is educated according to his infinitude', he declares (156). Becoming anxious is thus an adventure every person must go through in order to avoid perishing 'by never having been in anxiety or by succumbing in anxiety' (155). Vigilius thus concludes: 'Whoever has learned to be anxious in the right way has learned the ultimate' (155).

DESPAIR AS A SICKNESS OF THE HUMAN SPIRIT

If anxiety is the psychological precursor and consequent of freedom or spirit in a human being, despair is the psychological expression of the disparity or misrelation (*misforhold*) in a human being's relation to itself as spirit. Recognizing as early as 1836 that 'the present age is the age of despair', Kierkegaard analyses despair as a universal sickness of the human spirit in *The Sickness unto Death*, published in 1849 under the pseudonym Anti-Climacus and subtitled 'A Christian Psychological Exposition for Upbuilding and Awakening' (*JP* i. 737). Like Vigilius Haufniensis, Anti-Climacus engages in psychological analysis, but whereas the Watchman of Copenhagen does not claim to be anything more than a psychologist whose analysis of anxiety is only preliminary to dogmatics, Anti-Climacus is not only a psychological diagnostician but also a Christian. In fact, Anti-Climacus is a Christian 'on an extraordinarily high level', which qualifies him, unlike his alter ego Kierkegaard, to write about Christian concepts with authority (*JP* vi. 6439). But Anti-Climacus does not engage in theological reflection at 'a scholarly distance from life' as is commonly done in the discipline of theology; rather, what he writes is intended for the reader's personal upbuilding, to which, in his view, everything ought to serve or else is unchristian (*SUD* 5). Moreover, he claims that 'Everything essentially Christian must have in its presentation a resemblance to the way a physician speaks at the sickbed' (5). Anti-Climacus thus speaks as a Christian psychologist and bedside physician who diagnoses despair as a

[45] Cf. Hegel (1984–7: i. 385–9).

sickness of the human spirit that can be cured only by faith or a proper relation to God.[46]

The title of Anti-Climacus's Christian psychological exposition is taken from John 11: 1–6, which recounts the raising of Lazarus from the dead by Christ. The moral of this story is that physical death is not the end or sickness unto death but only a transition to eternal life, which is made possible by the coming of Christ. Anti-Climacus claims that 'Christianity has in turn discovered a miserable condition that the human being as such does not know exists', and it is this condition, namely despair, that constitutes the sickness unto death (*SUD* 8, 13, translation modified). Although despair is widely recognized as a psychological malady that afflicts many people, according to Anti-Climacus despair is not what we customarily think it is. Many people are in despair who are not aware of being in despair, and those who are aware of being in despair generally have a very superficial understanding of what despair truly is. They think they are despairing over some external disappointment or loss, whereas they are really despairing over themselves. For as Anti-Climacus sees it, despair is a sickness of the human spirit or self, which he defines à la Hegel as 'a relation that relates itself to itself' (13).[47]

In defining the self in relational terms, Hegel departed from the classical understanding of the self as a static, unchanging substance that underlies the changing accidents or attributes of the self. He envisioned the self as a dynamic subject engaged in purposive activity or a process of becoming in which the self unfolds or realizes itself through reflection or a mediation of what it is *in itself* as an immediate being with what it is *for itself* as a fully actualized being in self-conscious freedom. While Hegel has God or Absolute Spirit in mind as constituting the self, his definition also applies to human beings as rational beings or exemplifications of subjective spirit, which has its ground and *telos* in objective spirit or the social order and ultimately in absolute spirit as the mediation of subjective and objective spirit. As we saw in the previous chapter, however, Kierkegaard does not subscribe to the Hegelian concept of the divine, which he regards as pantheistic. Anti-Climacus's definition of the self thus applies only to the human self, which in his view is constituted by consciously relating itself to itself as a synthesis of the finite and the infinite, the temporal and the eternal, possibility and necessity in a continual process of becoming. Strictly speaking, as Anti-Climacus sees it, the self 'does not actually exist' but 'is simply that which ought to come into existence', and insofar as it 'does not become itself, it is not itself; but not to be itself is precisely despair' (*SUD* 30).

46 See also Evans (1990); Cappelørn and Deuser (1996); Perkins (1987); Nordentoft (1978).
47 Cf. Hegel (1977: 83–4); see also Taylor (1975: 94–108).

Despair, then, is the failure of the self to become itself, which is due to a disparity in relating to itself as a synthesis of the factors that make up the self. Before examining the precise nature of this disparity, however, we must note that for Anti-Climacus the self is not only a relation that relates itself to itself but also a relation that relates itself to God or that power which establishes it (*SUD* 13–14). This means that *one can become oneself only through a relation to God*, who defines what it means to be a human self and makes it possible for one to become that self (30). On this point, non-theistic existentialists who are otherwise deeply indebted to Kierkegaard's analysis of the human situation part company with him in the affirmation of the autonomous freedom of the human self to define and become itself. As Anti-Climacus sees it, however, despair signifies not only a disparity in one's relation to oneself but also in one's relation to God; in fact, all despair ultimately can be traced back to and resolved in the latter disparity (14). An understanding of despair in a theological context is thus central, not merely peripheral or non-essential, to Anti-Climacus's analysis. This is made immediately clear in his initial characterization of despair, which manifests itself in two basic forms: *despairingly not to will to be oneself* and *despairingly to will to be oneself* (14). Of the two, the first form of despair constitutes the formula for all despair inasmuch as the second form can be traced back to it; yet all despair ultimately can be resolved into the second form of despair, which is the expression for the disparity in the self's relation to God, namely its unwillingness to admit its 'complete dependence' upon God and its inability 'to arrive at or to be in equilibrium and rest by itself' (14, 20). These two forms of despair thus presuppose and implicate one another, so that both have to do ultimately with the self's relation to the divine as well as to itself. Moreover, as Anti-Climacus sees it, despair is completely rooted out only when 'in relating itself to itself and in willing to be itself, the self rests transparently in the power that established it', which is God, not the autonomous self or the social order (14).

While the possibility of despair marks the superiority of human beings over animals in that it indicates they are essentially spirit and not just physical and psychical beings, despair is dialectically 'the most dangerous of illnesses' to have inasmuch as the object of despair is not really over *something*, as is commonly believed, but rather over *oneself*, or more precisely, over the possibility of the eternal in oneself, which cannot be destroyed (*SUD* 19, 26). Thus the sickness unto death that constitutes despair is not a fatal sickness in the sense that one actually dies from it but rather in the converse sense of *being unable to die*: 'If a person were to die of despair as one dies of a sickness, then the eternal in him, the self, must be able to die in the same sense as the body dies of sickness. But this is impossible; the dying of despair continually converts itself into a living' in which one is unable to die or to destroy one's eternal self (18). Moreover, just as no living human being is likely to be diagnosed by a physician as being completely healthy, Anti-Climacus maintains that 'there is not one single living human being who does not despair a little, who does not secretly harbor an unrest, an inner strife, a disharmony, an anxiety . . . about himself' (22). Despair is thus a universal sickness or condition which every human being experiences and must contend with in one form or another, whether one is aware of it or not.

The Dialectical Constituents of the Self as a Synthesis

In order to awaken us to an understanding of what despair really is and the specific forms it can take in a human being, Anti-Climacus analyses despair first of all in terms of the dialectical constituents of the self as a synthesis of the temporal and the eternal, finitude and infinitude, necessity and possibility. Since the first pair of these constituents was introduced in *The Concept of Anxiety*, Anti-Climacus limits himself to a discussion of the disparity in the self's relation to the other two pairs (*SUD* 29–42). With regard to finitude and infinitude, he states that 'To become oneself is to become concrete', which means to become neither simply finite nor simply infinite but a synthesis or combination of both (30). This is done by first making an infinite movement away from oneself through reflection or imagination in order to form a conception of the ideal self one should become, and then by returning to oneself in a process of finitizing or actualizing that self within the context and limits of finitude. Despair, or a disparity in the proper relation of oneself to these factors, occurs whenever either of these movements is carried out to the exclusion of the other. Thus *infinitude's despair* is to lack finitude while *finitude's despair* is to lack infinitude. If one gets lost in infinitude, the self becomes fantastic and does not become itself. For example, if one constantly engages in daydreaming about what one is going to become in life but never actually takes any concrete steps towards realizing that goal, the self engages in 'a fantasized existence in abstract infinitizing' in which it moves further and further away from itself rather than becomes itself (32). Conversely, if one lacks infinitude, the self becomes completely finitized and reduced to a mere copy or number like others:

> But whereas one kind of despair plunges wildly into the infinite and loses itself, another kind of despair seems to permit itself to be tricked out of its self by 'the others.' Surrounded by hordes of human beings, absorbed in all sorts of secular matters, more and more shrewd about the ways of the world—such a person forgets

himself, forgets his name, divinely understood, does not dare believe in himself, finds it too hazardous to be himself and far easier and safer to be like the others, to become a copy, a number, a mass man. (*SUD* 33–4)

This form of despair was typical of the secular mentality of bourgeois society in Kierkegaard's time and is even more common in the present age.[48] Yet, as Anti-Climacus observes, it goes practically unnoticed in the world and is so far from being regarded as despair that a person in this kind of despair is thought to be 'just what a human being is supposed to be'—totally absorbed in temporal goals such as amassing money, carrying out secular enterprises, becoming a success in the world, gaining public esteem, and perhaps even making a name for oneself in history (34–5). But such a person lacks inwardness and is unwilling to venture everything in order to become a self in relation to God. Spiritually speaking, then, this person has no self, no matter how 'self-seeking' she or he otherwise is.

A comparable disparity occurs between the constituents of possibility and necessity in the synthesis of the self. Both possibility (freedom) and necessity (limitations) are 'equally essential' to becoming a self, but if one becomes lost in possibility, believing that everything is possible without having to submit to any limitations or constraints upon oneself, then one is in *possibility's despair* and lacks actuality (*SUD* 35–7). This form of despair is a common one, as individuals are often encouraged to think they can become and do anything they wish regardless of their personal, ethnic, cultural, social, and economic conditions and backgrounds. As noted in the previous chapter, Kierkegaard particularly associates the illusion that everything is possible with early nineteenth-century German romanticism, which is severely criticized in his academic dissertation for its negative attitude towards actuality in the affirmation of an unbounded freedom of the human imagination to create the self by experimenting with a multiplicity of poetic possibilities (*CI* 272–323).[49] As Anti-Climacus sees it, everything is possible for God, but there is much that is not possible for finite beings. Every individual is subject to personal and social limitations and is essentially defined as a self by God. Conversely, if possibility is lacking in a person's life, if from a merely human perspective there seems to be no hope and a personal collapse or downfall is certain, then the disparity takes the form of *necessity's despair* (*SUD* 37–42). Likening existence to respiration or breathing, in which one both inhales and exhales, Anti-Climacus associates this form of despair with determinism or fatalism, in which everything is necessary. The fatalist has no freedom or room to breathe and is suffocated by necessity. As Anti-Climacus sees it, however, an even more wretched

[48] Cf. Marcel (2006); Tuttle (2005); Marcuse (1964).

[49] See further Walsh (1994: 43–62).

expression of this form of despair can be seen in the philistine-bourgeois mentality, which is lost in triviality, probability, and spiritlessness and is bereft of the imagination required for becoming aware of God and the human self as spirit. The antidote for despair in this situation is a strong dose of possibility, namely the belief that for God all things are possible, precisely at that point where possibility seems impossible, which for Anti-Climacus is precisely what it means to have faith or to believe (38–9).

Unconscious Despair

Anti-Climacus identifies several forms of despair based on their differing levels of intensity, which are directly proportionate to the increase in a person's consciousness of being in despair and having a self: 'the greater the degree of consciousness, the more intensive the despair' (*SUD* 42). The lowest level of despair is that of being unconscious of being in despair and having a self that is eternal or spiritual in nature. This form of despair is equivalent to what was earlier identified in *The Concept of Anxiety* as spiritlessness, which in Anti-Climacus's view is the most common form of despair, particularly in classical paganism and the natural human being in Christendom. Comparing the human being to a two-storey house with a basement, Anti-Climacus suggests that 'all too regrettably the sad and ludicrous truth about the majority of people is that in their own house they prefer to live in the basement', that is, entirely in sensate categories, and are indignant if anyone suggests they should move to the upper floor (43).

Conscious Despair in Weakness

The next level of despair is conscious despair, in which one has a truer conception of despair and greater clarity about oneself as being in despair, although one may still have only 'a dim idea' of one's true state and self-identity at this level (*SUD* 48). Anti-Climacus basically distinguishes between two forms of conscious despair: *despairingly not to will to be oneself* (despair in weakness or 'feminine despair'), and *despairingly to will to be oneself* (defiant despair or 'masculine despair') (49). Although women can manifest masculine despair and men can exhibit feminine despair, these instances are exceptions to the rule, as feminine despair is typical of women, due to their natural or instinctive tendency to lose themselves in devotion to others, while masculine despair is commonly experienced by men, who are more egotistical and intellectual by nature and thus more prone to be self-assertive or defiant.[50] Despair in weakness manifests itself in two ways, either as *despair over the earthly or over something earthly* or as *despair of the eternal or over oneself*. The first is characteristic of people who live in a state of pure immediacy without any reflection at all or who have a modicum of reflection but 'no infinite consciousness of the self, of what despair is, or of the condition as one of despair' (50–1). According to Anti-Climacus, this is the most common form of despair in weakness (57). Purely immediate individuals may be conscious of being in despair but only as something that happens to them or affects them from outside, to which they passively submit. Thus, when they lose something of a worldly nature, such as money or a job, they are in despair but have no inkling that despair is really to lose the eternal. Insofar as they have a concept of self, it is defined by externals, such as the clothes they wear, and instead of willing to become themselves, they despairingly want to be someone else (52–3).

Despairing individuals who possess a degree of reflection are able to recognize that despair is not due to external circumstances but is brought on to a certain degree by their own actions. With this recognition and acceptance of personal responsibility for despair they begin to make a break with immediacy so as to acquire a sense of self apart from the environment and external events, and even to form 'a dim idea that there may even be something eternal in the self'—but only up to a certain point (*SUD* 55). They do not 'entertain the ludicrous notion of wanting to be someone else' like purely immediate individuals, but neither do they get very far in turning inward so as to become themselves (55). A common misperception about despair is that it belongs essentially to youth and thus is something left behind as an adult, but as Anti-Climacus sees it, that is far from being the case, as 'most people virtually never advance beyond what they were in their childhood and youth', which is immediacy with 'a little dash of reflection' (57–8).

According to Anti-Climacus, the second form of despair in weakness, despair *of* the eternal and *over* oneself, constitutes the formula for all despair (*SUD* 60). Even those persons who think they are despairing over something earthly are actually despairing of the eternal, which is what releases them from despair, and over themselves, which is what binds them in despair (60–1). Consciousness of despair at this level, however, constitutes an advance over the previous stage in that the person in despair understands that it is weakness to despair and is in despair over this weakness. One thus has a greater consciousness of the self, of what despair is, and of one's own condition as despair, yet is unwilling to acknowledge the self because of this weakness. Instead, one shuts oneself off from it in 'inclosing

[50] See further Walsh (1987: 121–34, or 1997: 203–15).

reserve', simultaneously loving and hating the self that one is unwilling to become (63). Although this form of despair is less common than despair over the earthly, it is generally undetectable and thus may appear in a person who otherwise leads a normal bourgeois life as a university graduate, parent, spouse, public officeholder, and nominal Christian. But the longing for solitude one frequently feels in this condition is a sign that there is a measure of spirit within oneself, unlike the 'superficial nonpersons and group-people' who 'promptly die the moment they have to be alone' and 'need the soothing lullaby of social life' in order to live (64). If one continues in inclosing reserve, however, Anti-Climacus warns that it could result in suicide or become intensified in a higher level of despair, namely defiant despair.

Defiant Despair

In defiant despair there is an even greater consciousness of the self, of what despair is, and of one's own state of despair as being self-initiated. One wants to become oneself, but one wants to become the self one wants to be rather than the self one is intended to be by God. As Anti-Climacus expresses it, 'the self in despair wants to be master of itself or to create itself, to make his self into the self he wants to be, to determine what he will have or not have in his concrete self' (*SUD* 68). Distinguishing between an acting self and a self being acted upon, Anti-Climacus elucidates this form of despair by way of an analogy to Greek mythology. Like Prometheus, the titan who stole fire from the gods for the benefit of humankind, the acting self steals the thought that God pays attention to the individual and egoistically pays attention to itself, recognizing no power over itself and relating to itself by imaginatively, hypothetically, arbitrarily constructing and deconstructing itself at will (68–9). However, if in the process of imaginatively constructing itself the despairing self is acted upon in such a way as to encounter a 'temporal cross' it cannot bear, then again like Prometheus (who was punished by Zeus for his theft by being chained to a rock while vultures ate his liver, which was rejuvenated daily to prolong his agony), the despairing self feels itself nailed to that cross, unable to do away with it yet unwilling to hope that it can come to an end (70). With respect to this particular 'thorn in the flesh', then, the despairing self does not will to become itself yet defiantly wills to be itself—not in spite of or without this suffering but along with it (70–1). Flouting and rebelling against all existence, the defiant self does not want to be helped temporally by the eternal but demonically prefers to be itself 'with all the agonies of hell' (71). Although this level of despair is a rarity in the world, it is virtually undetectable externally, as the intensified inclosing reserve that characterizes it is concealed in a world of its own, where it is 'restlessly and tormentedly engaged in willing to be itself' (73).

Despair as Sin

The psychological delineation of the foregoing forms of despair is preliminary to Anti-Climacus's ultimate goal, which is to provide a theological analysis of despair as sin for the edification of the single individual. Although despair is identified from the beginning as a disparity not only in one's relation to oneself but also to God, this latter disparity does not come to the fore until part 2 of *The Sickness unto Death*, where sin is associated with the intensification of the two forms of conscious despair (despair in weakness and despair in defiance) by virtue of being conscious of existing before God or with the conception of God (*SUD* 77). With this qualification the deliberation dialectically takes a new direction. The previous gradations in the consciousness of the self presuppose a merely human conception of the self, whose criterion for what it means to be a self is the human being itself. In becoming conscious of existing before God, the self acquires 'a new quality and qualification' as a *theological self* or *infinite self* in that it gains an infinite reality by having God as its qualitative measure and ethical goal (79). The greater the conception of God one has, the more self there is, and the more self there is, the greater one's conception of God (80). But the greater one's conception of self and God, the more intensified despair also becomes as a result of failing to become one's infinite self before God. Before God, therefore, despair is defined as sin or the wilful disobedience of God, which applies to all forms of sin. In agreement with Lutheran orthodoxy and against (Kantian) rationalist ethics, in which a conception of God is not necessary for the discernment of one's moral duty, Anti-Climacus claims that all sin is before God whether one is conscious of existing before God or not, although in a strict sense anyone who lives in despairing ignorance of God, such as the pagan and natural human being, does not sin since that person has a merely human conception of the self and does not consciously exist before God (80–1). Moreover, the pagan conception of sin as vice, the opposite of which is virtue, is contrary to the most decisive Christian definition of sin, according to which the opposite of sin is not virtue but faith, in which the self wills to be itself by resting transparently in God (82).[51]

[51] Some commentators nevertheless construe Kierkegaard as a virtue ethicist. See Gouwens (1996: 93–121); Davenport (2001); Roberts (1998).

The Christian qualification of the self as existing before God also presents the possibility of offence to the pagan and natural mentality. The notion that a human being has or should have an infinite reality before God is offensive because it 'makes too much of being human' (*SUD* 87). As Anti-Climacus sees it, the Aristotelian principle of the 'golden mean', *ne quid nimis* (nothing too much), is the *summa summarum* (sum total) of wisdom for the merely human mentality, which might be willing to go along with a lesser conception of the self before God, 'but too much is too much' (86–7)! Anti-Climacus thus claims that the real reason people are offended by Christianity is not because it is too dark, gloomy, and rigorous but because 'it is too high, because its goal is not a human being's goal, because it wants to make a human being into something so extraordinary that he cannot grasp the thought' (83, translation modified). Moreover, the very idea that a person exists directly before God as an individual human being whose sin is of concern to God runs counter to the speculative mind of Christian paganism, which universalizes the individual in the race and views sin as sin quite apart from whether it is before God or not (83). By contrast, Anti-Climacus claims that

> Christianity teaches that this individual human being—and thus every single individual human being, no matter whether man, woman, servant girl, cabinet minister, merchant, barber, student, or whatever—this individual human being exists *before God*, this individual human being who perhaps would be proud of having spoken with the king once in his life, this human being who does not have the slightest illusion of being on intimate terms with this one or that one, this human being exists before God, may speak with God any time he wants to, assured of being heard by him—in short, this person is invited to live on the most intimate terms with God! (*SUD* 85)

The Socratic versus Christian View of Sin

The difference between the Christian definition of sin and that of paganism, particularly the Socratic understanding of sin, is also made apparent by their respective views of what sin is. Lacking a notion of original sin as the antecedent state that explains the obscuring of human knowledge, Socrates identified sin with ignorance, by which he meant that one does the wrong because one does not know what is right.[52] If one knows the right, then one will do the right, as no one knowingly does the wrong. For Socrates, therefore, sin is due to a lack of knowledge. But if no one ever knowingly does the wrong, then sin does not exist, since for Anti-Climacus

[52] Cf. Plato, *Protagoras* 352b–358d (1997: 782–7).

sin is consciousness of doing wrong. He thus charges that 'Socrates does not actually arrive at the category of sin, which certainly is dubious for a definition of sin', and it is 'specifically the concept of sin . . . that most decisively differentiates Christianity qualitatively from paganism' (*SUD* 89). Christianly understood, sin is not a matter of knowledge but of the will, which was responsible for a much earlier obscuring of human knowledge in original sin, thus requiring a revelation from God in order to understand what sin is. In a certain sense, then, sin *is* ignorance inasmuch as Christianity regards human beings as being so deeply in sin that they do not know what sin is or that their condition is one of sin. In Christendom, where everyone presumably knows what sin is, Anti-Climacus charges that the problem of sin is not a matter of *not being able* to understand what is right due to ignorance, as in ancient paganism, but of *not being willing* to understand the right (95). One is unwilling to understand because one does not will what is right. Moreover, one sometimes does wrong even though one knows what is right. Yet modern philosophy, which in Anti-Climacus's estimation 'is neither more nor less than paganism', makes light of the transition from knowing to doing in the assumption that 'to think is to be' (Descartes's *cogito ergo sum*) and 'wants to delude us into believing that this is Christianity' (93).[53]

Sin is a Position

Anti-Climacus also subjects modern speculative theology to criticism for employing a duplicitous 'bait and switch' tactic with regard to the (Lutheran) orthodox Christian teaching that sin is a position. This teaching holds that sin is a reality or state of being that is wilfully brought into existence or 'posited' by the individual, not a negation in the form of a lack or defect in some given condition in the human personality such as weakness, sensuousness, finitude, or ignorance (*SUD* 96). The view that sin is a negation has its source in the Plotinian-Neoplatonic view of evil as a privation or lack of good and was taken over by St Augustine and later medieval scholastic theologians such as St Thomas Aquinas.[54] While agreeing with Lutheran orthodoxy that sin is a position, speculative theology nevertheless undermines this tenet, Anti-Climacus contends, by claiming to comprehend it logically, with the result that the concept of sin as a position is dialectically annulled by the higher position of comprehension in abstract thought. This issue is theologically important, as Anti-Climacus sees it, because Lutheran orthodoxy 'has correctly perceived that when sin is defined negatively, all Christianity is flabby and spineless' (96). Not only is

53 Cf. Descartes (1951).

54 Copleston (1953–75: i. 469–70; ii. 84–5, 371–4).

personal responsibility for sin compromised but the qualitative distinction between God and humanity is also blurred in that they tend to merge pantheistically into one in the medium of pure thought. Moreover, for Anti-Climacus the Christian teaching that sin is a position is a *paradox* that cannot be comprehended but must be believed, inasmuch as 'Christianity teaches that everything essentially Christian depends solely upon faith' (99).

The moral that follows from Anti-Climacus's analysis of sin as intensified despair before God is the strange conclusion that, in the strictest sense, sin is a great rarity in the world, since the lives of most people are too spiritless to be called sin, especially in Christendom, which in Anti-Climacus's view is 'not merely a shabby edition of the essentially Christian, full of printer's errors that distort the meaning and of thoughtless omissions and admixtures, but is also a misuse of it, a profanation and prostitution of Christianity' (*SUD* 102). This is made even more apparent in the intensification of sin into even deeper forms of despair through the continuation of sin.

Continuance in Sin

Unless one repents of one's sin before God and undergoes a radical 'upheaval' (*Omvæltning)* and 'about-face' (*Omvendelse*) so as to begin moving toward faith rather than further away from it in the consciousness of sin, one remains in the state of sin, which increases of its own accord so as to establish a consistency of sin (*SUD* 61 n., 65, translation modified; cf. *SV1*, xi. 173 n., 177). As a rule, Anti-Climacus observes, people are so completely under the power of sin that it has become second nature in them, making them blind to the continuity of sin in their lives (105). They associate sin with the committing of particular sins, which are merely expressions for a continuance in the state of sin. In the deepest sense, then, it is continuance in the state of sin, not the committing of new acts of sin as such, that constitutes new sin in a person's life. As Anti-Climacus sees it, 'every unrepented sin is a new sin and every moment that it remains unrepented is also new sin' (105). In this way the state of sin not only grows but undergoes an internal intensification so as to become the new sin of *despair over sin*. Whereas sin itself constitutes a break with the good, despair over sin signifies a break with repentance and grace, inasmuch as at this level of despair one wants nothing to do with the good and shuts oneself off from it in an even more inaccessible, demonic form of inclosing reserve that is totally absorbed in sin. Anti-Climacus notes, however, that 'despair over sin is not averse to giving itself the appearance of being something good' by claiming that one can never forgive oneself for sinning or that God can never forgive one for it (111). But in his view this is 'just a subterfuge' that at a still higher level of intensification becomes the sin of *despair of the forgiveness of sin* or *offence* (112).

Sin as Offence

While the basis for the definition of sin in the previous forms of despair was the theological or infinite self before God, the self in despair of the forgiveness of sin stands directly before Christ, who embodies 'the staggering reality' of the infinite self inasmuch as God only becomes the criterion and goal of the human self in him (*SUD* 114). Reconciliation with God is thus made possible through Christ, who offers the forgiveness of sin, but Christ's forgiveness may be rejected in either of the two ways previously identified as despair in weakness and defiant despair. Now, however, these forms of despair are the opposite of what they were previously, since the self is viewed not merely in terms of willing to be itself but of willing to be itself *as a sinner*, that is, from the standpoint of its imperfection (113). Despair in weakness, or not willing to be oneself, thus becomes defiant despair in the outright rejection of forgiveness because one is unwilling to accept oneself as a sinner. Correspondingly, defiant despair becomes despair in weakness by willing to be oneself as a sinner in such a way as to be beyond forgiveness or irredeemably a sinner.

Despair of the forgiveness of sin may also be characterized as *offence* inasmuch as Christ's claim to forgive sins was not only offensive to the Jews but presents the possibility of offence to Christendom as well. In fact, Anti-Climacus goes so far as to claim that 'the state of Christendom is actually despair of the forgiveness of sins', although it is so spiritless that, like paganism, it lacks a consciousness of sin and only imagines that it has gone beyond paganism by equating the 'pagan peace of mind' in which it lives with the consciousness of the forgiveness of sins (*SUD* 117). Not only has the qualitative difference between God and human beings been pantheistically abrogated by speculative philosophy and the common life in Christendom, the Christian doctrine of God's incarnation in Christ has also degenerated into a brazen identification of the mob with God and Christ as a result of 'the predominance of the generation over the individual' taught by speculative philosophy (118). As Anti-Climacus sees it, however, 'Christianity has protected itself from the beginning' with its teaching about sin, whose category is the category of individuality, which like sin is not accessible to speculative thought (119). Speculation thinks in terms of abstract universals, such as the concept of humanity, rather than the individual human being. Anti-Climacus thus claims that 'just as one individual person cannot be thought, neither can one individual sinner; sin can be thought (then it becomes negation), but not one individual sinner' (119). Speculative thought abstracts from actuality, whereas Christianity points in the opposite direction towards immersion in actuality. Christianly understood, 'Sin is a qualification of the single individual' and has its actuality only in the single individual (120). Anti-Climacus thus concludes that 'The dialectic of sin is diametrically contrary to that of speculation' (120). But he also goes beyond this to claim:

> By means of the teaching about sin and particular sins, God and Christ, quite unlike any kings, have protected themselves once and for all against the nation, the people, the crowd, the public, etc. and also against every demand for a more independent constitution. All those abstractions simply do not exist for God; for God in Christ there live only single individuals (sinners). (*SUD* 121)

As Anti-Climacus sees it, then, the Christian doctrine of sin, which pertains theologically only to the single individual, has political and social implications as well, particularly for democratic societies, inasmuch as in Christendom the category of the single individual has been subsumed under the Aristotelian category of the animal or the crowd (118).[55] In protest against this identification Anti-Climacus maintains that 'Being a human being is not like being an animal, for which the specimen is always less than the species. The human being is distinguished from other animal species not only by the superiorities that are generally mentioned but is also qualitatively distinguished by the fact that the individual, the single individual, is more than the species' (121 n., translation modified). The sociopolitical implications of Anti-Climacus's theological anthropology will be examined in a later chapter. Suffice it to remind the reader here that the Revolution of 1848, in which Denmark became a constitutional monarchy with universal male suffrage, occurred a year before the publication of *The Sickness unto Death*. Thus his comments should be read with that event particularly in mind, although their relevance extends far beyond the local context of that time.

[55] Cf. Aristotle, *Politics*, 3. 11 (1984: ii. 2033–5), where he argues in favour of the principle that 'the multitude ought to be in power rather than the few' because the many presumably make better judgments than individuals, who are only members of the whole, wherein power and a higher authority ought to reside. But Aristotle is somewhat ambivalent about this principle inasmuch as in his view 'the argument would equally hold about brutes'. Hence Anti-Climacus calls it 'the animal category' (*SUD* 118).

Sin Against the Holy Spirit

Anti-Climacus concludes his analysis of the continuance and intensification of sin with an account of 'sin against the Holy Spirit', which is identified in the New Testament as blasphemy or speaking against the Holy Spirit—a sin that can never be forgiven (*SUD* 125).[56] The intensity of despair reaches its highest level in this form of sin, in which the despairing individual positively abandons and discards Christianity by declaring it to be a lie and untruth. Anti-Climacus likens this sin to waging an offensive war against God in an outright attack upon Christianity, particularly against the paradox of God's incarnation in Christ, who presents a possibility of offence that cannot be removed. The lowest form of offence at Christ is to remain undecided or neutral about him, which for Anti-Climacus is tantamount to denying the divinity of Christ since the earnestness of existence requires that everyone *shall* have an opinion about him (129). At the next stage of offence at Christ one is preoccupied with making a decision about him but cannot bring oneself to believe and thus suffers inwardly from an unhappy relation to Christ. Sin against the Holy Spirit, which is the positive form of offence at Christ and thus the highest intensification of sin, involves the outright denial of Christ as the absolute paradox, either by denying the humanity of Christ in the docetic (from the Greek *dokein*, 'to seem') claim that he only appeared to be an individual human being or by rationalistically denying his divinity in the claim that he was merely an individual human being. The first form of denial corresponds to the Gnostic heresy that was rejected by the early church fathers; the second is particularly associated with an early Jewish Christian sect called the Ebionites, which Anti-Climacus explicitly identifies as holding this view in *Practice in Christianity*, another book attributed to him as 'author' (*PC* 123).[57] In that work, however, he suggests that the modern age suffers from a different confusion that is 'far more dangerous' than these early forms of offence (123). To see what that confusion is and how it is addressed in Kierkegaard's writings, let us turn next to his view of Christ.

[56] See Matt. 12: 31–2; Mark 3: 29; Luke 12: 10.

[57] On Gnosticism and Ebionitism see Grillmeier (1965: 90–101).

5

Christ as Absolute Paradox, Redeemer, and Prototype

The absolute paradox of Jesus Christ as the God-man, or more accurately the God-human being (*Gud-Mennesket*),[1] constitutes the heart of Kierkegaard's understanding of Christianity, for as he sees it, 'all Christianity is rooted in the paradox' (*JP* iii. 3083). In reflecting on the person and work of Christ as the absolute paradox, Kierkegaard was not interested in expounding the doctrines of the incarnation and atonement as such but in clarifying their meaning for the single individual who encounters Christ and must decide whether to believe or to be offended at him. A brief overview of the doctrine of the incarnation and its interpretation in the nineteenth century at the outset, however, will help to set his Christological reflection in historical and theological context.

THE DOCTRINE OF THE INCARNATION

The biblical basis for the doctrine of the incarnation rests principally on two passages from the New Testament.[2]

> And the Word became flesh and lived among us, and we have seen his glory, the glory as of a father's only son, full of grace and truth. (John 1: 14)

> Let the same mind be in you that was in Christ Jesus, who, though he was in the form of God, did not regard equality with God as something to be exploited, but emptied himself, taking the form of a slave, being born in human likeness. And being found in human form, he humbled himself and became obedient to the point of death—even death on a cross. (Philippians 2: 5–8)

The African church father Tertullian (*c.*160–220) laid the foundation for the understanding of Christ that eventually took hold in the Christian church with his view of the divine and human natures of Christ as 'two substances'

[1] Come (1997: 22 n. 53), points out that *Menneske* is a gender-neutral term for a human being, whereas 'man' is an ambiguous word that can refer either impersonally to humanity as a whole or personally to a member of the male sex, neither of which accurately expresses Kierkegaard's view of the incarnation.

[2] *The New Oxford Annotated Bible* (2001).

that were conjoined but not confused in 'one person' (*una persona*) who was at once God and man.[3] After centuries of Christological controversy in which one or the other of the two natures of Christ was either denied or compromised by various factions in the church, the early church fathers ratified the Christological definitions of the Councils of Nicaea (325) and Constantinople (381) at the Council of Chalcedon (451), declaring definitively that Christ was truly God and truly man, combining the two natures in one person without confusion, change, division, or separation.[4]

This definition has remained the orthodox view of Christ but has been subject to various modes of interpretation and criticism over the centuries. A popular mode of interpretation in the nineteenth century was the kenotic (from the Greek *kenosis*, 'self-emptying') theory of interpretation based on Philippians 2: 5–8 and dating from patristic times.[5] Reviving a seventeenth-century Christological debate within German Lutheranism over the question whether and how Christ used his divine powers of omnipresence, omnipotence, and omniscience during his earthly existence, some German Lutheran theologians of the mid-nineteenth century advocated a variant of this theory in the claim that Christ temporarily divested himself of these attributes of divinity in order to become fully human.[6] Although the kenotic theory remains controversial in the ongoing attempts of its modern supporters to explain the meaning of Christ's self-emptying in a manner consistent with the formula of Chalcedon,[7] it was indicative of a general emphasis in the nineteenth century on the humanity of Christ in Lutheran and Reformed (Calvinist) theology. While fully accepting the classical dogma of the incarnation, Martin Luther (1483–1546) had advocated a 'theology of the cross' emphasizing the humanity, lowliness, and suffering of Christ in opposition to a 'theology of glory' that attempts to behold God's invisible nature by unaided human power.[8] In the early nineteenth century, the Reformed theologian Friedrich Schleiermacher rejected the two-natures doctrine of Christ and made a new attempt to construct a Christology from below by relating everything to the redemptive activity of Jesus, who as a historical person exemplified ideal human nature through his perfect God-consciousness and sinlessness.[9] The nineteenth century also witnessed the blossoming of Hegelian speculative theology, which

[3] Grillmeier (1965: 140–57); Kelly (1968: 149–53).

[4] Grillmeier (1965: 175–302, 329–487); Kelly (1968: 280–343).

[5] See Gavrilyuk (2004: 135–71), on the kenotic Christology of the patristic theologian Cyril of Alexandria (*c*.378–444).

[6] See Thompson (2006); McGrath (1994: 78–80); Welch (1965); Schmid (1961: 389–93).

[7] See Evans (2006*a*).

[8] See Hinkson (2001); Althaus (1966: 25–34); Loewenich (1976: 17–49, 112–43).

[9] Schleiermacher (1956: 53, 376–424); see also R. R. Niebuhr (1964: 210–28).

interpreted the incarnation as the historical instantiation of the eternal unity of God and humanity. This movement culminated in the left-wing biblical criticism of David Strauss, whose *Life of Jesus* put the historical object of faith radically into question by viewing him essentially as a mythical representation of the philosophical idea of the eternal unity of the divine and human natures.

Like Luther, for whom paradox was also a hallmark of Christianity, Kierkegaard accepted the orthodox doctrine of the incarnation and stood squarely in the Lutheran tradition's emphasis on Christ's humanity, lowliness, and suffering.[10] But he did not get bogged down in the manner of Lutheran scholasticism with trying to explain how Christ can be both human and divine.[11] On the contrary, his point was precisely that the incarnation, like original sin, cannot be rationally explained but must be believed. With the advent of rationalist and speculative theology in the modern age, Kierkegaard was convinced that the paradox of the incarnation had been abolished altogether, either by making Christ's teachings rather than his person 'the principal thing', as in rationalism, or by construing the incarnation as the speculative unity of God and humanity rather than the unity of God and an individual human being, as in Hegelian speculative theology (*PC* 123). Over against these destructive Christological developments Kierkegaard sought to reaffirm Christ as the absolute paradox that cannot be eliminated or rationally comprehended.

A DIALECTICAL THOUGHT-PROJECT

Writing in the persona of Johannes Climacus in *Philosophical Fragments*, Kierkegaard first tackles this issue indirectly by proposing a 'thought-project' concerning the paradoxical question of whether truth can be learnt (*PF* 9–22). Paraphrasing Plato's *Meno*, the Socratic dialogue in which this question is raised, Climacus states the paradox thus: 'a person cannot possibly seek what he knows, and, just as impossibly, he cannot seek what he does not know, for what he knows he cannot seek, since he knows it, and what he does not know he cannot seek, because, after all, he does not even know what he is supposed to seek' (9).[12] The Platonic solution to this paradox was the doctrine of recollection noted earlier, namely that truth is immanent in human beings and needs only to be recollected in order to be known. As a teacher, then, Socrates did not bring the truth to others but merely played the role of a midwife who assisted them in 'giving birth to'

[10] Hinkson (2001). [11] Cf. Schmid (1961: 294–337).
[12] Cf. Plato, *Meno*, 80 e (1997: 880).

or remembering what they already knew but had forgotten. According to Climacus, both ancient and modern speculation repeat this idea by positing an eternal creation, emanation, or becoming of the deity that is known or comprehended on the basis of some prior state in human beings such as reason or self-consciousness (10 n.). Self-knowledge is thus equivalent to God-knowledge inasmuch as one is assumed to have an innate knowledge of and essential unity with the divine (11). Moreover, just as the teacher is only an occasion for recollecting truth in oneself, existence in time is only an occasion for coming to know the truth since one is presumed to be in possession of it from all eternity.

In contrast to this Platonic or speculative way of learning the truth, which can be understood as applying to all forms of natural theology, Climacus hypothesizes an alternative path to learning the truth which, in order to be truly different, must meet the following conditions:

(1) A particular moment in time, namely the coming into existence of the eternal, is decisive for coming to know the truth.
(2) The learner does not possess the truth, not even in the form of ignorance, nor seek the truth.
(3) Both the truth and the condition for understanding it must therefore be given to the learner by the teacher, who reveals to the learner that he/she exists in a state of untruth, for which the learner is responsible.
(4) The condition for understanding the truth must originally have been given to the learner in the creation, for otherwise the learner could not be held responsible for being in a state of untruth.
(5) The learner not only stands outside the truth but is polemical towards it since the condition for understanding the truth has been freely forfeited.
(6) Having forfeited the condition for understanding the truth, the learner is now bound and excluded from the truth, unable to free him/herself from bondage. (*PF* 13–17)

In this scenario the teacher cannot be merely a human being like Socrates but must be divine since the learner stands in need of being not merely *reformed* but *transformed* into a *new person* of a different quality, which only the god can do (*PF* 14, 18). The god is thus clearly more than a teacher and should be called *saviour*, *deliverer*, *reconciler*, and *judge* as well (17–18). The decisive moment of the god's coming into existence also deserves a special name: *the fullness of time* (18). The learner's state of untruth can likewise be given another name: *sin* (15). Similarly, the change undergone by the learner in receiving the condition for understanding the truth can be called a *conversion* and *rebirth* since it involves a conscious turning around by the learner, repentance or sorrow over his/her former state, and a transition from untruth to truth or non-being to being (18–19).

With the substitution of Christian terminology to characterize this alternative way of learning and acquiring the truth, it immediately becomes familiar, so familiar in fact that Climacus anticipates the objection that he has falsely claimed to invent a project that is common knowledge. He openly admits that it is not his own invention; nor is it the invention of any other human being—at least no one has stepped up to take credit for having invented it, which for Climacus is a test of 'the correctness of the hypothesis and demonstrates it' (*PF* 22). But the question he really wants to raise concerning the Christian hypothesis, particularly with regard to the notions of birth and rebirth, is not whether it is true or not but whether it is *thinkable*, and if so, who is supposed to think it—someone who has not undergone a conversion and been reborn or someone who has? For Climacus the correct answer to this question is clearly the latter person, as it would be unreasonable and ludicrous to expect persons who have not been reborn to think it or to find out by themselves that they do not truly exist. This means that the incarnation could not have been conceived by human reason but is thinkable only by virtue of a revelation from the god via an entry of the eternal in time that brings the truth to human beings.

A POETICAL VENTURE

Having dialectically distinguished Christianity from philosophical idealism and other immanent approaches to the knowledge and acquisition of eternal truth, Climacus embarks on a poetical venture in the imaginative construction of a poetic analogy to the human learner and divine teacher in the parable of the king and the maiden. To recap the parable briefly, the king/god is motivated out of love for a lowly maiden/learner to do away with the inequality between them in order to establish a happy love relation, 'for only in love is the different made equal, and only in equality or in unity is there understanding' (*PF* 25). The king/god determines that this equality cannot be brought about by an *ascent* of the maiden/learner, as that would involve only a deceptive 'change of costume', not a real change of station. He thus decides to bring it about by a *descent* on his part, becoming the equal of the lowliest of persons by taking the form of a servant, which for the god is 'not something put on like the king's plebeian cloak' or Socrates' summer cloak but is 'his true form' (31–2).[13] In appearing truly in the form of a servant, the god displays a boundlessness of love that neither the king nor Socrates was capable of showing, which according to Climacus 'is why their assumed characters were still a kind of deceit' (32).

In this imaginative portrayal of the incarnation in the form of a parable we get a first glimpse of Climacus's Christology, which clearly reflects Philippians 2: 5–8 in affirming Christ's divinity while stressing his humanity and lowliness in the form of a servant. That the god's appearance in the lowly form of a servant was his true form and not something merely put on, as in docetic views of the incarnation, is obviously very important to Climacus since he repeats it several times (*PF* 31–3, 55). For this reason, too, he insists that 'the god must suffer all things, endure all things, be tried in all things, hunger in the desert, thirst in his agonies, be forsaken in death' (32). As Climacus sees it, Christ's whole life, not merely his death, is a story of suffering that happens precisely because the god wills to be the equal of the lowliest of the lowly out of love. As in the case of his thought-project, Climacus readily admits that he is likely to be charged with 'the shabbiest plagiarism' in composing this imaginative parable or 'poem' as he calls it (35). But in this instance it is the god, not a human author, who has been robbed, since in Climacus's view 'it could occur to a human being to poetize himself in the likeness of the god or the god in the likeness of himself, but not to poetize that the god poetized himself in the likeness of a human being' unless there were some prior indication from the god of a need for a relation to human beings (36). In other words, while it is within the power of the human imagination to project a human likeness to God and vice versa, Climacus maintains that it is beyond the ability of human imagination as well as human reason to come up with the Christian idea of the incarnation without a revelation of God's love and desire for understanding and unity with human beings. Otherwise, he asks, 'how could it occur to a human being that the blessed god could need him?', since the divine is by definition self-sufficient and not in need of a relation to human beings in order to acquire self-understanding (24, 36, translation modified).

THE CONCEPT OF PARADOX

The stage is now set for the introduction of Christ as the absolute paradox. It is important first of all, however, to clarify what a paradox is before there

[13] Cf. Plato, *Symposium*, 220b (1997: 501).

can be any talk of an absolute paradox. Etymologically, this term is derived from the Greek words *para* ('beyond') and *doxa* ('opinion'), connoting something that goes beyond or is contrary to common opinion. A common misunderstanding of the concept of paradox is to regard it as a formal or logical contradiction.[14] A paradox contains two terms that stand in opposition to one another, both of which are affirmed as true, whereas in a logical contradiction each term necessarily excludes the other.[15] Although Climacus frequently speaks of paradox as a contradiction, claiming for example that 'the paradox specifically unites the contradictories', he clearly affirms the principle of contradiction, which holds that a statement cannot be both true and untrue at the same time (*PF* 61, 101, 108). Thus he does not understand a paradox to be a contradiction in that sense. In fact, Climacus enjoins us not to think ill of paradox inasmuch as in his view it constitutes 'the passion of thought' without which a thinker is like a 'lover without passion', namely 'a mediocre fellow' (37). Paradox, then, is an essential component of thought, not antithetical to it. The paradoxical passion that is 'fundamentally present everywhere in thought' is to will its own downfall by discovering something thought cannot think, namely the unknown (37). Another way of expressing this is to say that the understanding is always in hot pursuit of discovering its limit, whether that be in philosophy, religion, or science. Climacus stands squarely in the Kantian tradition here in recognizing the limits of thought and the paradoxical nature of that limit, which Kant calls antinomies or apparent contradictions that defy resolution on the basis of reason alone.[16] For Climacus the unknown against which thought ultimately collides and meets its limit is the divine. We have already seen the futility, for Climacus and Kierkegaard at least, of trying to prove the existence of God, who is absolutely different from human beings and thus unknowable because of their sinfulness. That which is absolutely different cannot be known or understood by thought, not even if revealed by the god, since there is no distinguishing mark by which it can be identified and assimilated into human thought. The only way of coming to know and understand the divine, therefore, is by the god annulling the absolute difference in absolute equality in the absolute paradox of the incarnation.

While there may be many relative paradoxes that appear to be contradictory or rationally inexplicable but ultimately can be explained, Climacus maintains that there is only one absolute paradox, which is absolute

[14] Cf. Knappe (2004: 15, 24). [15] See also Evans (1992: 96–109).

[16] See Kant (1956: 328, 384–484), and ibid. 7: 'Human reason has this peculiar fate that in one species of its knowledge it is burdened by questions which, as prescribed by the very nature of reason itself, it is not able to ignore, but which, as transcending all its powers, it is also not able to answer.'

precisely because it cannot be resolved or explained by the canons of reason. The absolute paradox is thus distinguished first of all by the fact that, as suggested in Climacus's thought-project and parable, it is *inconceivable* to the understanding: 'The understanding certainly cannot think it, cannot hit upon it on its own, and if it is proclaimed, the understanding cannot understand it and merely detects that it will likely be its downfall' (*PF* 47). In its paradoxical passion to discover that which thought cannot think, the understanding is naturally driven to will its own downfall yet has 'strong objections' to the absolute paradox because it is absurd and most improbable (47, 52). If the understanding chooses to will its own downfall and comes to an understanding with the absolute paradox by understanding that it is a paradox that absolutely cannot be understood, then a happy relation, to which Climacus gives the name *faith*, will result between them. But if the understanding's objections prevail, the encounter will result in an unhappy relation, taking the form of *offence*. Offence can be either active or passive in nature but in relation to the absolute paradox is essentially passive, which means that the absolute paradox is not something discovered by the understanding itself, as in the case of a relative paradox, but is announced or made known to the understanding by the absolute paradox itself. When the understanding proclaims that it has discovered the absolute paradox and declares it to be absurd, therefore, this is merely an 'acoustical illusion' or echo of the absolute paradox's claim that the offended consciousness is foolish and absurd because it has made an 'erroneous accounting' of the absolute paradox that is directed back upon the absolute paradox as an objection to it (51).[17] Does this mean then that the absolute paradox is not really absurd? This is a thorny question that must be considered in historical context.

CREDO QUIA ABSURDUM

In introducing the notion of the absurdity of the absolute paradox, Climacus alludes to Tertullian, who not only articulated the two-natures doctrine of Christ that was later adopted by the church but also made the following famous statement in defence of that doctrine: 'The Son of God was crucified; I am not ashamed because men must needs be ashamed of it. And the Son of God died; it is by all means to be believed, because it is absurd [*quia ineptum est*]. And He was buried, and rose again; the fact is certain, because it is impossible [*certum est quia impossibile*].'[18] Quoting

17 On the acoustical illusion of the absolute paradox, see further Walsh (2005: 54–62).
18 Tertullian (2004: 12); cf. Osborn (1997: 48–64); Rose (2001: 66–70).

1 Corinthians 6: 20, 'God has chosen the foolish things of the world, that he may put to shame the things that are wise', Tertullian observes that, from the standpoint of worldly wisdom, which is really foolishness in the eyes of God, the claim that the Son of God was truly born of a virgin with a body of flesh and was crucified, died, and resurrected is foolish and not to be believed. Thus, in order to become truly wise, one must become 'a fool in the world through believing the foolish things of God'.[19] Against the idea that the Son of God's birth is 'impossible or unseemly', Tertullian points out that 'to God nothing is impossible except what is against his will'.[20] If it had been against God's will to be born a human being, then he surely would not have given the appearance of becoming such, inasmuch as God is not a deceiver. For Tertullian, then, the incarnation is not really absurd or impossible, since for God all things are possible, but only from the standpoint of worldly wisdom. Thus he is not encouraging irrational belief in the incarnation because it is in fact absurd or impossible but only because it appears that way from the limited perspective of human beings.

Echoing Tertullian, Climacus claims that the absolute paradox is a paradox *quia absurdum* (because it is absurd) (*PF* 52). Thus it is not merely the understanding that is absurd, as suggested earlier in the text, but the absolute paradox itself is absurd and is the absolute paradox because it is absurd. When the understanding declares that the paradox is absurd, therefore, it is only parroting or caricaturing what the absolute paradox announces to the understanding about itself. This means that the absolute paradox proclaims itself as the absolute paradox and is not discovered to be such by the understanding itself. In the *Postscript* Climacus amplifies his view of the absolute paradox by contrasting it with a Socratic paradox (*CUP* i: 205–13). In the Socratic relation to truth, the eternal essential truth is not a paradox in itself but becomes paradoxical by virtue of being placed in relation to an existing individual who is passionately committed to eternal truth as an objective uncertainty. In the absolute paradox, by contrast, eternal truth itself is a paradox by virtue of having come into existence in time. It is therefore not merely *objectively uncertain*, as in the case of the Socratic paradox, but *objectively absurd* because 'it contains the contradiction that something that can become historical only in direct opposition to all human understanding has become historical', namely that 'the eternal truth has come into existence in time, that God has come into existence, has been born, has grown up, etc., has come into existence exactly as an individual human being, indistinguishable from any other human being' (210–11). This thesis, he claims, constitutes the absolute paradox *sensu strictissimo* (in the strictest sense) (217).

[19] Tertullian (2004: 17). [20] Ibid. 9.

These statements clearly identify the incarnation with the absolute paradox and the absurd. However, it must be remembered that Climacus professes (perhaps ironically or humorously) not to be a Christian and thus must be seen as construing Christianity from the standpoint of a person outside of faith.[21] In his journals Kierkegaard points out that the absurd functions as a 'negative criterion of that which is higher than human understanding and knowledge' and is 'the negative sign and predicate which dialectically makes sure that the scope of "the purely human" is qualitatively terminated' (*JP* i. 11; vi. 6598). In other words, the category of the absurd constitutes the negative limit of the understanding and reason with respect to the absolute paradox, which cannot be rationally understood or comprehended. Kierkegaard then goes on to make the following crucial statement:

> When I believe, then assuredly neither faith nor the content of faith is absurd. O, no, no—but I understand very well that for the person who does not believe, faith and the content of faith are absurd, and I also understand that as soon as I myself am not in the faith, am weak, when doubt perhaps begins to stir, then faith and the content of faith gradually begin to become absurd for me. (*JP* vi. 6598; cf. i. 10)

This statement makes it clear that the concept of the absurd is a category of the understanding rather than a qualification of the incarnation itself, which is not absurd to a believer because everything is possible for God (*JP* i. 9). But the absurd is a factor in faith inasmuch as 'the content of faith, seen from the other side, is the negative absurd' which stands in dialectical tension with it (*JP* i. 8). Only the passion of faith, not a higher understanding or mediation of the absolute paradox, is able to master the absurd, but one comes to faith only by way of the absurd and the possibility of offence, which remain negative possibilities in the life of faith.

'COME TO ME, ALL YOU WHO LABOUR AND ARE BURDENED'

If Climacus, who is presumably not a Christian, construes the incarnation from the obverse side of faith as the absolute paradox and the absurd, one might expect Anti-Climacus, who is a Christian to an extraordinary degree, to eschew the language of paradox in speaking of Christ since he speaks from the perspective of faith rather than that of an unbeliever. But that is far from being the case; if anything, Anti-Climacus heightens the paradox of Christ in his exposition of the incarnation in *Practice in Christianity*.

[21] On Climacus as a humorist, see Lippitt (2000); Walsh (1994: 210–17); Evans (1983: 185–205).

In agreement with Climacus, he states quite plainly: 'The God-human being [*Gud-Mennesket*] is the paradox, absolutely the paradox; therefore, it is altogether certain that the understanding must come to a standstill on it' (*PC* 82, translation modified; cf. 25, 30, 63, 123). With Anti-Climacus, however, we get a more biblically oriented, theological depiction of Christ in contrast to Climacus's poetical, philosophical portrayal. Anti-Climacus begins with Christ's invitation in Matthew 11: 28, 'Come to me, all you who labour and are burdened, and I will give you rest', interpreting it as an expression of the unconditional love extended to all human beings by Christ, who in order to be able to invite everyone in this way must 'live in the very same manner, poor as the poorest, poorly regarded as the lowly man among the people, experienced in life's sorrow and anguish, sharing the very same condition as those one invites to come to one, those who labor and are burdened' (13). In line with Climacus's parable of the king and the maiden, he explains: 'If someone wants to invite the sufferer to come to him, he must either alter his condition and make it identical with the sufferer's or make the sufferer's condition identical with his own, for if not, the contrast makes the difference all the greater' (13). Moreover, if one wants to invite *all* sufferers, then 'it can be done in only one way, by altering one's condition in likeness to theirs if it is not already originally so designed' (14). Reflecting the traditional Lutheran distinction between the two states of Christ (the state of humiliation during his lifetime and the state of exaltation in his resurrection, ascension, and coming again), Anti-Climacus points out that the person who issues this invitation is Jesus Christ in his abasement, which is an inverse sign of his state of glory, about which nothing can be known and must therefore be believed, but one becomes a believer only by coming to Christ in his state of abasement (24).[22]

DEMONSTRATING CHRIST'S DIVINITY FROM HISTORY

The first point Anti-Climacus wishes to make about Christ is that nothing can be known or demonstrated about him from history. This is a radical claim that must be carefully examined. Anti-Climacus is not saying that nothing can be known about the historical Jesus—a conclusion some nineteenth- and twentieth-century biblical scholars came to on the basis of a historical-critical study of the gospels, resulting in a radical separation

[22] On the two states of Christ see Schmid (1961: 376–407).

between the Jesus of history and the Christ of faith.[23] For Anti-Climacus the problem is not that we can know nothing about the historical Jesus but that whatever knowledge we do have about him reveals nothing about who he is in truth, which is God incarnate. Just as Climacus and Kierkegaard found it foolish and impossible to demonstrate the existence of God, Anti-Climacus asks rhetorically: 'Can any more foolish contradiction be imagined than this, to want to *demonstrate* . . . that an individual human being is God?' (26). In his view, the only thing that can be demonstrated about the incarnation is that it conflicts with all human reason, which makes it offensive in an eminent sense because it cannot be shown to be the rational actuality it is assumed to be. The so-called demonstrations of the divinity of Christ from scripture, such as the miracles, resurrection, and ascension of Christ, are only for faith and thus are not really demonstrations at all. Nor do they demonstrate a harmony of the scriptures with reason. Reprising Climacus's argument against 'the eighteen hundred years' as proof of the truth of Christianity, Anti-Climacus suggests that the most history can demonstrate about Jesus is that he was a great man. But one would be guilty of a gross *μετάβασις εἰς ἄλλο γένος* (shifting from one category to another) as well as blasphemy if one were to move from the quantitative epithets of 'great, greater, greatest' to the qualitative conclusion that 'ergo he was God' (27, 29). And if one begins with the assumption that Christ is God, then one has '*eo ipso* [for that very reason] crossed out, canceled, the eighteen hundred years as making no difference either way, demonstrating neither *pro* nor *contra*, because the certitude of faith is infinitely higher' (27).

Having shown the impossibility of rationally demonstrating that Christ is God, Anti-Climacus examines the blasphemous idea that the results of Christ's life were more important than his life. This idea, he thinks, is 'what lies at the base of this whole enterprise' of demonstrating the divinity of Christ from history (30). Anti-Climacus does not deny that the results of Christ's life were extraordinary, but if one wants to make the claim that Christ's life was extraordinary because of the results of his life, this is once again to make a mockery of God. Unlike other great figures in history, Christ's life is extraordinary in itself, not because he accomplished great things. Anti-Climacus asks us to imagine a person—Martin Luther King, Jr. would be a good example—who suffered wrong from his contemporaries but was justified by history and shown to be the extraordinary person he was on the basis of the results of his life. But the same does not apply to Christ, for two reasons. First, we cannot know anything about who Christ really was from the historical results of his life. Second, to judge Christ on

[23] See Schweitzer (1961); Kähler (1964); Bultmann (1958). See also Paget (2001); Theissen and Merz (1998); Funk and the Jesus Seminar (1998); Evans (1996); Funk *et al.* (1993).

the basis of the results of his life is to make his abasement into something accidental rather than a self-willed condition which, together with his divinity, constitutes a 'dialectical knot' that cannot be untied until his coming again in glory (33). The calamity of Christendom, Anti-Climacus observes, is that 'Christ is neither the one nor the other, neither the person he was when he lived on earth nor the one he will be at his second coming . . . but is someone about whom we have learned something in an inadmissible way from history' (35).

THE LIFE OF JESUS

Anti-Climacus thus emphasizes once again that it is the abased Christ who issues the invitation to all to come unto him, and it is precisely this combination of abasement and divinity that creates the possibility of offence at him. To illustrate this claim, he constructs an imaginative mini-history of the life of Jesus divided into two periods (*PC* 40–56). In the first period Jesus is portrayed as being idolized by the crowd but doubted, scorned, and scoffed at by the established order, represented in Anti-Climacus's account by persons from the (Danish) cultured elite: the sagacious and sensible person, the clergyman, the philosopher, the sagacious statesman, the solid citizen, the witty scoffer. These personages are mystified by Jesus but nevertheless reject him because he does not conform to their various preconceptions of what an extraordinary person should be like or do and because it is 'sheer madness' and a 'delusion' on his part to consider himself to be God (43, 49). In the second period of Christ's life all their predictions come true, as the people turn away from him and he comes to no good end, walking straight into the trap laid for him by the established order. Assuming for the moment that Christ was only a human being, Anti-Climacus asks how 'this frightful inverted relation' can be explained, inasmuch as no one, or practically no one, accepted the invitation of Christ but opposed him and put him to death (57). The answer, Anti-Climacus suggests, is to be found in the fact that Christ did not conform to the merely human conception of compassion and human misery but exhibited divine compassion in the 'unlimited *recklessness*' with which he concerned himself with the suffering of others (58). People are prepared to show compassion to others 'to a certain degree', he notes, but 'To make oneself quite *literally one with the most wretched* (and this, this alone is *divine* compassion)' is 'too much' for them (59). They are thus offended at the loftiness of Christ, which they are prepared to believe in at a distance for an hour or so when a poet or orator depicts it to them but certainly not when it is manifested in actuality, in their daily life.

CHRIST AS THE UNITY OF GOD AND AN INDIVIDUAL HUMAN BEING

Having introduced the possibility of offence at Christ, Anti-Climacus enters into a fuller exposition of this distinctively Christian category, which brings us to the heart of his paradoxical view of the incarnation: 'Offence is essentially related to the composite [*Sammensætningen*] of God and human being (*Menneske*), or to the God-human being [*Gud-Mennesket*]', who is 'the unity of God and an individual human being [*et enkelt Menneske*]', not God and man or the human race (*PC* 81–2, translation modified; cf. *SV1* xii. 79). Theologically, this is the main bone of contention between Anti-Climacus and the speculative Christologies of his time, which in his view are not Christian but another expression of the ancient pagan claim of kinship between God and humanity. Anti-Climacus does not mention any speculative thinkers in particular who are guilty of this modern confusion, which in his estimation is 'far more dangerous' than the fallacies of interpretation in the early period of Christendom, but there are several candidates who fit the description in one way or another (123).

The first candidate is Hegel, who affirms an implicit unity of divine and human nature on the basis of the principle of identity or the unity of thought and being.[24] This implicit unity comes to consciousness in humanity 'in such a way that a human being appears to consciousness as God, and God appears to it as a human being'.[25] But for Hegel it is essential that the consciousness of this divine–human unity, which is known philosophically in the form of *thought*, be brought forth for humanity in the form of *sense certainty*, that is, as an immediate sensible intuition that can be perceived. It was therefore necessary for God to appear in the world in the flesh, and for the sake of sense certainty, which cannot perceive the thought of humanity, to appear in '*just one human being*'.[26] This person is Jesus Christ, the God-man, whom Hegel recognizes as being 'a monstrous compound [*ungeheure Zusammensetzung*] that directly contradicts both representation and understanding [*Verstand*]'—which is the closest he comes to the notion of paradox.[27] As mediator of the divine–human unity, however, the idea of the God-man stands in need of mediation itself. For Hegel, this occurs religiously through the death of Christ, socio-culturally through the formation and subsistence of the community of faith, and philosophically through the higher comprehension of reason (*Vernunft*).[28] Hegel thus agrees with Anti-Climacus that the God-man appeared in the form of an individual human being, but for him the incarnation is not

24 Hegel (1984–7: iii. 312; cf. Hodgson (2005: 156–74). 25 Hegel (1984–7: iii. 312).
26 Ibid. 313. 27 Ibid. 315. 28 Ibid. 322–47; see also Taylor (1980).

unique or limited to Christ, since it represents the historical process of the reconciliation of humanity as such with the divine.

Another candidate is the Danish speculative theologian Martensen. While affirming that Christ 'can indeed be said to have descended from heaven and thereby has a supernatural character', Martensen follows Schleiermacher in viewing Christ as the Second Adam, 'the first perfect creation of *human nature*' and 'the holy root which invisibly bears the entire human race' and is its 'purest and most noble flower'.[29] But Martensen's Hegelian roots are still evident as he goes on to state: 'One must, to be sure, maintain the *fact* of the incarnation, but ... in doing so, one must not forget that this fact has as its presupposition the originally existing, eternal unity of divine and human nature.'[30] On this basis Martensen argues that the incarnation is the mediation of the divine and the human, which invalidates the principle of contradiction or law of the excluded middle in Christian theology, whose task in his view 'has always been to grasp the identity of what is contradictory for the understanding'.[31] He thus concludes: 'The central point of Christianity—the doctrine of Incarnation, the doctrine of the God-man—shows precisely that Christian metaphysics cannot remain in an either/or, but that it must find its truth in the third which this law excludes.'[32] The 'third' of which he speaks, of course, is the mediation of speculative theology and philosophy. Like Hegel, Martensen also holds that 'the union of the divine and human natures demands realization in an actual personality'.[33] Thus we must continue to look elsewhere for a speculative thinker who denies Anti-Climacus's fundamental claim that the incarnation is the unity of God and an individual human being.

That person is David Friedrich Strauss, the left-wing Hegelian whose seminal work *The Life of Jesus Critically Examined* (1835) caused a stir not only in German biblical and theological circles but also in Denmark and elsewhere. Strauss's critique of the New Testament gospels radically undermined the historical character of the Christian faith by exposing the presence of many mythical elements in the biblical narratives about the life of Jesus. In the 'Concluding Dissertation' of this work he also takes into consideration the dogmatic import of the life of Jesus, reviewing and critiquing the history of Christology from its orthodox formulation to the present age. This leads him to pose the following questions: 'is not the idea of the unity of the divine and human natures a real one in a far higher sense, when I regard the whole race of mankind as its realization, than when I single out one man as such a realization? is not an incarnation of God from eternity,

[29] Martensen (2004: 592; 1866: 259); cf. Schleiermacher (1956: 62–5, 367–8, 389).
[30] Martensen (2004: 596); cf. Martensen (1866: 258).
[31] Martensen (2004: 588). [32] Ibid. [33] Martensen (1866: 261).

a truer one than an incarnation limited to a particular point of time.'[34] Strauss then goes on to state:

This is the key to the whole of Christology, that, as subject of the predicate which the church assigns to Christ, we place, instead of an individual, an idea; but an idea which has an existence in reality, not in the mind only, like that of Kant. In an individual, a God-man, the properties and functions which the church ascribes to Christ contradict themselves; in the idea of the race, they perfectly agree. Humanity is the union of the two natures—God become man, the infinite manifesting itself in the finite, and the finite spirit remembering its infinitude; . . . It is Humanity that dies, rises, and ascends to heaven, for from the negation of its phenomenal life there ever proceeds a higher spiritual life . . . By faith in this Christ . . . that is, by the kindling within him of the idea of Humanity, the individual man participates in the divinely human life of the species.[35]

It is here, I submit, that we find the speculative viewpoint that Anti-Climacus specifically has in mind when he insists that the incarnation is a unity of God and an individual human being, which Strauss explicitly denies.[36] That Strauss is the person Anti-Climacus is chiefly opposing is also evident in his charge that 'speculation takes away from the God-human being the qualifications of temporality, contemporaneity, and actuality', since for Strauss the God-man is the idea of humanity, not an actual human being (*PC* 81, translation modified). But Strauss is not the only left-wing Hegelian who associates the incarnation with humanity or the human species rather than a particular human being. Feuerbach also interprets Christ as 'nothing but an image, under which the unity of the species has impressed itself on the popular consciousness'.[37] For Feuerbach the unity of the species is realized in the whole human race, not in a single individual. Feuerbach thus concludes that 'where there arises the consciousness of the species as a species, the idea of humanity as a whole, Christ disappears, without, however, his true nature disappearing; for he was the substitute for the consciousness of the species, the image under which it was made present to the people, and became the law of the popular life'.[38] While not associating the species with the figure of Christ, Marx also affirms the consciousness of 'species-being' as constituting authentic human nature and existence, from which modern workers are alienated by the subhuman material conditions and status of their lives as productive labourers.[39]

We shall have occasion in a later chapter to consider the sociopolitical implications of affirming the species over the single individual. It should

34 Strauss (1973: 780). 35 Ibid.

36 See also Pattison (2007; 2005: 150–6); Come (1997: 22–3).

37 Feuerbach (1989: 268); cf. Harvey (1995: 114–19). 38 Ibid. 269.

39 Marx (1963: 120–34).

be pointed out here, however, that in a journal entry from 1850, the same year *Practice in Christianity* was published, Kierkegaard reaffirms the view in *The Concept of Anxiety* that the single individual is more and higher than the race or species, inasmuch as the single individual is 'the whole race and also the individuation', whereas the race is merely an animal qualification and as such is not akin to or identical with God (*JP* ii. 2024; cf. 2071). As Kierkegaard sees them, human beings are not merely 'animal copies' (*Dyre-Exemplarer*) or particular specimens of the race but spiritual beings who are created in the image of God and thus are higher than the race (2024, cf. 2048). Consequently, he contends that '*here* is where the battle must really be fought' (*JP* ii. 1614). Christ is not the human race nor does he save the human race, only single individuals.

FORMS OF OFFENCE AT CHRIST

Over against the speculative mediation of the Hegelians Anti-Climacus continues to stress the paradoxical contradictoriness of the incarnation: 'Humanly speaking, there is no possibility of a crazier composite than this either in heaven or on earth or in the abyss or in the most fantastic aberrations of thought' (*PC* 82). He then proceeds to identify three forms of offence occasioned by Christ, two of which constitute essential offence, or offence in the strictest sense, while the third concerns Christ as an individual who comes into conflict with the established order. Elucidating the third form first, Anti-Climacus observes that this form of offence is not limited to Christ, as any person who is unwilling to be subordinate to the established order can become the object of offence. From the perspective of the established order, insubordination implies that one is God or at least more than a human being, whereas in Anti-Climacus's view it is actually the established order that has deified itself as 'a totality that recognizes nothing above itself' (91). When the established order thus accuses Christ or some other single individual of blasphemy for presumably wanting to be God or more than human, we have here another instance of an 'acoustical illusion' in which the established order hears its own claim to be divine as if it were being made by an individual about him/herself (88). That this form of offence can be expected to occur in the present age is made apparent to Anti-Climacus by the fact that Hegel's *Philosophy of Right*, the foremost statement on civil society and the state in the modern age, makes the individual conscience 'a form of evil' because the established order has been deified in it (87).[40] The consequence of such deification, as

[40] Cf. Hegel (1991*a*: 167–84).

Anti-Climacus sees it, is that everything becomes secularized, including the relationship to God, just as the religious secularization of Judaism brought Jesus into conflict with the established order of his time, creating the possibility of offence at him because he emphasized inwardness in contrast to the external piety of the scribes and Pharisees (89, 91–2).

Whereas the possibility of offence at Christ occasioned by his conflict with the established order of his time was a 'vanishing possibility' that ended with his death, the two forms of essential offence identified by Anti-Climacus are transhistorical in character; that is, they 'will continue until the end of time' and have to do specifically with Christ as the God-human being (*PC* 94). The first possibility of essential offence is posed by the *loftiness* or divinity of Christ and is occasioned by the fact that he speaks and acts as if he were God (cf. Matthew 11: 6; Luke 7: 23) and on one occasion even declares himself to be God (John 6: 51–61). Since the claim that Christ was God cannot be demonstrated and the individual who speaks this way about himself looks just like everyone else, the possibility of offence at Christ's loftiness cannot be avoided and must be encountered by everyone, even those who do not take offence at him but believe. The second possibility of essential offence has to do with Christ's *lowliness* or the fact that 'the one who passes himself off as God proves to be the lowly, poor, suffering, and finally powerless human being' (102). The possibility of offence in this instance is occasioned not by Christ's claim to be God but by 'the boundless self-contradiction' that 'God should be a mortal man like this' (102). However, it is the combination of loftiness and lowliness in Christ that presents the possibility of offence, for neither loftiness nor lowliness by itself is offensive.

CHRIST AS A SIGN OF CONTRADICTION

The possibility of essential offence at Christ is thus occasioned by the fact that he is a 'sign of contradiction' (*PC* 124). To be a sign means that something is different from what it immediately is; to be a sign of contradiction means that it contains a contradiction in its composition, that it is the opposite of what it immediately is or appears to be. In the case of Christ, this means that his lowliness is inversely a sign of his loftiness. Christ's lowliness poses the possibility of offence solely because it is a sign of his loftiness, for if he were merely a lowly man there would be no reason to be offended by him. But a sign is a sign only to the person who knows that it is a sign and what it means; otherwise it becomes the opposite of a sign, 'an unconditional concealment' (125). Consequently, there must be something that draws attention to the contradiction, such as a miracle or direct claim to be God, but which is not enough in itself to cancel the contradiction, thus occasioning the possibility of offence. Anti-Climacus makes it quite clear that the kind of contradiction Christ exemplifies as a sign of contradiction is not a *logical* contradiction, which applies only in the realm of thought, but a *qualitative* contradiction: 'In Scripture the God-human being is called a sign of contradiction—but what contradiction, if any, could there very well be in the speculative unity of God and humanity? No, there is no contradiction in that; but the contradiction, and it is the greatest possible, is the qualitative contradiction between being God and being an individual human being' (125, translation modified). From the perspective of speculative theology, there is no contradiction, or more precisely, the apparent logical contradiction of the incarnation is annulled or mediated in the higher comprehension of the eternal unity of God and humanity. From Anti-Climacus's perspective, however, such a unity does not have 'the remotest resemblance to the essentially Christian' but is 'a fantastic unity that has never existed except *sub specie aeterni* [under the aspect of eternity]' or in the realm of pure thought (126). The qualitative contradiction pertaining to Christ, by contrast, is the greatest possible contradiction because it combines qualitative opposites in existence, not merely in thought, and therefore cannot be mediated by abstract thought.

CHRIST'S INCOGNITO

As a sign of contradiction Christ is not directly recognizable as God but takes on 'the most profound incognito' in assuming the form of a servant as a lowly individual human being (*PC* 128).[41] In Anti-Climacus's estimation, however, the modern age has abolished Christ, accepting only his teachings or else making him into a fantastic being who was God 'to such a degree' that he would have been immediately and directly recognizable if one had lived contemporaneously with him, whereas the truth is that he was God 'to such a degree' that he was unrecognizable as such to his contemporaries (128). Although Christ freely willed 'from eternity' to be incognito, in choosing to be born as an individual human being he became subject to 'the power of his own incognito', trapped or bound, as it were, in an 'omnipotently maintained unrecognizability' that was the basis of his purely human suffering (128–9, 132). As Anti-Climacus sees it, Christ's incognito is characterized by 'a strange kind of dialectic' in which 'he, omnipotent, binds himself and does it so omnipotently that he actually feels bound, suffers under the consequences of his loving and free

[41] For a comparison of Kierkegaard and Luther on the incognito or hiddenness of God in Christ, see Hinkson (2001).

decision to become an individual human being' (132). Here one can detect a version of the Lutheran doctrine of *communicatio idiomatum* (impartation of properties), which in its orthodox formulation affirmed a full imparting of the attributes of deity to the humanity of Christ. In some seventeenth- and nineteenth-century Neo-Lutheran kenotic reformulations of this doctrine, however, it was modified so as to involve a self-limitation with regard to the use of certain divine attributes such as omnipotence, omniscience, and omnipresence in Christ's earthly existence.[42] Anti-Climacus likewise embraces the notion of the self-limitation of the divine but understands it *paradoxically* inasmuch as Christ is seen to employ omnipotence in the very binding of himself to the limitations and suffering of human existence rather than refraining from the use of his omnipotence or temporarily abandoning it altogether as proposed in some kenotic theories.[43]

CHRIST'S INDIRECT COMMUNICATION

Being the sign of contradiction also means that it is impossible for Christ to communicate who he is directly to human beings, but in Anti-Climacus's view Christ employs a form of indirect communication that is different from the one identified by Johannes Climacus in the *Postscript*. In that book, it may be recalled, indirect communication takes the form of a double reflection in which the communicator becomes a cipher or 'nobody' in order to set the recipient free 'to untie the knot himself' (*PC* 133; cf. *CUP* i. 72–7). But indirect communication can also occur in such a way as to require the communicator's presence through reduplication of the communication in the communicator's own existence. As Anti-Climacus sees it, all communication concerning what it means to exist requires a communicator who exists in what has been understood (134). In order for a communication to be truly indirect, however, the communicator must be 'dialectically defined' as a contradiction, so that even when the communicator speaks directly, as when Christ claims to be God or the Son of God (John 10: 30–6), the communication is not direct but indirect, since 'it is not entirely direct that an individual human being should be God' (134). The recipient of the communication is thus confronted with a choice of whether to believe in him or to be offended. Anti-Climacus

42 See Thompson (2006: 76–87); McGrath (1994: 78–81); Welch (1972: 235–40).

43 See also *JFY* 172–3, where Kierkegaard suggests that Christ 'hides' the use of his powers of omnipotence from the crowd, thus reflecting the 17th-century *krypsis* (concealment) school of Tübingen rather than the *kenōsis* (renunciation) school of Giessen as suggested by Gouwens (1996: 169 n.). On these schools see McGrath (1994: 79–80); Schmid (1961: 390–3). On Kierkegaard's kenotic Christology, see also Law (1993: 183–9), and Rose (2001: 107–14).

thus concludes his exposition of the possibility of offence at Christ by re-emphasizing its importance as 'the negative mark' without which Christ would not be the object of faith, for without the possibility of offence, the divinity of Christ would be directly recognizable, which is paganism (143). To abolish the possibility of offence, then, is to abolish not only faith but Christ and Christianity as well.

CHRIST AS REDEEMER

For all Kierkegaard's emphasis upon Christ as the absolute paradox and sign of contradiction, the dual roles of Christ as the redeemer and prototype of human beings are equally if not more important in his understanding of Christ. Although the role of Christ as prototype is stressed in Kierkegaard's later works and journals, it always stands in a complementary dialectical relation to his role as redeemer. Thus each role must be viewed in tandem with the other. For the purpose of analysis, however, I shall begin with the role of Christ as redeemer, who makes his first appearance, it may be recalled, in *Philosophical Fragments* under the guise of the unnamed teacher who brings the truth as well as the condition for understanding it to human beings, who are so immersed in sin that they are unaware of lacking the truth. The first thing Christ does, then, is to help individuals to recollect that they exist in a state of untruth. But this much, Climacus points out, even a Socratic teacher can do: 'To this act of consciousness, the Socratic principle applies: the teacher is only an occasion, whoever he may be, even if he is a god, because I can discover my own untruth only by myself, because only when *I* discover it is it discovered, not before, even though the whole world knew it' (*PF* 14). Since the whole point of Climacus's thought-project is to conceive, if possible, a situation that is different from the Socratic immanent way to the truth, he is quick to point out that this is the 'one and only analogy to the Socratic' in this alternative scenario (14). Where the unnamed teacher and the Socratic teacher truly differ is that the former actually brings the truth and the condition (faith) for understanding it to human beings, whereas the Socratic teacher is only a midwife who assists persons in recollecting the truth themselves. The unnamed teacher is thus far more than a teacher, because in order to bring the truth to human beings he must first transform them, which only the god is capable of doing. The unnamed teacher, then, is the god, but he is also a *saviour*, *deliverer*, and *reconciler* (17). With these epithets, Climacus clearly alludes to the work of Christ in his role as redeemer, but it is primarily in Kierkegaard's later devotional writings that the redeeming work of Christ through his suffering, death, and atonement for sin is spelt out.

CLASSICAL THEORIES OF ATONEMENT

Before turning to these writings, however, let us briefly review the Christian doctrine of atonement concerning God's redeeming and reconciling activity in and through the suffering and death of Christ. Several types of atonement theory have emerged in the Christian tradition to explain how and why Christ's atonement took place and what it accomplished. The earliest type, known as the classic or dramatic theory, was first worked out by the Greek church father Irenaeus, whose interpretation became the dominant view among both Eastern and Western theologians in the patristic period and, according to one school of interpretation at least, was later revived and deepened by Luther.[44] The central claim of this theory is that a cosmic drama took place between God and Satan, the power of evil that held humankind in bondage and suffering in the world. Atonement or reconciliation between God and the world was initiated and effected by God through the death of Christ as a ransom or payment to Satan in order to secure the freedom of humankind from sin, death, and the devil. The second type, dubbed the Latin or legal theory, introduced by Anselm (1033–1109), archbishop of Canterbury, in his treatise *Cur Deus Homo* (Why God Became Human), can be found in medieval, Reformation, and post-Reformation Protestant theology.[45] According to Anselm, Christ came not to make satisfaction to Satan but to God, whose honour was violated by the transgressions of humankind, thereby requiring a penalty to be paid for the remission of sin.[46] Since no human being is worthy to be an acceptable sacrifice to God, Christ voluntarily makes satisfaction for sin in our stead by his sinlessness and perfect obedience unto death.[47] A variant of the penal theory, called the sacrificial theory, is based on the New Testament book of Hebrews and the Old Testament tradition of making a sin-offering or sacrifice to expiate (atone for) rather than to propitiate (appease God for) the sins of humankind.[48] In this version, found in both patristic and Reformation theology, Christ is viewed as the representative of and substitute for human beings. He is both the High Priest and the sacrificial victim through whose death humankind is redeemed and a new covenant is mediated between God and his chosen people. The final type, variously identified as the exemplar, subjective, or moral influence theory, was formulated by Peter Abelard (1079–1142), a younger contemporary of Anselm who was critical of both the legal and classic theories of atonement. Abelard's alternative emphasizes the role of Christ as example and teacher whose life

[44] Cf. Aulén (1950: 20–76, 119–38). Contra Aulén on Luther, see Althaus (1966: 218–23); Siggins (1970: 108–43).

[45] Aulén (1950: 97–111, 139–49).

[46] Anselm (1962: 202–3, 206–10).

[47] Ibid. 192–4, 198, 232–4, 237.

[48] Richardson (1976: 23–4).

of love, forgiveness, suffering, and death stirs the hearts of human beings to repentance and love in response, which become the basis for their reconciliation with God.[49] This theory took hold in liberal Protestant theology of the nineteenth and twentieth centuries, most notably in Schleiermacher and his followers.[50]

Of course, many theologians cannot be pigeon-holed as advocating a single type of atonement theory, and it is to be expected that Kierkegaard will defy classification as well. Moreover, speaking in the voice of a pseudonym, Kierkegaard observes that dogmatic theologians seek to comprehend the mystery of the atonement by pondering and illuminating its eternal significance, whereas the believer is commanded to believe rather than to try to comprehend it; thus 'the death of the Holy One has a totally different meaning for him' (*WA* 58–9). Like the believer, Kierkegaard is content to rest in faith and concern himself only with the meaning of the death and atonement of Christ for the believer, which is the believer's personal reconciliation with God in and through Christ.

HOLY COMMUNION

For Kierkegaard the longing for reconciliation with God begins with the consciousness of sin, in which one becomes aware of one's distance from being a self before God.[51] But the consciousness of sin is dialectical in character, inasmuch as it may lead one further away from faith in the continuation and intensification of sin, as described in *The Sickness unto Death*, or it may become further qualified so as to function as an indirectly positive aid in bringing a person to faith.[52] In the latter instance, the consciousness of sin takes the form of a *contrite or anguished conscience* that sorrows over sin, openly confesses it, and seeks forgiveness from Christ, who takes away the consciousness of sin and replaces it with the consciousness of forgiveness (*JP* iii. 2461; iv. 4018; *UDVS* 14, 18–19, 246; *WL* 201). The place where this happens is in the rite of Holy Communion. It is thus in the posture of penitence and confession, culminating in a heartfelt longing for communion with Christ at the altar, that reconciliation with God in and through Christ's atonement takes place (*CD* 251–61, 264–5, 269). Communion in the Danish Evangelical Lutheran Church during Kierkegaard's time was commonly preceded by a public service of confession in which general confession was made by the participants and absolution or assurance of the pardoning of their sins was given by

49 Fairweather (1956: 283–4). 50 Aulén (1950: 112–13, 149–54, 149–56).

51 On the longing for reconciliation with God, see Cappelørn (2007).

52 See further Walsh (2005: 20–47); Cappelørn (2004).

the priest before they received communion, which was offered on Fridays, Sundays, and holidays at the cathedral Church of Our Lady in Copenhagen where Kierkegaard communed.[53] Kierkegaard composed a baker's dozen of discourses for the communion on Fridays, which was his favourite time to attend communion. It is primarily in this liturgical context and in these communion discourses that his views on the atonement of Christ are expressed. The event for which these discourses were written also accounts for the very personal nature of the reflection one finds in them.

In one of these discourses Kierkegaard speaks of Christ as a faithful friend whose death 'has atoned for my every slightest actual sin, but also for the one that may lurk most deeply in my soul without my being aware of it' (*CD* 260). As he sees it, Christ did not sacrifice his life 'for people in general, nor did he want to save people in general'; rather, 'he sacrificed himself in order to save each one individually' (272, cf. 293–4). For Kierkegaard, therefore, the atonement is an intensely personal matter, not an objective, impersonal cosmic event or transaction that takes place between God and the devil, nor was it 'a bygone event' that is 'finished and done with' (278). The generation that crucified Christ was not solely to blame for his death, as it is the human race, to which all of us belong, that is responsible. As Kierkegaard sees it, therefore, we are not merely 'spectators and observers at a past event' but 'accomplices in a present event' (278).

By his death Christ 'performs love's miracle, so that, without doing anything—by suffering he moves every person who has a heart!' (*CD* 280). This statement resonates with Abelard's moral influence theory in its emphasis on the atonement as an act of love that elicits love in return. But in line with the Latin or legal perspective, Kierkegaard also describes Christ's death as 'the sacrifice of Atonement' that 'makes repayment' for the sin of the world and for betraying and crucifying him, in return for which Christ institutes 'the meal of love' or 'the meal of reconciliation for all' (280; cf. *JP* i. 342; ii. 1223, 1423; iv. 4038). Reflecting Luther's view of the real presence of Christ in communion, Kierkegaard claims that Christ is personally present at the communion table and knows each person who belongs to him.[54] Using the analogy of the sun, whose rays penetrate everywhere, he describes Christ as 'humankind's eternal sun' which shines everywhere (272). Unlike the sun, however, Christ makes a distinction between those he knows and those he does not know. If one is not known by him, communion is received in vain, but if one is known by him and belongs to him as a follower, he is always present and accompanies one wherever one goes. Kierkegaard thus says: 'It is not as if everything were settled by someone's going to Communion on rare occasions; no, the task

[53] Cappelørn (2006).

[54] On Luther see Althaus (1966: 375–403).

is to remain at the Communion table when you leave the Communion table' (274). Reconciliation with Christ at the communion table, then, is not finished there but only just begun.

A recurring theme in Kierkegaard's communion discourses is that we are incapable of doing anything at all to make satisfaction for our sin, not even so much as to be able to hold fast the thought of our unworthiness so as to make ourselves receptive to Christ's blessing: 'If at the Communion table you want to be capable of the least little thing yourself, even merely to step forward yourself, you confuse everything, you prevent the reconciliation, make the satisfaction impossible' (*CD* 298–9; cf. *WA* 140, 155). Consequently, Christ must do everything in that regard. This is perhaps best illustrated in two communion discourses on the woman who was a sinner in Luke 7: 36–50. This woman is seen as a 'prototype of piety' because of her unconditional sorrow over her sin, her self-forgetfulness and open confession of sin, and especially her love of Christ, which is expressed by the fact that she said nothing and did nothing except weep and kiss his feet in the realization that she was capable of doing literally nothing at all to make satisfaction for her sin, whereas Christ was capable of doing 'unconditionally everything' (*WA* 140–1, 149, 155–7).[55]

HOW CHRIST ATONES FOR SIN

Exactly how Christ makes satisfaction for sin is explained in a substitutionary manner by Kierkegaard. Using the figure of Christ as high priest in the New Testament epistle to the Hebrews, he portrays Christ as the high priest who puts himself completely in our place in several ways (*WA* 113–24). First, he who was God put himself in our place by becoming a human being in order truly to be able to sympathize with us, which only divine sympathy is capable of doing. Second, unlike a merely human sympathizer, who has 'the universal and common limitation of being unable to put himself completely in another's place', the high priest of true sympathy is able to put himself completely in the sufferer's place in the sense of really being able to understand what the sufferer is going through and to comfort that person regardless of the nature of his or her sufferings (115). Christ is able to do this because he has suffered more than any other human being ever has or ever will suffer and has been tempted and even abandoned by God. Yet he is without sin, which is the only way Christ cannot put himself in our place and is infinitely different from us, who are all sinners. But Christ is able to put himself completely in our place in yet another way, namely

[55] On the woman who was a sinner see further Walsh (2006). On the dialectic of divine and human agency in the communion discourses, see Barrett (2007).

by making satisfaction for our sin and guilt through his own suffering and death, suffering in our place the punishment for sin so that we may be saved and live (123). Addressing the reader directly, Kierkegaard asks:

> Here it is indeed even more literally true that he puts himself completely in your place than in the situation we described earlier, where we indicated that he could completely understand you, but you still remain in your place, and he in his. But the satisfaction of Atonement means that you step aside and that he takes your place—does he not then put himself completely in your place? (*WA* 123)

When 'punitive justice here in the world or in judgment in the next' looks for us in the place where we stand as sinners, therefore, it will not find us, because we are no longer there and someone else stands in our place (123). Kierkegaard thus asks rhetorically: 'What is the Redeemer but a substitute who puts himself completely in your place and in mine, and what is the comfort of Redemption but this, that the substitute, atoning, puts himself completely in your place and in mine!'

Another way of expressing what happens in the atonement is to say that Christ hides or covers a multitude of sins through his sacrificial love. Kierkegaard devotes several discourses to the topic of hiding a multitude of sins in Christian love by Christ's followers (*EUD* 55–78; *WL* 280–99). In the communion discourse on this topic, however, he focuses exclusively on Christ's love, which hides a multitude of sins by his death. Even though we may be able to hide our sins from the world, we cannot hide them from ourselves or from the conscience that dwells deep within us, leading us to wish: 'Would that there were a forgiveness, a forgiveness that does not increase my sense of guilt but truly takes the guilt from me, also the consciousness of it' (*WA* 184). For Kierkegaard, Christ's love does just that. Christ stands at the altar and invites those who want to flee from the consciousness of sin to his arms and literally hides their sin, transforming it into purity and enabling them to believe themselves justified and pure. Just as a mother hen gathers her chicks under her wing and covers them in hiding from the enemy (cf. Matthew 23: 37), so Christ hides our sins with his death, which pays the penalty for sin (185–6). Christ died only once for our sins and for those of the whole world, but the pledge that he died for us is repeated at the communion table, where he gives himself to us as a safe hiding place. Kierkegaard points out that only Christ can do this, for even the most loving person can only mitigate or extenuate our sins, not hide them. In receiving the pledge that Christ died for us, we receive Christ himself, but 'Only by remaining in him, only by living yourself into him are you under cover, only then is there a cover over the multitude of your sins' (188). Kierkegaard thus concludes:

This is why the Lord's Supper is called communion with him. It is not only in memory of him, it is not only as a pledge that you have communion with him, but it is the communion, this communion that you are to strive to preserve in your daily life by more and more living yourself out of yourself and living yourself into him, in his love, which hides a multitude of sins. (188)

As Kierkegaard sees it, then, the atonement or satisfaction wrought by Christ's death is 'the ultimate pledge' that our sins have been forgiven (*WA* 159). While Christ can be said to have borne the sins of the world even in his lifetime through his life of suffering, we have a comfort that his contemporaries lacked in that 'his death becomes the infinite comfort, the infinite headstart' for those who follow him (159). But a word of judgement also accompanies this word of comfort in that, just as those who love Christ much are forgiven much, so too those who love him little are forgiven little. Forgiveness is a totally unmerited gift of grace that places the sinner in an infinite debt of gratitude to Christ, but Christ's innocent death, which was 'love's sacrifice', also passes judgement on the lack of love for him in response to his offer of forgiveness (171–2). In this sense, Kierkegaard observes, love is more severe than justice, which denies forgiveness because one has sinned too much rather than loved too little. With justice there is no forgiveness at all, whereas with love everything is forgiven, with the result that if one is then forgiven little it is because one has loved little in return, thereby incurring new sin and guilt for one's lack of love.

But does this not revert back to 'the baleful region of meritoriousness' with the forgiveness of sins being based on love rather than works (*WA* 176)? Kierkegaard thinks not, as that is prevented by 'the blessed recurrence of salvation in love', in which forgiveness is given in response to loving much or little, not as a meritorious consequence of love (176). Love and forgiveness stand in a reciprocal as well as proportional relation to one another, each eliciting and increasing the other, so that if one is forgiven little, it is because one has loved little, not because one has not merited forgiveness. Regardless of whether one is forgiven much or little, everything remains within the sphere of love. In emphasizing a reciprocal relation between love and forgiveness, Kierkegaard again reflects an Abelardian subjective approach to the atonement, but the substitutionary perspective is clearly dominant in his soteriology.

CHRIST AS PROTOTYPE

Recognizing that 'times are different and different times have different requirements', Kierkegaard observes that in the Middle Ages the gospel of grace was changed into a new law more rigorous than the old and everything became a matter of works and merit (*FSE* 15). Then Luther appeared on the historical scene with the corrective that a person is saved by faith alone, strategically shoving aside the New Testament epistle of James with its warning that faith without works is dead in order to restore faith to its rightful place. The secular mentality, however, was quick to take Luther's words in vain, appropriating grace in such a way as to free itself from works altogether. In the present age, in which everyone is a Christian as a matter of course, Kierkegaard imagines that if Luther were alive today he would no doubt bring the Apostle James forward a little, not against faith and grace but for their sake, so that the need for them might be felt more deeply and not taken in vain (*FSE* 24; cf. *JFY* 192–4).

Similarly, with respect to Christ, Kierkegaard remarks in his journals: 'It is entirely clear that it is Christ as the prototype which must now be stressed dialectically, for the very reason that the dialectical (Christ as gift), which Luther stressed, has been taken completely in vain, so that the "imitator" in no way resembles the prototype but is absolutely undifferentiated, and then grace is merely slipped in' (*JP* ii. 1862). Kierkegaard is quite conscious of having moved 'in the direction of Christ as pattern' in his writings and even cautions himself not to 'go astray by all too one-sidedly staring at Christ as the prototype' (*JP* iii. 2503; ii. 1852). Thus, while recognizing that 'the present situation calls for stressing "imitation" ', he insists that 'the matter must above all not be turned in such a way that Christ now becomes only prototype and not Redeemer, . . . No, *the Atonement and grace are and remain definitive*', for several reasons (*JP* ii. 1909, emphasis added). One is that all our striving will be shown to be 'sheer paltriness' when we stand before God for judgement at the moment of death (1909). Another is that grace is needed in order to prevent our striving from being transformed into an 'agonizing anxiety' that prevents us from striving (1909). Perhaps the most important reason, however, is that we continue to sin while striving and therefore remain in unconditional need of the atonement. Kierkegaard even interprets the atonement itself as pointing to Christ as our prototype and example inasmuch as the vicarious satisfaction with which we 'put on Christ' means not only to appropriate his merit for the forgiveness of our sins but also to seek to be like him, to borrow his clothes, so to speak, so as 'to *re-present* him' (*JP* ii. 1858). Another reason why Christ as prototype must be advanced in the present age is because Christianity has been turned into a doctrine, throwing the situation in Christendom into 'utter confusion' and making the definition of what it means to be a Christian 'almost indistinguishable' (*JFY* 209). Consequently, the *prototype* must be advanced in order at least to procure some respect for Christianity, to make somewhat distinguishable what it means to be a Christian, to get Christianity moved out of the realm of scientific scholarship and doubt and nonsense (objective) and into the realm of the subjective, where it belongs just as surely as the Savior of the world, our Lord Jesus Christ, did not bring any doctrine into the world and never delivered lectures, but as the *prototype* required *imitation*, yet by his *reconciliation* expels, if possible, all anxiety from a person's soul.

(*JFY* 209)

MEDIEVAL AND MODERN VIEWS OF CHRIST AS PROTOTYPE

But what does it mean for Christ to be a prototype and in what sense is imitation of him required? Let us begin to tackle these questions by first noting the historical background within which these ideas became prominent in the Christian tradition. The notion of a prototype is associated with being an archetype or original pattern, model, form, or ideal of some kind. In the Christian tradition the notion of Christ as a prototype and example for the Christian life through his perfect obedience, self-giving love, self-denial, and suffering has both biblical and patristic roots but came to the fore in the Middle Ages in the strict discipline and asceticism associated with the imitation of Christ in monastic orders and by religious figures and mystics of the period such as St Bernard of Clairvaux, St Francis of Assisi, Thomas à Kempis, and Johannes Tauler. Kierkegaard owned works by or about most of these figures and was acquainted with the medieval ascetic tradition of the imitation of Christ.[56]

Closer to Kierkegaard's own time, Kant also viewed Christ as the prototype or ideal of moral perfection. As Kant sees it, only human beings who have a moral disposition would be able to believe and trust that 'under similar temptations and afflictions' they would 'steadfastly cling to the prototype of humanity and follow this prototype's example in loyal emulation' so as to become pleasing to God.[57] But while Kant does not deny the historical appearance of this ideal in the person of Christ as the Son of God, in his view 'There is no need ... of any example from experience to make the idea of a human being morally pleasing to God a model to us', since it is already present in our reason.[58] Moreover, Kant holds that 'each and every human being should furnish in his own self an example of this idea' inasmuch as 'outer experience yields no example adequate to

[56] Rohde (1967: nos. 245–7, 272–4; 282, 427); see also Dewey (1968: 111–16).

[57] Kant (1998: 80–1). [58] Ibid. 81.

the idea' because 'it does not disclose the inwardness of the disposition but only allows inference to it, though not with strict certainty'.[59] We cannot be certain, therefore, that Christ is in fact an example of moral perfection or that he is divine. Indeed, even if his divinity could be proven, in Kant's view it would be of no practical moral benefit, since 'the prototype which we see embedded in this apparition must be sought in us as well'.[60] Moreover, Christ's purity of will and sinlessness as a superhuman being would make him so infinitely distant from us that he could no longer be held up as an example for our moral development. The most the thought of such a divine human being can do, then, is to excite *admiration* in us, not *emulation*.[61] Ironically, then, even though Kant affirms Christ as a prototype, he ends up vitiating Christ's historicity and divinity in favour of a universal rational ideal within human beings that can and should be conformed to for the sake of attaining moral perfection.

Another modern thinker in whose theology the notion of Christ as prototype figures importantly is Schleiermacher, who views the historical Jesus as being both the ideal embodiment of absolute perfection (*Urbildlichkeit*), by virtue of which he is the redeemer who brings the life-giving and person-forming power of God to the human race, and the exemplar (*Vorbild*) of perfected human nature by virtue of the constant potency of his God-consciousness.[62] As exemplar of what it means to be a human being, Christ enters into the corporate life of humanity in every way except its sinfulness, which does not belong to human nature in its original perfection or possibility for a continuous and universal God-consciousness.[63] Christ's God-consciousness had to undergo a gradual process of development in the context of the environment in which he lived, but at every moment of this development he was free from sin, due to the implantation of a higher God-consciousness within him originally and to the fact that his life issued solely from human nature in general and not from 'the narrow circle of descent and society' to which he belonged.[64] What Christ exemplifies for Schleiermacher, therefore, is the actualization of the original possibility of a sinless development in an individual human being.[65] In his capacity as exemplar, Christ thus constitutes the second Adam, who manifests in his perfect God-consciousness the original spirituality that was insufficiently present in the first Adam, in whom 'the spirit remained sunk in sensuousness'.[66]

[59] Kant (1998: 81–2). [60] Ibid. 82. [61] Ibid. 83.

[62] Schleiermacher (1956: 377–89); see also R. R. Niebuhr (1964: 210–28), and Mariña (2005*a*).

[63] Schleiermacher (1956: 244–7, 381). [64] Ibid. 388. [65] Ibid. 381–3.

[66] Ibid. 389.

CHRIST AS PROTOTYPE IN KIERKEGAARD'S WRITINGS

Like Kant and Schleiermacher, Kierkegaard views Christ as the prototype (*Forbillede*) of 'essential human perfection' who defines what it means to be a human being and exemplifies 'the lofty creation' that the human being essentially is and was destined to become (*UDVS* 197). In his view, the human race is related to God, otherwise 'there could be no such prototype for it' (231). Since human beings are created in the image of God, who is Spirit and thus invisible, to resemble God means to be spirit, which constitutes the invisible glory of being human (192–3; cf. *SUD* 13). Ever mindful of the infinite qualitative difference between God and human beings due to sin, however, Kierkegaard maintains that 'the human being and God do not resemble each other directly but inversely; only when God has infinitely become the eternal and omnipresent object of worship and the human being always a worshiper, only then do they resemble each other' (193). The divine conception of what it means to be a human being, spirit, or self, it may be recalled, is to become a theological self, that is, a human self whose qualitative criterion and ethical goal is God, but *'only in Christ is it true that God is the human being's goal and criterion'* (*SUD* 79, 113–14, emphasis added). A relation to Christ is thus crucial for becoming a self before God.

In order to be and to portray the truth as a human being, Christ had to undergo a process of development during his earthly life, learning perfect obedience through suffering before being exalted as the prototype (*UDVS* 250–63; *PC* 181–4). The life of the prototype thus can be depicted in two ways, either through the image of lowliness and abasement or through the distant image of his loftiness (*PC* 184). It is decidedly the former, however, that is the basis of imitation, discipleship, or, more literally, following after Christ (*Kristi Efterfølgelse*)[67] in Kierkegaard's theology, although Christ's abasement must always be understood inversely as a sign of his loftiness (238–9). Whereas human beings ordinarily form, via the imagination, an image of perfection or ideal self which they strive to become in life, the Christian's image of perfection is Christ, whose perfection or loftiness appears inversely in the world as lowliness or abasement (186–99). Since for Kierkegaard it holds that 'As was the prototype, so must the imitation [*Efterfølgelsen*] also be', to follow Christ means 'to deny oneself' and 'to *walk the same road* Christ walked in the lowly form of a servant, indigent,

[67] See Dewey (1968: 119–61), who opposes translating this term as 'imitation' in order to distinguish Kierkegaard's view from medieval ascetic and facsimile forms of imitation. On discipleship, see also Law (2002*a*).

forsaken, mocked, not loving the world and not loved by it' (*UDVS* 221, 223; cf. *JP* ii. 1867). This, Kierkegaard says, both 'the mightiest and the lowliest', 'the wisest and simplest', in short, 'every human being can do' (*UDVS* 226).

This way of following Christ is narrow, difficult, rigorous, and strenuous, inevitably entailing voluntary suffering and perhaps even persecution and martyrdom on the part of the Christian striver who undertakes to become a witness to the truth. But Kierkegaard is careful to distinguish his view of imitating or following Christ from the ascetic forms of imitation practised in the Middle Ages, which in his view merely copied (*copierede*) Christ rather than imitated or followed after (*efterfulgte*) him (*JP* ii. 1893, 1922). The basic mistake of the Middle Ages, Kierkegaard contends, was naively to believe that one could actually resemble the prototype by engaging in such practices as entering a monastery, giving everything to the poor, fasting, and engaging in various forms of self-flagellation (*JP* ii. 1857, 1866, 1893, 1905, 1914; *JFY* 192). Kierkegaard does not oppose asceticism and monasticism *per se*, which in his view were 'still an expression of an infinite passion and of Christianity's heterogeneity with the world', but he does object to the merit, honour, admiration, and extraordinary religious status associated with them and which made them homogeneous with the world and the secular mentality of the age (*JP* iii. 2760, 2762, 2764). While he agrees that there ought to be striving towards likeness to Christ, in his view Christ does not function altogether *literally or directly* as a pattern or example for human beings (*JP* ii. 1921–2). The ideality of Christ as the prototype is so infinite that he is 'heterogeneous to an ordinary human being by a full quality' (*JP* ii. 1922; cf. 1432). Consequently, 'the prototype is so far in advance that the believer is demolished', even though 'in spite of the infinite imperfection there is nevertheless a slight advance' in striving to be like him (*JP* ii. 1861).Yet, as Kierkegaard sees it, 'Every step forward toward the ideal is a backward step, for the progress consists precisely in my discovering increasingly the perfection of the ideal—and consequently my greater distance from it' (*JP* ii. 1789). Paradoxically, then, Christian perfection consists inversely in the 'deep recognition of the imperfection of one's striving' rather than in a direct perfection of striving to be like Christ (*JP* ii. 1482).

Thus, in accordance with the second use of the law in Lutheran doctrine, the chief function of Christ as prototype for Kierkegaard is 'to teach us how infinitely far away we are from resembling the ideal' and thus 'to teach us how greatly we need *grace*' (*JP* i. 334; ii. 1922; cf. 1905–6).[68] Here we see the dialectical alternation between the two roles of Christ as redeemer and

[68] See Barrett (2002); Hall (2002: 12–22); *The Book of Concord* (2000: 311–12); Schmid (1961: 508–20).

prototype in his theology, which is perhaps best expressed in the following journal entry: 'when we are striving, then he is the prototype; and when we stumble, lose courage, etc., then he is the love which helps us up, and then he is the prototype again' (*JP* i. 334; cf. i. 349, 692; ii. 1857, 1863, 1877, 1884; *JFY* 147). Grace does not mean that we are exempt from striving but rather that we are treated gently when we fail to measure up and are freed from 'the anxiety of meritoriousness' associated with trying 'to earn salvation by suffering' (*JP* ii. 1868). In line with his Lutheran heritage, Kierkegaard affirms that salvation is by grace alone, but one still must strive to conform one's life to the prototype, not as a 'kind of extorted discipleship', but *out of gratitude*, for if following Christ does not come as 'a glad fruit of gratitude', it is not imitation but 'a perverted mimicking' and grace is taken in vain (*JP* ii. 1892; cf. 1886).[69]

IMITATION VERSUS ADMIRATION OF CHRIST

In the present age, especially in Protestantism, Kierkegaard contends that the prototype has become so far removed from the single individual that 'it has become merely an idea of the race', with the result that 'it never occurs to him in the remotest way to want to strive toward likeness' (*JP* ii. 1873; cf. 1904). Imitation or following after Christ thus has been done away with and replaced with aesthetic admiration of him, as in Kant's view (*JP* ii. 1895). The person specifically indicted for bringing about a 'fundamental change' in established Christendom in Denmark, particularly with regard to the proclamation of Christian truth in preaching, is Bishop Mynster, whose sermons or 'observations' are interpreted by Anti-Climacus as encouraging the listener to become an admirer rather than an imitator of Christ (*PC* 233–57). The difference between these two ways of relating to Christ, as Anti-Climacus sees it, is this: 'An imitator *is* or strives *to be* what he admires', whereas 'an admirer keeps himself personally detached, consciously or unconsciously does not discover that what is admired involves a claim upon him, to be or at least to strive to be what is admired' (241). While there are many things that properly may be admired, such as beauty, wealth, talent, great achievements, masterpieces of art, and good fortune, and that involve no obligation of imitation on our part, Anti-Climacus contends that admiration is 'totally inappropriate' in relation to the ethical, which requires self-reflection and reduplication of the universally human

[69] Barrett (2002: 105) identifies the imitation of Christ in Kierkegaard's theology as 'the functional equivalent of the third use of the law' in Lutheran doctrine in that it serves as 'a stimulus and guide for the good works that are the fruit of faith'. Contra this interpretation, see Hall (2002: 16–22). See also *The Book of Concord* (2000: 502–3).

in one's existence (242). The admiration of Christ in Christendom is even more strongly denounced by Anti-Climacus as a lie, deceit, sin, and paganism, especially as it is expressed in Christian art, which promotes artistic indifference in the artist and viewers and turns the suffering of Christ into money and admiration for the artist (243, 254–6). Although Anti-Climacus does not want to be judgemental towards art, even admitting that the abolition of Christianity in Christendom will soon have gone so far that 'people must make use of art in the most various ways to help get Christendom to show at least some sympathy with Christianity', he is convinced that the most art can do is to elicit admiration of Christ, whereas 'only the imitator is the true Christian' (254–6). To speak of imitation, however, is already to anticipate the subject of the next chapter—Kierkegaard's view of the Christian life—to which I shall now turn.

6

The Christian Life of Faith, Hope, and Love

For Kierkegaard the Christian life is a new life pre-eminently characterized by faith, hope, and love, but according to the inverse dialectic that informs his understanding of Christianity, these positive passions are always experienced and known indirectly and inversely through negative qualifications such as the consciousness of sin, the possibility of offence, self-denial, and voluntary suffering in likeness to Christ.[1] Consequently, thinking theologically about the trilogy of faith, hope, and love in the Christian life will require us also to take into account the negative factors through which these positive passions are experienced and known. Kierkegaard's primary criticism of Christendom was that it had a confused, superficial, lenient, merely positive understanding of what it means to be a Christian, with the result that the 'major premise' of grace and faith in Lutheran doctrine was being taken in vain because its 'minor premise'—works of love, witnessing, and suffering for the truth—had been abolished (*JFY* 24).[2] A large part of his theological reflection on the Christian life, therefore, consists in bringing the qualifications that constitute the minor premise once again into view so that a true understanding and expression of the Christian life can emerge in the modern age.

REFLECTING ON FAITH

In a journal entry from 1850 Kierkegaard testifies to the centrality of the question of faith in his pseudonymous works and to the importance of employing dialectical reflection to illuminate it, which he claims to have done with unparalleled devotion and accuracy:

> In many forms and under several pseudonyms, a whole pseudonymous literature is chiefly concerned with illuminating the question of faith, with discerning the sphere belonging to faith, with determining its distinction from other spheres of the intellect and spirit, etc. And how is all this done? By dialectic, by reflection. I venture to claim that it would be hard to find an author who has been so devoted to

[1] See Walsh (2005).

[2] On the relation of faith and works in Kierkegaard, see also Barrett (2002) and Rae (2002).

reflecting on faith—although certainly not speculating unceremoniously on particular dogmas; for I 'reflected,' yes, I thought (and that was, after all, reflection) that the first thing to be done was to clear up the whole question of faith. I venture to claim that in my writings the dialectical qualifications of specific points are set forth with an accuracy such as has not been known before. (*JP* vi. 6595)

The starting point for Kierkegaard's reflection on faith, however, was not in his pseudonymous writings but in his early upbuilding discourses, the very first one of which focuses on the concept of faith. In this discourse faith is seen as being qualitatively different from all other good things of life such as health, happiness, prosperity, power, good fortune, and fame, in that it is not only the highest good but a good in which all human beings can share:

The person who wishes it for another person wishes it for himself; the person who wishes it for himself wishes it for every human being, because that by which another person has faith is not that by which he is different from him but is that by which he is like him; that by which he possesses it is not that by which he is different from others but that by which he is altogether like all. (*EUD* 10)

First and foremost, then, faith is a possibility for every human being that is based on and gives expression to our common humanity rather than our differences as single individuals. But faith cannot be had by just wishing for it, nor is it something one can procure for others; rather, faith is gained only by personally willing it, which all individuals must do for themselves. Like hope, faith is directed towards the future in that it constitutes the power of the eternal within us through which everything, including the past, present, and future, can be fathomed as a whole (19). Only by conquering the future, then, can we understand the past, find meaning in the present, and face the future without anxiety and despair. That is done, Kierkegaard claims, by expecting *victory* in the certitude that 'all things must serve for good [for] those who love God' (cf. Romans 8: 28; *EUD* 19–23, 26–8). The first condition for arriving at faith, therefore, is to become aware of whether one has it or not, which is disclosed by how one relates to the expectation of victory in the eternal—an expectancy which for Kierkegaard is never disappointed, regardless of whether it is substantiated in time by something in particular.[3]

[3] See Walsh (2000) on Regine Olsen as the unnamed intended recipient of this discourse, which was written specifically to encourage her not to lose faith as a result of their broken engagement.

The Paradox of Faith

One of Kierkegaard's pseudonyms who is acutely aware of the fact that he lacks faith is Johannes de silentio (John of Silence), the 'author' of *Fear and Trembling*.[4] In this early pseudonymous work, Kierkegaard's literary persona laments the tendency of modern philosophy—by which he means Hegelian speculative philosophy, most notably that of the Danish Hegelians and Martensen in particular—to 'go further' than faith by presumably comprehending it conceptually in a philosophical system (*FT* 3–4). As Johannes sees it, faith is a lifelong task that is not achieved in a matter of days or weeks nor can it be comprehended by reflection: 'Even if one were able to convert the whole content of faith into conceptual form, it does not follow that one has comprehended faith, comprehended how one entered into it or how it entered into one' (5). For an exemplar of faith Johannes looks to Abraham, traditionally regarded as the father of faith because he did not doubt when tested by God's command to sacrifice his son Isaac, who had been given to Abraham and his wife Sarah in their old age in order to fulfil the Lord's promise to make Abraham the father of a great nation (cf. Genesis 12: 1; 22: 1–19). Abraham believed *by virtue of the absurd* that God would fulfil his promise in spite of the divine command to sacrifice Isaac, either by rescinding the command or by providing a new Isaac if he were sacrificed, which Abraham was willing to do in obedience to God even though it stood in stark contradiction to his love for Isaac and to the divine promise. To Johannes, therefore, the faith of Abraham is a paradox that goes against all human understanding and expectation, a paradox that can be entered into only with much anxiety, fear and trembling, and courage.

Sacrifice or Murder?

These emotional qualifications are requisite because what Abraham was about to do, considered from an ethical standpoint, was to commit *murder*. Thus Kant, for example, explicitly condemned Abraham's intended action on ethical grounds, saying: 'if something is represented as commanded by God in a direct manifestation of him yet is directly in conflict with morality, it cannot be a divine miracle despite every appearance of being one (e.g. if a father were ordered to kill his son who, so far as he knows, is totally innocent)'.[5] Unless the killing of Isaac can be justified on religious grounds

[4] See Lippitt (2003) for a handy guide to this work and various ways of interpreting it. See also Evans (2004: 61–84); Mooney (1991); Perkins (1993; 1981).

[5] Kant (1998: 100, cf. 180; and 1996: 124, 204, 282–3).

as a *sacrifice*, then, Abraham would have been guilty of a monstrous crime if he had gone through with it and should have been tried as a murderer rather than lauded as the father of faith. The contradiction contained in this dilemma, Johannes observes, is enough to make a person reflecting on it sleepless with anxiety, yet rarely is there anyone in his age (or ours) who is made sleepless by it or who is willing to do what Abraham was prepared to do in obedience to God's command. Should anyone wish to emulate Abraham after hearing him praised in the local parson's sermon, that person undoubtedly would be immediately condemned and chastised by the very parson who had praised Abraham. This contradiction further underscores for Johannes what a prodigious paradox faith is and how difficult it is to arrive at faith, let alone 'go further' by comprehending it.

The Double Movement of Faith

For Johannes, however, the great and remarkable thing about Abraham that makes him the father of faith is not that he was willing to sacrifice Isaac but that he believed throughout the whole ordeal that he would get Isaac back: 'For it is great to give up one's wish, but it is greater to keep a firm grip on it after having given it up; it is great to lay hold of the eternal, but it is greater to stick doggedly to the temporal after having given it up' (*FT* 15). Abraham did not expect to be reunited with Isaac in the afterlife but believed precisely that God—for whom all things are possible, even that which from a human standpoint is clearly impossible—would restore Isaac to him in this life. Abraham thus performed what Johannes calls 'the double movement' of faith (29).[6] The first movement is one of infinite resignation, exemplified by Abraham's willingness to give Isaac up if demanded by God; the second is the movement of faith by which he miraculously and joyfully receives Isaac back. It is the latter movement that is so amazing to Johannes, leading him to exclaim:

> The dialectic of faith is the finest and most remarkable of all; it has an elevation of which I can certainly form a conception, but nothing more. I can make the great trampoline leap whereby I pass over into infinity; my spine is like a tightrope

[6] Cf. Hegel (1984–7: ii. 441–54), on the faith of Abraham and the Jewish cultus as a double movement of absolute negation and affirmation. For Hegel the first moment of negativity consists in the infinite surrendering of all particular interests and 'everything ephemeral and contingent' in fear of the Lord. From this there arises a second moment of affirmation in the form of an abstract, absolute trust or infinite faith in God, which is then mediated in the determinate form of a 'particular kind of existence' embodied in the family, people, and land. Whereas Hegel views the double movement of faith as being mediated in a third form of concrete faith that is identical to the ethical, Johannes sees it as a paradoxical, unmediated movement that is higher than the ethical.

walker's, twisted from my childhood. Thus it is easy for me to go one, two, three, and turn a somersault in existence, but the next movement I cannot make, for the miraculous I cannot perform but only be amazed by it. (*FT* 30)

The Knight of Faith versus the Knight of Infinite Resignation

Johannes candidly admits that he is incapable of making the movement of faith whereby, by virtue of the absurd, the finite is regained in its entirety after having been renounced in infinite resignation, but he does claim to be able to describe this movement. Although he has never come across an authentic exemplar of faith in his own time, he can very well imagine what one would be like. As Johannes envisions him, the knight of faith bears 'a striking resemblance' to a *bourgeois philistine*, that is, someone who belongs entirely to finitude, enjoying and taking part in everything 'with a persistence that characterizes the worldly person whose heart is attached to such things' (*FT* 32).[7] In other words, he looks and behaves just like a typical middle-class citizen of nineteenth-century Denmark: 'No heavenly look or any sign of the incommensurable betrays him. If one did not know him, it would be impossible to distinguish him from the rest of the crowd' (33). Unlike the bourgeois philistine, however, the knight of faith does everything by virtue of the absurd, having resigned the finite infinitely and received it back again. Likening the knight of faith to a ballet dancer who is able to make the movement of infinity with 'such precision and proficiency that he constantly gets finitude out of it', Johannes observes: 'It is supposed to be the most difficult task for a dancer to leap into a particular posture in such a way that there is no second when he grasps at the position but assumes it in the leap itself. Perhaps no dancer can do it—but that knight does' (34). Unlike most people, who are 'wallflowers who do not join in the dance', the knight of infinite resignation is also a dancer who makes the leap upwards into infinity and then back down again into finitude (34). But there is always a slight hesitation in resuming the posture of finitude which reveals that the knight of infinite resignation is really a stranger in the world, whereas 'to be able to land in such a way that it looks as if one were simultaneously standing and walking, to transform the leap of life into a gait, absolutely to express the sublime in the pedestrian—that only the knight of faith can do—and that is the only miracle' (34).

In Johannes's view, faith is often confused with infinite resignation in that it is thought to be other-worldly rather this-worldly in orientation.

[7] The knight of faith as described by Johannes is a man, but women can also become knights of faith (see *FT* 37–8).

The movement of infinite resignation is a prerequisite of faith inasmuch as it is only through this movement that we become transparent to ourselves in our eternal validity as human beings in relation to God by giving up the finite for the infinite, the temporal for the eternal. Until that happens there can be no question of receiving the finite back again in faith. But infinite resignation is a movement we can make on our own, whereas getting the finite back again is entirely beyond human power and understanding and thus is possible only by virtue of the absurd or the fact that for God everything is possible. At the same time, however, the *impossibility* of this possibility, humanly speaking, must be acknowledged or else we are self-deceived and have not even attained infinite resignation, let alone faith, which in Johannes's view is not an 'aesthetic emotion' or 'spontaneous inclination of the heart' but the paradox of existence (*FT* 40–1). To illustrate this difference, Johannes contrasts the movement of faith to the naïve conviction of a young girl who believes her wish will be fulfilled despite all difficulties but dares not 'look the impossibility in the eye in the pain of resignation' (40). 'Fools and young people chatter about everything being possible for a human being', he observes, but 'that is a great misapprehension. Spiritually speaking, everything is possible, but in the finite world there is much that is not possible' (37). Knights of infinite resignation make the impossible possible by expressing it spiritually, renouncing the content of their wishes in time while recollecting them inwardly in an eternal sense. Knights of faith, by contrast, believe in the possibility of giving their wishes expression in time, should the moment ever come allowing that to happen, even though they are acutely aware that, humanly speaking, it is impossible. Whereas 'A purely human courage is required to renounce the whole of temporality in order to gain the eternal, . . . it takes a paradoxical and humble courage . . . to grasp the whole of temporality by virtue of the absurd, and this is the courage of faith', Johannes claims (41). He thus concludes: 'Temporality, finitude is what it is all about' (42). Even though he lacks the courage of faith himself, he is able to appreciate the difficulty and greatness of it and encourages others to do the same, enjoining us to 'either forget Abraham or else learn to be horrified by the prodigious paradox that is the meaning of his life, so that we may understand that our age, like every age, can be joyful if it has faith' (45).

Dialectical Problems Relating to Faith

To further show what a prodigious paradox faith is, Johannes poses three dialectical problems or questions implicit in the story of Abraham: (1) 'Is there a teleological suspension of the ethical?' (2) 'Is there an absolute duty to God?' (3) 'Was it ethically defensible of Abraham to conceal his undertaking' from his family? (*FT* 46, 59, 71) The main backdrop for the discussion of these problems is Hegel's view of the ethical in *The Philosophy of Right*.[8] According to Hegel, the ethical life (*Sittlichkeit*) consists in the fulfilling of one's duties to oneself and others through conformity with the objective laws and customs of a rational social order or state. This view of the ethical is set over against a purely personal morality (*Moralität*) emphasizing the subject's own subjective, particular will and conviction in determining and willing the good, which Hegel regards as abstract and arbitrary.[9] Although Hegel does not discuss Abraham in this text, Johannes seeks to draw out the implications of Hegel's view of the ethical with respect to Abraham, whose act of faith, as Johannes sees it, cannot be explained or justified in terms of *Sittlichkeit* or *Moralität*.

Each of the problems posed by Johannes begins with an equation of the ethical with the universal, which means that it applies to everyone and remains in force at every moment.[10] Understood in a Hegelian fashion as being immanently complete in itself, the ethical is the *telos* for everything outside itself, including the single individual, whose ethical task is constantly to annul his or her particularity in order to be fulfilled in the universal. Whenever one asserts oneself over against the universal after having entered into it, then, one is guilty of moral evil or sin and can only be brought back into the fold of the ethical by 'repentantly surrendering [oneself] as the particular to the universal' (*FT* 46–7, 54). But if that is so, Johannes contends, then Hegel was wrong in not speaking out (as Kant did) against Abraham being lauded as the father of faith, since his proposed action was not for the sake of the universal, as in the case of several classical tragic heroes whom Johannes cites as performing personal sacrifices in service to the state, but was a purely private undertaking for which he ought potentially to have been charged with murder (47, 50–2).

The Teleological Suspension of the Ethical

Over against a Hegelian conception of the single individual as subordinate to the universal, Johannes asserts just the opposite with respect to Abraham and faith:

[8] On Kantian elements in this work as well, see Green (1992: 86–91, 183–205); Knappe (2004: 12–13, 77–97).

[9] Hegel (1991*a*: 129–40). On Hegel's ethics, see Wood (1990; 1993*b*).

[10] Cf. Kant (1990: 24); Hegel (1991*a*: 64, 189–98).

> Faith is exactly this paradox, that the single individual is higher than the universal, but in such a way, mind you, that the movement is repeated, so that after having been in the universal he now as the particular keeps to himself as higher than the universal. If this is not faith, then Abraham is lost and faith has never existed in the world precisely because it has always existed. (*FT* 47)

In overstepping the ethical by relating himself as the single individual to a *telos* higher than the ethical, Abraham stands in an absolute relation to the absolute in the recognition of an absolute duty to God that cannot be mediated or reconciled with the ethical or universal. He thus performs what Johannes calls a 'teleological suspension of the ethical', which does not mean that the ethical is abolished but rather that it is relativized and given expression in a paradoxical or opposite manner from the way it is normally expressed in human relations (61). In being willing to sacrifice his son at divine command, Abraham does not cease to love Isaac, which is the highest ethical duty of a father to his son; on the contrary, Johannes contends that one's absolute duty to God may 'bring one to do what ethics would forbid, but it can never make the knight of faith stop loving' (65). That is the crucial difference between Abraham and a murderer, political terrorist, or religious fanatic, with whom he is often confused:[11]

> The moment he is willing to sacrifice Isaac, the ethical expression for what he does is this: he hates Isaac. But if he really hates Isaac, he can be sure that God does not ask it of him, for Cain and Abraham are not identical. He must love Isaac with all his heart; inasmuch as God demands Isaac, Abraham must love him, if possible, even more dearly, and only then can he *sacrifice* him, for it is indeed this love for Isaac which by its paradoxical opposition to his love for god makes his act a sacrifice . . . Only at the moment when his act is in absolute contradiction to his feeling, only then does he sacrifice Isaac, but the reality of his act is that by which he belongs to the universal, and there he is and remains a murderer. (*FT* 65)

Faith as a Second Immediacy

The contradiction between Abraham's inner feeling of love for Isaac and the outward act of violence he was willing to perform for God's sake and his own sake as a test of faith leads Johannes to make a second point about

[11] See e.g. Stewart (2003: 321–3), who proposes as an analogue to Abraham's situation the political assassination of a Russian noble by a German theology student named Karl Ludwig Sand, who was presumably 'inspired by the higher calling of German nationalism' during the period when Hegel was writing his *Philosophy of Right*. But this example is not analogous to Abraham for at least two reasons: (1) Sand's presumed higher calling was not from God but inspired by a political ideology; and (2) He did not love the man he killed. See also Perkins (2006*b*).

faith in contrast to Hegelian philosophy, namely that *inwardness is higher than outwardness*. For Hegel, the inner and the outer stand in a reciprocally opposed relation of identity, the inner constituting the abstract ground of the outer, which gives concrete content and actuality to it.[12] For instance, a child, who is inwardly preoccupied with its own immediate feelings and natural abilities, finds its outward rational fulfilment as an adult who has been educated to identify his or her personal interests with those of the universal. From a Hegelian standpoint, then, the outer is higher than the inner, with the result that the ethical task is to divest oneself of inwardness by giving it expression in an outward form. Whenever one fails to do that and slips back into 'the inward qualification of feeling, mood, etc.' after having entered the universal, one 'commits an offense and stands in temptation' (*FT* 60). As Johannes sees it, however, in identifying inwardness with the immediacy of feeling and mood, recent philosophy makes faith equivalent to the aesthetic, whereas the paradox of faith is that 'there is an inwardness that is incommensurable with the outer, an inwardness that, mind you, is not identical with that first one but is a new inwardness', which Kierkegaard elsewhere calls a 'second immediacy' or 'spontaneity after reflection' (*FT* 60; cf. *CUP* i. 347; *JP* i. 49; ii. 1123; v. 6135).[13] In other words, the inwardness or immediacy of faith is not a given condition or natural capacity of human consciousness but commences paradoxically by virtue of the absurd after a conscious movement of infinite resignation has been made. Nor is it identical to the 'mediated immediacy' or 'mediated knowledge' that Hegel and the Hegelians call faith, since for Kierkegaard reflection does not issue in a higher conceptual cognition or identification of faith with knowledge but enables us to understand that we cannot understand the content of faith and therefore must simply believe it in the passion of faith.[14]

The Silence of Abraham

Much of the inner distress and anxiety associated with the passion and paradox of faith as exemplified by Abraham derives from the fact that he is utterly unable to make himself intelligible to anyone, including his own family, inasmuch as he stands outside the universal in an absolute relation to God that commands him in a particular instance to do what ethics would forbid. Unlike aesthetics, in which concealment plays an essential role in

[12] Cf. Hegel (1991*b*: 204–13).

[13] Cf. Hegel (1991*b*: 108–24; 1984–7: i. 385–96, 407–16); Martensen (2004: 597); Schleiermacher (1956: 5–18).

[14] On 'mediated immediacy' see Perkins (2006*b*) contra Stewart (2003: 97–100, 386–7).

both ancient and modern drama, ethics demands disclosure of oneself in the universal and recognizes no justified concealment or incommensurability. But if that is so, Johannes reiterates his charge that Hegelian philosophy is wrong or 'befuddled' in speaking about faith and regarding Abraham as the father of faith inasmuch as faith is once again confused with the first immediacy of the aesthetic, whereas it is properly viewed paradoxically as a second immediacy that cannot be mediated in the universal (71). Unlike the tragic hero and a host of other poetic personages conjured up by Johannes as possible analogies to the knight of faith, Abraham cannot speak because he cannot make himself intelligible to others, whereas the aesthetic hero who remains silent is able to speak but will not. Just as Abraham stands outside the ethical, then, he also does not fall within the scope of the aesthetic. The only possible justification for his silence, therefore, is that he stands in an absolute relation to the absolute that cannot be mediated by the universal or reduced to the aesthetic, leading Johannes to conclude: 'Either there is then a paradox, that the single individual as the particular stands in an absolute relation to the absolute, or Abraham is lost' (106).

The Faith of Abraham versus Christian Faith

There is a difference, however, between the faith of Abraham and Christian faith and between believing by virtue of the absurd and believing the absurd or the absolute paradox of the incarnation. In an unpublished response to a contemporary review of *Fear and Trembling*, Kierkegaard explains that Abraham is called the father of faith because he exemplifies the formal definition and passion of faith, which is to believe against the understanding, whereas Christian faith is essentially related to a later historical event, namely the entry of the eternal in time in the figure of Jesus Christ, who is the object of faith (*JP* i. 11; vi. 6598). Thus there is no conflict between the pseudonyms on the nature of faith and the absurd, only a difference in the content of faith, which is not absurd to the believer but only to those who stand outside of faith as non-believers or third parties, for whom the category of the absurd functions as a negative sign and criterion of that which is beyond human understanding and reason (*JP* i. 7–12; vi. 6598). Thus, in the works by Johannes Climacus, who like Johannes de silentio does not profess to have faith, Christian faith is illumined, as it were, from the other side, from the standpoint of a person who is not a believer but nevertheless discerns a great deal about the conditions for faith, what faith is, and what it is not.

Contemporaneity with Christ

In his journals Kierkegaard states that 'before there can even be any question about having faith, there must be the *situation*. And this situation must be brought about by an existential step on the part of the individual . . . The requirement is that you must venture out, out into water 70,000 fathoms deep. This is the situation' (*JP* ii. 1142). As Johannes Climacus sees it, the situation that results in either the happy passion of faith or the unhappy passion of offence is occasioned by an encounter of the understanding with the absolute paradox, which came into existence in a decisive moment of time, thereby providing a historical point of departure for the eternal happiness of both contemporary and later followers of Christ. The immediate contemporary and the follower 'at second hand' thus stand essentially in the same situation of contemporaneity with this 'absolute fact', which is different from all other historical facts in that relations to it are not apportioned by time (*PF* 67, 91–100). This means that genuine contemporaneity is determined not by immediate historical contemporaneity with the absolute paradox but by receiving the condition of faith from the god in the encounter of the understanding with the absolute paradox. If the understanding comes to an understanding with the absolute paradox, that is, comes to understand that it is the absolute paradox and thus steps aside, allowing the absolute paradox to give itself, the condition in which this occurs is *faith*, which must be provided by the absolute paradox itself since the individual is not already in possession of the condition. The follower thus owes everything to the absolute paradox, even the condition of faith, which according to Climacus is just as paradoxical and miraculous as the absolute paradox itself, inasmuch as the condition for eternal happiness is now given in time through a relation to the eternal in time rather than immanently in human consciousness itself.

Faith versus Knowledge

Climacus proceeds to distinguish faith from *what it is not* as well as to state more explicitly *what it is*. First and foremost, he denies that faith is knowledge, since 'all knowledge is either knowledge of the eternal, which excludes the temporal and the historical as inconsequential, or it is purely historical knowledge, and no knowledge can have as its object this absurdity that the eternal is the historical' (*PF* 62). Here Climacus again applies the basic distinction of Leibniz, Lessing, and Hume between two types of knowledge: necessary, rational (demonstrative) eternal truths and contingent, empirical (probable), historical truths of fact.[15] As Climacus sees it, faith does not fit into either of these categories, inasmuch as the object of Christian faith is not an eternal truth that can be rationally known and comprehended, nor does it have the probability that is required for historical knowledge. On the contrary, 'the paradox specifically unites the contradictories, is the eternalizing of the historical and the historicizing of the eternal', which is not only objectively uncertain but objectively absurd from the standpoint of all human understanding (*PF* 61; *CUP* 210).

But if faith is not knowledge, it likewise does not lead to knowledge or a higher understanding that resolves the paradox, as the understanding that faith arrives at regarding the absolute paradox is precisely that it cannot be understood. In rejecting the notion of a higher understanding of the content of faith, Climacus joins Kierkegaard in setting himself against the classic formula of the Middle Ages, *credo ut intelligam* (I believe in order to understand), which in Kierkegaard's view simply reinstates the Greek view of faith in Plato and Aristotle, for whom faith belongs in the sphere of the intellectual rather than the existential (*JP* i. 180; ii. 1148, 1154; iii. 3023).[16] Climacus also parts company with modern speculative thinkers such as Hegel and Martensen, for whom the goal of theology is the mediation of faith in knowledge.[17] As Climacus sees it, the object of faith is not a *teaching* about Christ that is to be comprehended through philosophy or theology but rather the *teacher* himself, who is the absolute paradox and thus not subject to mediation or a higher understanding in knowledge. He thus concludes:

> Faith, then, is not a lesson for slow learners in the sphere of intellectuality, an asylum for dullards. But faith is a sphere of its own, and the immediate identifying mark of every misunderstanding of Christianity is that it changes it into a doctrine and draws it into the range of intellectuality. What holds as the maximum in the sphere of intellectuality, to remain completely indifferent to the actuality of the teacher, holds in just the opposite way in the sphere of faith—its maximum is the *quam maxime* [in the greatest degree possible] infinite interestedness in the actuality of the teacher. (*CUP* i. 327)

The Role of the Will in Faith

Faith is also not an act of the will, since for Climacus the condition of faith is given by the god or absolute paradox in a personal encounter (*PF* 62). But this does not mean that the will is totally inoperative in faith, for

[15] Leibniz (1965: 11, 13); Lessing (2005: 85); Hume (1988: 71–83).

[16] See also Pedersen (1980).

[17] Cf. Hegel (1984–7: i. 347); Martensen (2004: 597–8; 1997: 78–9).

that would negate human freedom. On the contrary, once the condition is given, the will plays an important, even decisive, role in the life of faith for both Climacus and Anti-Climacus (*PF* 63; cf. *PC* 186).[18] While faith is a gift, it is not something imposed against our wills but must be either received in faith or rejected in offence through a resolution of the will. The reception of faith takes place in what Climacus in the *Postscript* calls 'the leap', which is 'the category of decision' that carries the individual across the 'ugly broad ditch' between the historical and the eternal (*CUP* 1: 98–9). As Anti-Climacus expresses it: 'Faith is a choice, certainly not direct reception—and the recipient is the one who is disclosed, whether he will believe or be offended' (*PC* 141). Regardless of whether one chooses to believe or to be offended, however, one cannot avoid the possibility of offence, which is the 'crossroad' at which one turns either to offence or to faith. One may choose not to be offended, but 'one never comes to faith except from the possibility of offense' (81).

Faith versus Doubt and Offence

Climacus also distinguishes between two senses of faith (*Tro*): *faith in the ordinary sense*, or belief concerning the coming into existence of anything historical, and *faith in an eminent sense*, which is based solely on the contradiction that the god has come into existence (*PF* 87). The first form of faith pertains to the immediate apprehension of anything that has come into existence or become historical, such as a star or an event, inasmuch as its coming into existence is uncertain or elusive to the senses, thus requiring a basic belief that it has occurred:

> belief believes what it does not see; it does not believe that the star exists, for that it sees, but it believes that the star has come into existence. The same is true of an event. The occurrence can be known immediately but not that it has occurred, not even that it is in the process of occurring, even though it is taking place, as they say, right in front of one's nose. (*PF* 81–2)

Climacus elucidates this ordinary sense of belief in order to show that there is an element of belief involved in all our knowledge of the historical, even in immediate sensation and cognition. But he is also motivated by a desire to clarify the relation of belief to doubt, particularly as exemplified in Greek scepticism and its modern counterpart in the Cartesian/Hegelian claim

[18] On volitional versus non-volitional interpretations of the role of the will in faith for Kierkegaard, see Jackson (1998); Come (1997: 320–36); Gouwens (1996: 137–8); Evans (1992: 115–16, 138–42); Ferreira (1991).

that everything must be doubted.[19] According to Climacus, the Greek sceptics 'doubted not by virtue of knowledge but by virtue of the will', that is, by withholding assent, which 'implies that doubt can be terminated only in freedom, by an act of the will' (82). The Greek sceptics tried to avoid error and find tranquillity of mind by suspending judgement or not drawing a conclusion (*Slutning*) about immediate sensation and cognition, thereby keeping doubt in play, whereas belief comes to a resolution (*Beslutning*) or termination of doubt in the decision to believe (84). As Climacus sees it, then, belief and doubt are opposite passions, neither of which is a cognitive act: 'Belief is a sense for coming into existence, and doubt is a protest against any conclusion that wants to go beyond immediate sensation and immediate knowledge' (84).

Faith or belief in the ordinary sense is likewise required with respect to the coming into existence of the absolute paradox. But this particular historical fact has the 'unique quality' of being based upon the self-contradiction that the eternal has come into existence, thus requiring faith in an eminent or higher sense that applies only to this historical fact (*PF* 87). This is what properly constitutes faith for both Climacus and Anti-Climacus (cf. *PC* 141). Here the opposite of faith is not doubt but offence, as 'the relation of personality to Christianity, is not to doubt or to believe, but to be offended or to believe' (*PC* 81 n.). Faith in an eminent sense is also 'specifically qualified differently from all other appropriation and inwardness' by the fact that it is an 'objective uncertainty with the repulsion of the absurd, held fast in the passion of inwardness, which is the relation of inwardness intensified to its highest' (*CUP* i. 611). 'This formula', Climacus declares, 'fits only the one who has faith, no one else, not even a lover, or an enthusiast, or a thinker, but solely and only the one who has faith, who relates himself to the absolute paradox' (611).

Faith and Becoming a Self

Whereas Climacus articulates the formula for faith in relation to the absolute paradox, in which the passion of faith is infinitely interested in an actuality that is not one's own (*CUP* i. 323–4), Anti-Climacus defines faith in relation to the task of becoming a self. Although *The Sickness unto Death*

[19] See e.g. Sextus Empiricus (2000); Descartes (1951: 17–22); Hegel (1955: i. 406). In an unpublished MS titled 'Johannes Climacus or *De Omnibus Dubitandum Est*', Kierkegaard explores the Cartesian thesis that everything must be doubted in a narrative about Johannes Climacus as a young student of philosophy. After dutifully examining the historical and philosophical basis of this claim, Johannes decides to bid the philosophers farewell and go his own way because, in his view, they avoid the existential difficulties of doubting everything, which ultimately leads to despair (*JC* 113–72, 234–5).

progressively tracks the movement away from faith in the consciousness of despair or sin, which is the opposite of faith, it also suggests that these negative factors can function dialectically in an indirectly positive manner so as to become *the first element in faith* inasmuch as one acquires the possibility of being cured from despair and sin by becoming conscious of oneself as existing before God and Christ (*SUD* 49, 82).[20] Faith is thus defined *ideally* by Anti-Climacus as that condition of the self in which there is no despair at all: 'in relating itself to itself and in willing to be itself, the self rests transparently in the power that established it' (49, 82, 131). But 'the battle of *faith*' is fought in the existential realm, where faith becomes a struggle for possibility, which in Anti-Climacus's view is 'the only salvation' for despair (38). The critical decision of faith, however, does not occur until one has been brought to the utmost extremity where, humanly speaking, there is *no* possibility. Then the question is whether one will believe that for God everything is possible, which for Anti-Climacus is 'the very formula for losing the understanding' (38). More closely defined, then, 'to believe is . . . to lose the understanding in order to gain God' (38).

HOPING AGAINST HOPE

Just as Christian faith goes against the understanding by believing in possibility in the face of impossibility, Christian hope is a 'hope against hope' that also goes against the understanding by hoping at precisely that point where, humanly speaking, there is no hope and all purely natural hope has been changed into hopelessness or despair (*EUD* 94–5; *FSE* 82; *SUD* 18).[21] Christian hope is thus a gift of the Spirit that comes only after one has 'died to' the understanding's merely human view of hope, which is associated with a multiplicity of expectations that often do not materialize but result in suffering and hardship that end in the loss of hope. In Kierkegaard's view, however, hardship does not take away hope but actually procures it (*CD* 106–13). Reversing Hegel's association of childhood with the inner and adulthood with the outer, Kierkegaard suggests that childhood is best characterized as 'a dream-life' in which our innermost being is asleep and we are turned entirely outward, open to every sense impression and confusing ourselves with it, so that 'inwardness is outwardness' at this stage of life (107–8). Although it is possible to remain in such a dream-like state in adulthood, hardship helps in an indirect or repelling manner to awaken us to the possibility of eternity's hope by drowning out and

[20] See further Walsh (2005: 29–32); Cappelørn (2004: 95–124).

[21] See also Gouwens (1996: 153–85).

silencing all external voices, enabling us to turn inward and listen to the voice of eternity planted deep within our innermost being:

> People continually think that it is the world, the environment, the circumstances, the situations that stand in one's way, in the way of one's fortune and peace and joy. Basically it is always the person himself who stands in his way, the person himself who is bound up too closely with the world and the environment and the circumstances and the situations so that he is unable to come to himself, to find rest, to hope. (*CD* 109–10)

Kierkegaard thus asserts: 'The only person hardship can depress is the person who refuses to be helped eternally' and 'The only person from whom hardship can take away hope is the person who does not want to have the hope of eternity' (113). For the person who truly wants it, however, hardship procures the hope of eternity.

Hoping All Things Always

Kierkegaard defines more explicitly what it means to hope in a Christian sense in *Works of Love*. Christianly understood, 'hope is composed of the eternal and the temporal', which means that its task is both to *hope all things* (the expression for its eternal aspect) and *to hope always* (the expression for its temporal aspect), which together express the same thing: 'at every moment always to hope all things' (*WL* 249). The only point at which the eternal, which simply *is* and thus not subject to temporal becoming, can be present in or intersect with the temporal realm is in *the future*, for otherwise a meeting in the present, which is so fleeting that it does not actually exist or is already past, would then be the eternal.[22] In relation to time, then, the eternal is the future or *the possible*, which is always a duality, containing both 'the possibility of advance or of retrogression, of rising or falling, of good or of evil' (249). We relate to the possible through *expectation*, which contains the same duality as the possible, so that what one expects depends upon a *choice* between these two equal but opposite possibilities. To hope, Kierkegaard says, is 'To relate oneself expectantly to the possibility of the good', which is the eternal (249). Hope is therefore different from temporal expectancy, which is not really hope, even though it is commonly called that, but 'a wish, a longing, a longing expectation now of one thing, now of another, in short, an expectant person's relationship to the possibility of multiplicity' (250). This sort of expectancy is particularly associated with

[22] On the present or instant in Kierkegaard's early pseudonymous writings, see Kangas (2007).

youth, which is full of expectation and possibility and then declines as we become older and settle into a life of 'dull repetition and paraphrasing of the same old thing' (250–1). 'Without the eternal', Kierkegaard observes, 'one lives with the help of habit, sagacity, aping, experience, custom, and usage', from which one may get a variety of things but not the possibility of the good or hope (251). Authentic hope is not associated with a certain age or period of life but extends over the whole of life, so that one's whole life is a time of hope, and 'anyone who refuses to understand that', he adds, 'is veritably in despair... whether he is conscious of it or not' (252).

Hoping for Others

As Kierkegaard sees it, hope in the possibility of the good is inherently related to love, so that it is impossible to hope for oneself without also hoping for others:

> No one can hope unless he is also loving; he cannot *hope for himself* without also being loving, because the good has an infinite connectedness; but if he is loving, he also hopes for others. In the same degree to which he hopes for others, he hopes for himself, because in the very same degree to which he hopes for others, he is one who loves. And in the very same degree to which he hopes for others, he hopes for himself, because this is the infinitely accurate, the eternal like for like that is in everything eternal. (*WL* 255)

Thus the task of hope from an eternal point of view is not merely to hope all things but *lovingly* to hope all things, which means that we hope for others as well as ourselves, or more accurately, we hope for ourselves only to the degree that we hope for others. Love is 'the middle term' between hope for oneself and hope for others, for 'without love, no hope for oneself; with love, hope for all others' (260). Whereas the person in despair assumes the impossibility of the good and hopes nothing at all for others, the loving person hopes all things for others and does not give up on them as being hopelessly lost, since from the standpoint of the eternal there is always the possibility of good for them. But loving and hoping for others is often sorely put to the test by a host of worldly passions and mentalities such as sagacity, anger, bitterness, envy, malice, small-mindedness, and worldly conceit that threaten to weigh us down and tempt us to expect the downfall and perdition of others (257–8). Yet, even if we can do nothing at all for others, we can still lovingly hope for them, for 'love alone hopes all things' (259).

THE WORKS OF LOVE

Kierkegaard's theology of hope thus anticipates the third term in the trilogy of passions that pre-eminently characterize the Christian life, namely love, which for Kierkegaard is the only thing that makes life worth living and is the only true sign that one is a Christian (*WL* 375). Kierkegaard's most substantive contribution to Christian thought is perhaps to be found in *Works of Love* (1847), in which Christian love is profoundly probed in distinction from pagan, worldly, natural, and merely human forms of love such as erotic love and friendship.[23] There really is nothing comparable to this work in the history of Christian thought, yet it is still relatively unknown and unexplored in contemporary Christian theology and ethics. Here, however, I shall touch on only a few of the main themes and distinctions of this work, particularly as they relate to two budding sociopolitical movements of the time, namely communism and the emancipation of women.

The Origin and Nature of Christian Love

Like a spring whose source is hidden and impenetrable, human love has its abode in and flows from the secret, innermost being of a person, where it originates even more hiddenly and mysteriously in the unfathomable, deep spring of God's love, without which there would be no love (*WL* 8–10). The conviction that human love has its source in divine love underlies Kierkegaard's whole theology of love and forms the basis for his understanding of Christian love as well as other forms of love from which it must be distinguished. For Kierkegaard, the Christian doctrine of love is summed up in the first and second commandments of the Old Testament (Deuteronomy 6: 5; Leviticus 19: 18) and New Testament (Mark 12: 28–31; Matthew 22: 37–9; Luke 10: 27): 'to love God with one's whole heart and the neighbour as oneself' (44). The first thing to be said about Christian love, therefore, is that it is *commanded* love, which makes it a duty to love.[24] In Kierkegaard's view, the 'very mark' and 'distinctive characteristic' of Christian love is that it contains the apparent contradiction that to love is a duty (24–5). Love is commonly thought to be a matter of inclination or feeling that cannot be commanded, whereas duty, as construed in Kantian

[23] Cf. Nygren (1954). For critical studies of *Works of Love*, see Ferreira (2001); Walsh (2005: 93–112); Perkins (1999*b*); Cappelørn and Deuser (1998); Løgstrup (1997: 218–64); Adorno (1940).

[24] See Evans (2004: 112–222), and Quinn (1998) vs. Ferreira (2001: 40–2), on the interpretation of this work as espousing a divine command theory of moral obligation.

ethics for example, has its ground in the rational will, which for Kant is self-legislating.[25] As Kierkegaard sees it, however, Christian love is not a natural inclination but a passion that has undergone a fundamental change so as to become a matter of conscience, which means that it is consciously based on a relation to God or the eternal. Moreover, in his view Christian love 'did not arise in any human being's heart' but has its origin in divine revelation, through which 'Everything has become new' in the duty to love (24–5).

Loving the Neighbour

In line with the second commandment of the Bible, Kierkegaard defines Christian love *(Kjerlighed)* as love for the neighbour. But who is our neighbour and what does it mean to love the neighbour as oneself? Kierkegaard begins to unpack the meaning of this commandment by pointing out that the term 'neighbour'*(Næste)* is derived from the word 'nearest' (*Nærmeste*), suggesting that the neighbour is the person who is or ought to be nearest to us—just as near as we are to ourselves (*WL* 21). Philosophically, the concept of neighbour corresponds to 'the other',[26] which in Kierkegaard's view includes all people but need be only one person in order to fulfil the commandment, for 'if there is one other person whom you in the Christian sense love *as yourself* or in whom you love *the neighbour*, then you love all people' (21). Christianly understood, loving the neighbour involves a 'redoubling' or duplication of oneself in the other in such a way as to test and do away with selfishness in one's self-love (21). In commanding love of the neighbour as oneself, Christianity presupposes that we love ourselves; thus it does not oppose self-love *per se* but seeks only to purge it of selfishness in order to teach us to love ourselves in the right way. This is done, Kierkegaard contends, not by loving another person 'more than oneself', which in his estimation is only a poetic intoxication and projection of oneself in an 'other I' or 'other self', but by duplicating oneself in the other in such a way as to transform self-love into love for the other regarded as an 'other you' who is independent and distinct from oneself (18–19, 53). In the latter mode of redoubling, which is the Christian mode, what one selfishly would have desired only for oneself is now desired for the other, and instead of making demands upon the other, all the demands are placed upon oneself. Loving oneself in the right way thus corresponds perfectly to loving the neighbour; indeed, for Kierkegaard they are fundamentally 'one and the same thing' (22).

[25] Kant (1990: 13–15, 48–50).

[26] Cf. Hegel (1969: 117–18).

Christian Love as Self-Denial

Another way of expressing this is to say that Christian love is *self-denial's love*, which is the boundless and passionate giving of ourselves to others in such a way as to drive out selfishness in ourselves by placing the neighbour as a middle term or third party between self-love and its 'other I' in the beloved or friend (*WL* 54). As Kierkegaard sees it, self-denial is 'Christianity's essential form' and is what distinguishes Christian love most of all from other forms of love such as erotic love (*Elskov*) and friendship (*Venskab*) (56). These forms of love are based on personal preference and thus are exclusive in nature, loving one person above or in contrast to all others, whereas 'self-denial's boundlessness in giving itself means not to exclude a single one' (52). 'The Christian doctrine', Kierkegaard asserts, 'is to love the neighbor, to love the whole human race, all people, even the enemy, and not to make exceptions, neither of preference nor of aversion' (19).

Yet Christian love is not a separate type of love in contrast to other types of love; rather, in Kierkegaard's view Christianity recognizes only one form of love, spiritual love, which can and should 'lie at the base of and be present in every other expression of love' (66, 146). Thus Christianity does not seek to do away with other forms of love but undertakes to bring about a 'change of infinity' or transformation of the eternal in them so that the other, including the spouse and friend, is loved first and foremost as a neighbour or human being, which is the fundamental category of every individual: 'Each one of us is a human being and then in turn the distinctive individual that he is in particular' (139, 141).

The Equality of Love

A central feature of Kierkegaard's understanding of Christian love is its emphasis on our common humanity and universal equality as human beings. In contrast to paganism, in which, according to Kierkegaard, 'people are inhumanly separated one from another by the dissimilarities of earthly life' and individuals are taught to disclaim kinship with one another, Christianity affirms the eternal equality and kinship of all human beings before God (*WL* 69; cf. *EUD* 141–5). It teaches us to shut our eyes to or to look away from the dissimilarities of earthly life, to lift ourselves above them and let them 'hang loosely' so as to allow the essential likeness or 'eternal resemblance' common to all individuals to show through (68, 72, 88). At the same time, however, Christianity does not seek to do away with dissimilarities, which in Kierkegaard's view are inherent to earthly existence:

No person has ever lived in Christendom, any more than in paganism, who is not dressed or cloaked in the dissimilarity of earthly life. Just as little as the Christian lives or can live without his body, so little can he live without the dissimilarity of earthly life that belongs to every human being in particular by birth, by position, by circumstances, by education, etc.—none of us is pure humanity. (70)

Nor does Christianity seek to establish temporal similarity or one temporal condition among all people, which in Kierkegaard's view is the preoccupation and goal of a pious, well-intentioned worldliness but not of Christianity, which maintains strict neutrality towards all earthly dissimilarities (71). In Kierkegaard's estimation, the achievement of 'worldly similarity' (*verdslige Lighed*) is impossible, but even if it were possible, it would not be the same as 'Christian equality' (*christelige Ligelighed*), which is essentially an inward, spiritual qualification of human beings that is possessed eternally, not an external social condition, although in his view spiritual equality can be preserved 'in any externality whatever' (*WL* 72; *EUD* 143).

Christian Love versus Communism

In distinguishing Christian equality from external or social equality, Kierkegaard sets himself squarely against two budding egalitarian social movements of the time: communism and the emancipation of women. Although he does not explicitly mention Marx in any of his works or journals, he possessed and apparently read a book published in 1843 by the left-wing Hegelian Arnold Ruge that contained a short article by Marx written under a pseudonym.[27] That Kierkegaard was familiar with communism at the time *Works of Love* was written, however, is evident from a journal entry of 1847 in which he mentions that one of its deliberations is 'rightly turned against communism' (*JP* iv. 4124; cf. 4111). But more than one deliberation, if not, according to one commentator, the whole book, is clearly polemical towards communism.[28] Kierkegaard's knowledge of socialism/communism (they are synonymous to him) at this point appears to have been gleaned mainly from Copenhagen newspaper accounts of French socialists of the time, although he was aware as early as 1834 of the Saint-Simon movement, an early socialist sect which, long after its demise in the early 1830s, had a strong ideological impact on Young German left-wing Hegelian sociopolitical thought in the 1840s (*EPW* 4).[29] There were also a few lonely voices crying in the wilderness over social problems,

[27] Malantschuk (1980: 76–82); Rohde (1967: no. 753); Marx (1972: 23–5).
[28] Malantschuk (1980: 8–9).
[29] Ibid. 11; Breckman (1999: 18, 106–7, 214–20, 151–64, 282–4).

particularly the plight of the poor, in Scandinavia in the 1830s and 1840s, most notably Niels Treschow (1751–1833) in Norway and Frederik Dreier (1827–53) in Denmark, the latter being an openly avowed socialist who founded a society for relief of the poor in 1847.[30]

The first edition of Marx's *Communist Manifesto* appeared in 1848, a year after *Works of Love* was published. That same year Kierkegaard recorded in his journal: 'The idea of genuine equality, essential equality, has been given up; equality has now become a political question discussed throughout Europe', and he specifically refers to communism as leading to a new form of tyranny—the fear of men or the crowd (*JP* iv. 4131). In a preface to 'A Cycle of Ethical-Religious Treatises' (also written in 1848) he predicts the disintegration of European society into anarchy or 'a world of atoms' in which no one would be able to rule except God—a circumstance which in his view would actually constitute an advance inasmuch as the deity would then become a schoolmaster who 'watches over everyone, each one individually' (*BA* 236). But Kierkegaard has no idea what concrete shape the world would assume in the event of this impending disintegration, readily admitting that:

> Here thinking halts. The shape of the world would resemble—well, I do not know to what I should compare it—it would resemble an enormous Christiansfeldt [a small Danish town in south Jutland founded by the Moravians], and then the two most powerful opponents would be present, contending with each other over the interpretation of this phenomenon—*communism*, which would say: This is secularly right; there must be no distinction whatever between persons; wealth and art and science and scholarship and government, etc. etc. are of evil; all people should be alike as workers in a factory, as the inmates in a workhouse, dressed alike, eating the same food (made in one enormous pot) at the same stroke of the clock, in the same measure, etc.—*pietism*, which would say: This is Christianly right; there must be no distinctions between persons; we should be brothers and sisters, have everything in common; wealth, position, art, science, scholarship, etc. are of evil; all people should be alike as once was the case in the little Christiansfeldt, dressed alike, praying at specified times, marrying by drawing lots, going to bed by the clock, eating the same kind of food out of one big dish in a definite rhythm, etc.
>
> (*BA* 236)

Whether communist or pietist in organization, then, a society based on worldly similarity would be virtually the same, ironically resulting in a loss of individuality. But in Kierkegaard's estimation neither form of social organization would be equivalent to Christian equality, which affirms our common humanity and spiritual equality in the context of individual and social dissimilarities.

[30] Hovde (1943: ii. 625–34).

The Emancipation of Women

Kierkegaard's negative attitude towards social equality also led him to oppose the emancipation of women, the subject of his very first publication in a newspaper article while still a university student (*EPW* 3–5).[31] In the 1830s there was already a women's liberation movement brewing in Scandinavia and elsewhere in Europe which continued to gather steam in the 1840s, particularly after the political revolutions of 1848.[32] Viewing Christianity as seeking to bring about only the change of infinity within individuals, not a change in their external social status or privileges, in *Works of Love* Kierkegaard advises a poor charwoman, for example, to be content with her socio-economic situation:

> Christianity's divine meaning is to say in confidence to every human being, 'Do not busy yourself with changing the shape of the world or your situation, as if you (to stay with the example), instead of being a poor charwoman, perhaps could manage to be called "Madame." No, make Christianity your own, and it will show you a point outside the world, and by means of this you will move heaven and earth; yes, you will do something even more wonderful, you will move heaven and earth so quietly, so lightly, that no one notices it.' (*WL* 136)

In like manner, while objecting to the abominable treatment of women almost as animals or disdained beings of another species in the history of male–female relations, Kierkegaard makes the following observation concerning women's rights:

> What battles there have been to establish in a worldly way the woman in equal rights with the man—but Christianity makes only infinity's change and therefore quietly. Outwardly the old more or less remains. The man is to be the woman's master and she subservient to him; but inwardly everything is changed, changed by means of this little question to the woman, whether she has consulted with her conscience about having this man—as master, for otherwise she does not get him. Yet the conscience-question about the conscience-matter makes her in inwardness before God absolutely equal with the man. (*WL* 138)

This aspect of Kierkegaard's view of Christianity and Christian love reveals the degree to which, on the woman question at least, he was a man of his time, limited by the patriarchal perspective and practices that prevailed in both religion and culture of that period.[33] But there are deeper implications of Kierkegaard's social views that serve to temper and qualify the negative viewpoints noted above. Christian love is an inward concern or passion for the other as a neighbour, but it is not such a hidden feeling that it has

[31] See Watkin (1999). [32] Hovde (1943: ii. 680–93).

[33] See Léon and Walsh (1997) for a variety of feminist critiques of Kierkegaard.

no outward expression and consequences. On the contrary, the 'essential mark' of Christian love is that it bears fruit and is made recognizable in *works of love* (*WL* 10–11). 'Indeed,' Kierkegaard says, 'if there could actually be such a self-contradiction in love, it would have to be the greatest torment that love insisted on keeping love hidden, insisted on making love unrecognizable' (*WL* 11). Thus, while there is no work or act that unconditionally demonstrates the presence of love, which depends solely on the inward motivation or *how* a work is done, love for the other as one's neighbour or spiritual equal will or should express itself in outward forms and ways that seemingly would preclude patriarchal and other structures of domination between men and women, even if they are allowed to stand externally.

That Kierkegaard would affirm this interpretation is supported by the fact that he credits Christianity with having done away with the institution of slavery: 'The times are past when only the powerful and the prominent were human beings—and the others were bond servants and slaves. This is due to Christianity' (*WL* 74). Moreover, he encourages an active concern for the material plight of the poor and needy among us—not at a distance but close at hand and without condescension.[34] In this way Christianity 'quietly' goes about bringing change in the temporal sphere externally in social relations as well as internally in the individual. Kierkegaard states:

> Christianity has not wanted to topple governments from the throne in order to place itself on the throne; it has never contended in an external sense for a place in the world... and yet it has infinitely changed everything it allowed and allows to continue. In other words, just as the blood pulses in every nerve, so does Christianity want to permeate everything with the relationship of conscience.
>
> (*WL* 135)

God as the Middle Term in Human Love Relations

Central to the possibility of Christian love is a relationship to God, which for Kierkegaard is 'the mark by which the love for people is recognized as genuine', even in special relations to spouses and friends (*WL* 120). Kierkegaard contends that:

> However beautiful a relationship of love has been between two people or among many, however complete all their desire and all their bliss have been for themselves in mutual sacrifice and devotion, even though everyone has praised this relationship—if God and the relationship with God have been omitted, then this, in the Christian sense, has not been love but a mutually enchanting defraudation of love. (*WL* 107)

[34] See Ferreira (2001: 57–62); Barrett (1999).

If a love relation does not contain a relation to God or lead both parties in the relation to God, it is not true love but only a worldly alliance or what the world calls love, which is the opposite of Christian love. What the world regards as love is, at best, 'to love the good and humanity, yet in such a way that one also looks to one's own earthly advantage and that of a few others' (123). Christian love, by contrast, includes God as a third party or middle term in every love relation and actually makes God, who is love, the sole object of those relations. This is one of the most profound insights in Kierkegaard's understanding of Christian love, which goes beyond the mutuality that characterizes merely human love to require 'threeness' or the presence of God as that which not only binds us in love but teaches us what it truly means to love ourselves, to love others, and to be loved in return, which is to love God: 'To love God is to love oneself truly; to help another person to love God is to love another person; to be helped by another person to love God is to be loved' (107, cf. 130). Since God is love, this means that the object of every love relation, including the relation to one's own self, is God or love itself rather than either party in the relation. In other words, Christianity seeks to make every love relation an expression of sacrificial love by teaching both parties to help the other to love rather than seek to be loved in and through their relation to one another.

The Double Danger of Christian Love

If we venture to mediate our love relations in this way, however, conflict with the world is inevitable because Christian love is the opposite of pagan, worldly, merely human conceptions of love (*WL* 118, 121, 123). As Kierkegaard sees it, the Christian life is exposed to 'double danger', involving struggle on two fronts, first of all *inwardly* in striving to develop a Christian disposition within oneself, and then *outwardly* with the world, which rewards the true expression of love to others with 'hate, contempt, and persecution' (76, 81–2, 191–2). Ironically, the more we succeed in the first struggle, the worse it goes for us in the second. In Kierkegaard's view, opposition from the world is essential, not merely accidental, to Christianity since they are qualitatively heterogeneous to one another, and anyone who does not encounter opposition 'is obliged to be a bit dubious' about his or her self (194). It is thus essential for those who choose Christianity to know what they are getting into: 'A young person should not be promised anything other than what Christianity can keep, but Christianity cannot keep anything other than what it has promised from the beginning: the world's ingratitude, opposition, and derision, and continually to a higher degree the more earnest a Christian one becomes' (194). Thus, if 'the last difficulty' or second danger of becoming a Christian is suppressed, there can be 'no talk of Christianity', which in Kierkegaard's view is 'essentially abolished' unless it can be demonstrated that the world has become 'essentially good' and therefore no longer heterogeneous to Christianity as it was originally assumed to be (194).

Although Christendom imagines that it is Christian, Kierkegaard charges that it has in fact done away with the possibility of offence, which is essential to Christianity, in the illusion that what it calls self-denial is Christian self-denial, whereas true Christian self-denial always bears the mark of double danger (*WL* 194–5). Labelling the worldly or merely human conception of self-denial as 'counterfeit self-denial', Kierkegaard maintains that 'as soon as the double mark is missing the self-denial is not Christian self-denial' (195). The worldly or merely human idea of self-denial is to 'give up your self-loving desires, cravings, and plans—then you will be esteemed and honored and loved as righteous and wise'; conversely, the Christian idea of self-denial is to 'give up your self-loving desires and cravings, give up your self-seeking plans and purposes so that you truly work unselfishly for the good—and then, for that very reason, put up with being abominated almost as a criminal, insulted and ridiculed' (94). Whereas merely human self-denial is done with the expectation that it will be positively rewarded by the world, Christian self-denial not only expects opposition from the world but *freely chooses it*, which for Kierkegaard is 'the very assurance' that one stands in a genuine relation to God (195).

In recognizing that the Christian life involves double danger and the practice of self-denial not only internally in the overcoming of selfishness and worldliness within ourselves but also externally in voluntary submission to being maltreated by the world, Kierkegaard arrives at the key insight that governs all his later religious writings, which increasingly emphasize *voluntary suffering* in imitation of Christ as the distinctive mark of what it means to be a Christian in contrast to paganism, Judaism, and ordinary human sufferings such as sickness and adversity. This does not mean, however, that there is no joy or consolation in the Christian life. On the contrary, just as the Christian life is characterized by the passions of faith, hope, and love, so too joy is experienced in the strife of suffering and consolation for one's own internal and external suffering is gained in and through consoling others (cf. *CD* 95–159).[35]

[35] See Nelson (2007); Bøgeskov (2007); Walsh (2005: 123–6, 141–6).

The Question of Martyrdom

Nor does voluntary suffering for the sake of Christ necessarily require martyrdom, although that must remain a possibility in every Christian's life. Speaking in the voice of Anti-Climacus in *Practice in Christianity* (1850), Kierkegaard states:

> I have never asserted that every Christian is a martyr, or that no one was a true Christian who did not become a martyr, even though I think that every true Christian should—and here I include myself—in order to be a true Christian, make a humble admission that he has been let off far more easily than true Christians in the strictest sense, and he should make this admission so that, if I may put it this way, the Christian order of rank may not be confused and the no. 1 place completely disappear as place no. 2 takes over its position. (*PC* 226–7)

But Kierkegaard seems to be of two minds on this issue, inasmuch as in *Two Ethical-Religious Essays* (1849), H.H., the anonymous 'author' of that work, maintains that no one has the right to allow oneself to be put to death for the truth as Christ did since no one possesses absolute truth and authority to atone for this misdeed as he did (*WA* 49, 83–4, 86).[36] The martyrdom of the apostles constituted an exception, inasmuch as over against the non-Christian world they may be said to have possessed absolute truth. In relation to other Christians, however, there is only a relative difference between persons since every human being is a sinner. Thus one dare not let others become guilty of murder by allowing them to put one to death for the sake of truth. Even if one assumes that 'so-called Christendom is not Christian at all' but 'far more pagan than paganism was', one dare not accuse others face to face of not being Christians, since only God knows the human heart (87). Thus one cannot justify letting others put one to death on the basis of their presumed paganism. In the spirit of *Works of Love*, H.H. argues that love for others as neighbours will prevent one from allowing that to happen, for by 'lovingly considering their cause', just as Christ 'lovingly bore in mind his enemies' cause', one comes to recognize through self-examination that one is not superior to others in the possession of truth and therefore must 'keep watch' so that they do not falsely become more guilty than they deserve (88). The upshot of the matter for the present generation of Christians, therefore, would seem to be that they dare not allow themselves to be martyred for the truth. But this conclusion saddens Kierkegaard's anonymous 'author', who wonders how a religious awakening can be brought about 'if one does not dare to use the only true means of awakening, to let oneself be put to death

[36] See also Burgess (2006) and Barrett (2006).

for the truth' (84). He nevertheless suggests that in a society ruled by a tyrant, whether that is an individual or the crowd, it is not inconceivable that, ironically, one might be put to death simply because one defends the view that one does not have the right to let oneself be put to death for the truth. Thus the possibility of martyrdom is not entirely ruled out. Indeed, we shall have occasion to revisit this issue in the next chapter in light of the Danish political revolution of 1848 and Kierkegaard's final attack on Christendom.

7

Religion, Culture, and Society

Kierkegaard's critique of Christendom in all its aspects—philosophical, theological, ecclesiastical, cultural, and sociopolitical—began in his earliest writings and was sustained throughout his authorship, culminating in the attack literature of the last year of his life. The most concentrated discussion of the relation of religion, culture, and society in his writings, however, appears in *Two Ages: The Age of Revolution and the Present Age, A Literary Review* (1846).[1] The subject of this review was a novella titled *Two Ages*, published anonymously in 1845 by Madam Thomasine Gyllembourg, the mother of J. L. Heiberg, the leading light of Danish culture both aesthetically and philosophically in Kierkegaard's time. In 1833 Heiberg had issued *On the Significance of Philosophy for the Present Age*, a prospectus for a series of popular lectures intended to introduce Hegelian philosophy to the cultured elite (including women) of Copenhagen. In this work Heiberg characterized the present age as a period of transition and crisis due to the previous age of rationalism, which in his view had led to a discarding of religion by the cultured elite or 'humanity's upper house', leaving it for the edification of the uncultured masses while the cultured few busied themselves with politics.[2] In the 1830s, it may be recalled, a liberal movement arose in Denmark supporting freedom of the press and representative government in opposition to the conservatives, who favoured the continuation of an absolute monarchy. It was also during this period that the peasant awakening movement, which had pushed for economic and agrarian reforms in the 1820s, made significant gains in land ownership and political representation in the provincial estates or advisory assemblies established by the king. Moreover, disagreements over the legal and political status of the mostly German-speaking duchies of Slesvig and Holstein in southern Jutland in this decade fed German and Danish nationalism. So there was considerable political ferment in Denmark at that time. In Heiberg's judgement, however, it was 'the very political character of the age' that constituted its crisis, inasmuch as 'after having cast out religion, that is, knowledge of the

[1] See Cappelørn and Deuser (1999) and Perkins (1984) for critical essays on this work. On Kierkegaard's social and political thought in general, see Kirmmse (1990), Pattison and Shakespeare (1998), Connell and Evans (1992), Westphal (1991), Nordentoft (1973).

[2] Heiberg (2005: 94–5).

infinite, the age has only finite determinations left'.[3] His solution to the confusion and chaos of the present age was to unify it through *philosophy*, which in his view was 'truth itself'.[4] 'Only philosophy can go into the many details of our finite goals, particularly our political ones', Heiberg declared, for 'only philosophy can see their tendency toward the infinite and, with this knowledge, clarify their obscure aspects'.[5] Thus the most immediate demand of the time, as he saw it, was to arrive at a higher understanding and unity of religion, art, poetry, politics, and science through Hegelian philosophy, which by virtue of being recognized as the most comprehensive philosophical system laid claim to being 'the age's own'.[6]

THE PHENOMENON OF LEVELLING IN THE PRESENT AGE

By 1846, however, a new era had dawned with different demands of the time, creating a generation gap between the aristocratic conservatism of the older generation and the bourgeois liberalism of the younger. Although still a young man, Kierkegaard did not align himself with the latter, but neither did he embrace the cultural elitism of the former. Rather, he deftly crafted a critique of both parties while setting forth a different vision of what the age needs in his review of Madam Gyllembourg's novella. In the preface to this work the anonymous author states that she has not set out to portray the great political events 'that so violently shook the close of the previous century' in the age of revolution, namely the French Revolution, nor the political agitation it continues to spawn in the present age, but to present 'the domestic reflexion' of these two ages in family life, personal relations, and individuals in order to illumine the 'glaring contrast' between them (*TA* 153). Analysing this contrast in his literary review, Kierkegaard identifies the distinctive character of the age of revolution as consisting above all in *passion*, in contrast to which the present age shows itself to be essentially a 'sensible, reflecting age devoid of passion, flaring up in superficial, short-lived enthusiasm and prudentially relaxing in indolence', thereby lacking decision and action (68, 71). The present age does not seek to overthrow the established order and abolish the monarchy as in a revolutionary age but lets everything stand, 'subtly drain[ing] the meaning out of it' and gradually transforming the monarchy into 'make-believe' (77, 80–1). An age without passion, Kierkegaard observes, has 'no assets of feeling in the erotic, no assets of enthusiasm and inwardness in politics and religion, no assets of domesticity, piety, and appreciation in

[3] Heiberg (2005: 95). [4] Ibid. 98, 115. [5] Ibid. 101. [6] Ibid. 115, 117.

daily life and social life' (74). Consequently, 'there is no hero, no lover, no thinker, no knight of faith, no great humanitarian, no person in despair' to vouch for the validity of their words and observations on the basis of a primitive experience (75). Lacking passion or inwardness, individuals in the present age are spectators rather than participants in social relations; they do not relate to one another with the intensity of a mutual devotedness but watch each other in the tension of reflection, which imprisons them in a state of envy or selfishness that in Kierkegaard's estimation has become the 'negatively unifying principle' of the age (81). The more dominant reflection and indolence become in the present age, the more dangerous envy becomes, finally taking the form of *levelling* in the reduction of the single individual to a nonentity in the faceless abstraction of the public or crowd.

For Kierkegaard, the phenomenon of levelling is of 'profound importance' because it heralds 'the ascendancy of the category "generation" over the category "individuality" ' in the present age (*TA* 84). In his view, levelling constitutes the 'basic tendency' of the modern age, which has gone through various concrete upheavals that approximate levelling but do not qualify as genuine levelling because they are not sufficiently abstract (90). As Kierkegaard understands it, levelling is not equivalent to the elimination of class or economic differences between individuals but has to do fundamentally with the loss of individuality in the abstraction of the public or crowd.[7] Although oriented towards social equality, the modern age goes astray in the implementation of this ideal by giving it expression in the form of levelling, which in Kierkegaard's view is the very opposite of equality because it does not value individuals. Rather, levelling constitutes 'abstraction's victory over individuals' by reducing their significance to the mathematical equality and equivalence of numbers (84–5). Only the crowd or public is significant, and the greater its number the more significance and abstract power it has. Individuals dare not take the lead in levelling or venture anything on their own for fear of being judged for setting themselves above or apart from the crowd. Consequently, in Kierkegaard's estimation the individual 'does not belong to God, to himself, to the beloved, to his art, to his scholarship; no, just as a serf belongs to an estate, so the individual realizes that in every respect he belongs to an abstraction in which reflection subordinates him' (85). This serfdom of the individual leads Kierkegaard to view the principle of sociality in the modern age as a 'consuming, demoralizing principle' that has its basis in a 'disregard for the separation of the religious individual before God' (86). In a passage excised from the final text, he states:

[7] See also Tuttle (2005) and Perkins (1999*c*).

Leveling is the counterfeit anticipation of eternal life, which has been abolished as other-worldly and nowadays is supposed to be actualized here *in abstracto*. When everyone, each one separately, is essentially a part of the divine totality, yes, then there will be the consummation of equality. But if the dialectic turns away from inwardness and wants to depict equality by the negative principle that they who individually are inessential are equals in a union of externalities, this is leveling.

(*TA* 134)

THE PHANTOM OF THE PUBLIC

In Kierkegaard's view, levelling is made possible through the rise and agency of the 'monstrous nonentity' or 'phantom' of the public, which in turn is possible only in a passionless, reflective age by the aid of the press when it has become a phantom itself through the practice of journalistic anonymity (*TA* 90–1, 93, cf. 138–9).[8] The concept of the public could not have appeared in antiquity, Kierkegaard argues, because in that time

the people were obliged to come forward *en masse in corpore* [as a whole] in the situation of action, were obliged to bear the responsibility for what was done by individuals in their midst, while in turn the individual was obliged to be present in person as the one specifically involved and had to submit to the summary court for approval or disapproval. (91)

'Only when there is no strong communal life', Kierkegaard claims, is it possible for the press to create the phantom of the public, which is made up of 'unsubstantial individuals who are never united or never can be united in the simultaneity of any situation or organization and yet are claimed to be a whole' (91). The public is supposed to include everyone but cannot 'be called up for inspection' or held responsible because it exists only in abstraction; it is not a people, a generation, an age, a congregation, or an association—all of which are concretions of one sort or another (91–3). To illustrate how this nebulous nonentity goes about levelling or reducing individuals to insignificance and nothingness in modern society, Kierkegaard alludes to his experience with the scandalous tabloid *The Corsair*, characterizing it as a 'dog' that is kept for the amusement of the public (95). The dog is goaded by the public to attack a man of distinction, tearing at his coat tails and engaging in all sorts of tricks until the public finally becomes tired and calls the dog off. But since it was a third party, namely the dog, that actually did the dirty work of levelling, the public assumes no responsibility, claiming that it is merely a 'subscriber', not the owner of the 'bad dog', which it now wants exterminated (95).

[8] See Pattison (2002: 64–71) for a comparison of Kierkegaard and Heiberg on the public.

RESISTING LEVELLING

Because levelling is the product of a superior abstract power or demonic force, in Kierkegaard's judgement it cannot be controlled or halted by any age, heroic individual, assemblage, or national individuality but is here to stay (*TA* 86–8). Living in an age of levelling can nevertheless be genuinely educative for individuals, inasmuch as the rigorous personal testing to which they are subjected in the process of levelling can serve as the point of departure or inspiration for a higher life in the religious. We can either resist levelling or succumb to it and become part of the crowd. Levelling can be halted only on an individual basis by each person entering into a relation to God, through which the single individual becomes an essential human being in the full sense of equality before God and in relation to other human beings. Kierkegaard thus urges the single individual to make 'the inspired leap of religiousness' over the blade of levelling into 'the embrace of the eternal' (89, 108). Every person must make this momentous leap alone, as no one can help others; even women must make the leap by themselves, so that 'God's infinite love will not become a second-hand relationship for them' (108–9).

Although reflection functions as a snare or mental prison that often prevents individuals from deciding and acting on their own in an age of reflection, encouraging them to do only what is prudent and safe like everyone else, Kierkegaard maintains that 'reflection itself is not the evil'; rather, it is 'stagnation in reflection' that is the culprit (96). Indeed, as he sees it, 'considerable reflectiveness is the condition for a higher meaningfulness than that of immediate passion', but an infinite enthusiasm or passion for the religious must intervene in order to persuade the reflective powers to decide and to act (96). For Kierkegaard, therefore, it is not philosophy or a higher form of reflection that is needed to counter levelling in the present age but the passion and essentiality of the religious in the single individual who is reflective enough to perceive what the prudent thing to do is but passionate enough to reject it in order to gain the highest enthusiasm and equality of the religious.

THE PRINCIPLE OF ASSOCIATION

If the present age cannot be saved by philosophy, it likewise cannot be redeemed by the idea of sociality or the principle of association, which in Kierkegaard's view serves in an inversely dialectical manner to weaken and vitiate individuals while seeking to strengthen them by sticking together in numbers (*TA* 106). Inspired by the Saint-Simon movement of the 1820s and 1830s, for whom the forming of associations was a central strategy for alleviating the plight of the poor by organizing stock corporations with communal ownership of property and dividends, Scandinavian socialists in the 1840s addressed the severe problems of pauperism in their generation in a similar manner.[9] In Denmark Frederik Dreier founded the Craftsman's Educational Society for relief of the poor, while Marcus Thrane (1817–90) formed a number of Workmen's Associations in Norway.[10] Danish liberals also formed an alliance with the peasant movement in 1846 through the establishment of the Society of the Friends of the Peasant.[11] Although Kierkegaard admits that the principle of association 'can have validity with respect to material interest', the levelling that comes with it leads to a loss not only of individuality but also of genuine community, which requires a strong sense of individuality in order to be viable: 'Not until the single individual has established an ethical stance despite the whole world, not until then can there be any question of genuinely uniting; otherwise it gets to be a union of people who separately are weak, a union as unbeautiful and depraved as a child-marriage' (106). Only when one is turned inward in passionate self-concern as a single individual can one form a proper relation to and with others: 'If the essential passion is taken away, the one motivation, and everything becomes meaningless externality, devoid of character, then the spring of ideality stops flowing and life together becomes stagnant water' (62).

One of the characteristics of the age of revolution admired by Kierkegaard is that both individually and corporately individuals of that age were passionately related to an idea ('freedom, equality, fraternity') that bound them together, yet not so close as to become a herd, which Kierkegaard, alluding to Aristotle, regards as an animal category, not a human one.[12] 'When individuals (each one individually) are essentially and passionately related to an idea and together are essentially related to the same idea', he observes, 'the relation is optimal and normative', involving both individual separation in inwardness and corporate unanimity in relation to the idea (*TA* 62). As Kierkegaard sees it, both elements are necessary for genuine community, for 'if individuals relate to an idea merely *en masse* (consequently without the individual separation of inwardness), we get violence, anarchy, riotousness' (63). Without a common idea to bind and inspire individuals together, everything devolves into crudeness or a lack of culture. Ideally, then, the proper relation of the

[9] Breckman (1999: 151–64); Woszek (1987).

[10] Hovde (1943: ii. 626, 635–41.

[11] Kirmmse (1990: 57).

[12] Cf. Aristotle, *Politics* 3. 11, 1281a40–3–1281b15–20. See also *UDVS* 190; *SUD* 118; *JP* iii. 2986.

individual and society may be summed up in the following astronomical metaphor: 'The harmony of the spheres is the unity of each planet relating to itself and to the whole' (63).

The structure of the relation between the individual and society in an age of levelling, however, will be different from that of previous ages, in which the leaders of society were recognizable individuals who exercised authority in their various positions of rank, thereby supporting and being supported by the whole. Now, like 'plainclothes policemen' or 'secret agents', they will be *unrecognizable* individuals who lead *without authority*, giving support to the universal in a negative and indirect manner by *repulsion*, that is, by exposing the evil of levelling in society and defeating it through *suffering* rather than by an external victory (107–9). As Kierkegaard envisions them, 'not one of the unrecognizable ones will dare give direct help, speak plainly, teach openly, assume decisive leadership of the crowd'; rather, they must learn to love others infinitely by constraining themselves rather than constraining and domineering over others (108–9). In a journal entry of the following year Kierkegaard observes:

> There never has been and there cannot be a Christian reformation which turns against authority as if all would then be well; that would be much too secular a movement. No, the essentially Christian reformation means to turn against the mass, for the essentially Christian reformation means that each person must be reformed, and only then is the most ungodly of all unchristian categories overthrown: the crowd, the public. (*JP* iii. 2929)

UNUM NORIS OMNES

The view set forth in *Two Ages* on the difference between the sociality of the crowd or public and genuine community is further confirmed and given its most incisive expression in a journal entry from 1850:

> In the 'public' and the like the single individual is nothing; there is no individual; the numerical is the constituting form and the law for the coming into existence of a *generatio aequivoca* [spontaneous generation]; detached from the 'public' the single individual is nothing, and in the public he is, more basically understood, really nothing at all.
>
> In community the single individual *is*; the single individual is dialectically decisive as the presupposition for forming community, and in community the single individual is qualitatively something essential and can at any moment become higher than 'community', specifically, as soon as 'the others' fall away from the idea. The cohesiveness of community comes from each one's being a single individual, and then the idea; the connectedness of a public or rather its disconnectedness consists in the numerical character of everything. Every single individual in

community guarantees the community; the public is a chimera. In community the single individual is a microcosm who qualitatively reproduces the cosmos; here, in a good sense, it holds true that *unum noris omnes* [if you know one, you know all]. In a public there is no single individual and the whole is nothing; here it is impossible to say *unum noris omnes*, for here there is no: one. 'Community' is certainly more than a sum; but it is truly a sum of ones; the public is nonsense: a sum of negative ones, of ones who are not ones, who become ones through the sum instead of the sum becoming a sum of the ones. (*JP* iii. 2952, translation modified)

Here Kierkegaard reaffirms the notion of *unum noris omnes* introduced earlier in *The Concept of Anxiety*. In that work, we may recall, this expression was used to assert the solidarity of Adam and the race with regard to hereditary sin; here it is seen as providing the basis for genuine community, which affirms the individual in contrast to the crowd and the numerical.[13] As Kierkegaard continues to reflect on the concept of the individual in relation to the numerical in his late journals, he associates the deepest fall of the human race with the fact that 'there are no individualities any more, but in a wretched sense everyone has become two' (*JP* iii. 2993). Turning the tables on Marx, who regarded religion as the opiate of the people, he further suggests that it is the numerical which has a drugging effect upon people, destroying the human spirit as a result:

... the numerical transfers a human being to an exalted state just as opium does—and then he is tranquilized, tranquilized by the tremendous trustworthiness of millions. And yet in truth millions are just as untrustworthy, entirely just as untrustworthy as one. But one does not have the drugging effect that millions have—and thus it is clear to see, one is entirely trustworthy. That is, 'millions' transfer a human being into a drugged state; he sinks under the force of numbers; he expires *qua* spirit ... (*JP* iii. 2980, translation modified)

THE EUROPEAN CRISIS OF 1848

The forced but peaceful transition from an absolute monarchy to a constitutional monarchy in Denmark in 1848, together with the violent political revolutions in France and Germany that same year, confirmed in Kierkegaard's mind the validity of his diagnosis of the sickness of the present age and his predictions about the future articulated two years earlier in *Two Ages* (*JP* iv. 4167; *BA* 315–16). Personally, he regarded this event as something to weep over, as to him it represented the victory of irrationality

[13] It also undergirds the proper relation of the individual and the state, which in Kierkegaard's view was given ideal expression in Plato's *Republic*, in which the state is not higher than the individual but constructed 'for the individual, *unum noris omnes*' (*JP* iii. 3327).

and the 'rabble tyranny' of the crowd over rational government and the possibility of any stable government at all, since the same forces of levelling that brought down the old government could be expected in turn to overthrow the new one as well (*JP* iv. 4127, 4134, 4149; *BA* 319–20). At a deeper level, Kierkegaard saw the political change as an expression of the same demoralization and internal disintegration that Denmark and all of Europe were undergoing as a result of the lack or loss of spirit or true religiousness in the individual and society (*JP* iv. 4127, 4149; vi. 6255). In his view, the root corruption or evil was not the government but the crowd, which with the aid of the liberal press had established itself as the authority, truth, and god, equating its will with the will of God and pantheistically confusing *vox populi* (the voice of the people) with *vox dei* (the voice of God) (*JP* iii. 2933, 2942; vi. 6255). This is not to say, however, that the crowd altogether lacks validity, as Kierkegaard admits that 'with regard to all temporal, earthly, worldly goals, the crowd can have its validity, even its validity as the decisive factor, that is, as the authority', but it 'becomes untruth when it is carried over into the realms of the intellectual, the spiritual, and the religious' (*PV* 106 n., 109).

The crisis of 1848 also helped Kierkegaard to understand his own position and purpose better and to discern more clearly what the age needs and where it is heading (*BA* 228–9). Theologically, he concludes that 'The conflict about Christianity will no longer be doctrinal conflict' between orthodoxy and heterodoxy but about 'Christianity as an existence'—a conflict occasioned not only by the political crisis of 1848 but also by the socialist and communist movements of the time (*JP* iv. 4185). In his view, the crisis of 1848 was the introduction to a new era that would not begin until 'this convulsive seizure', as he called it, had run its course, which was likely to take a generation or two, and until the age had come to understand 'what *the question* is about' (*BA* 229–30). 'Europe as a whole ... has *worldly* lost its way in problems that can be answered only *divinely*', Kierkegaard contends, especially the problem of human equality, which in his view is 'the problem which confronts the whole generation' (229; *JP* vi. 6340). People have wanted to solve this problem in the medium of worldliness, whose essence is difference, whereas, as pointed out in *Works of Love*, Christian equality is not the same as worldly similarity, which cannot be achieved in the temporal realm. Consequently, as Kierkegaard sees it, what appears to be a political question in the present age is really a religious question that can only be answered by procuring a new point of departure *from above*, that is, from God, rather than *from below* via the crowd (*BA* 317). Inversely to the Reformation, which in his view seemed to be a religious movement but turned out to be a political one, Kierkegaard predicts that when the real question underlying the catastrophe of 1848 became apparent, what appeared to be a political movement would turn out to be a religious movement instead (*JP* vi. 6256).

MARTYRS AND/OR PASTORS AS REFORMERS OF THE CROWD

Due to the advance of civilization, urbanization, centralization, and the rise of the press as the means of communication that 'corresponded to all this and essentially produced it', Kierkegaard was convinced that personal existing had vanished and daily life had been given a wrong direction in the modern age (*JP* iv. 4166). Insofar as there was any reform, it had been directed one-sidedly against the government by the press and its minion, the crowd. But no one had thought of reforming the crowd, which in his view 'is what it really means to reform' and where 'the real scene of martyrdom' takes place (ibid.). 'In order to recover eternity,' he writes in 1848, 'blood will again be required, but blood of another kind, not that of battle victims slain by the thousands, no, the more costly blood, of the single individuals—of the martyrs', who conquer not by putting others to death but by being put to death themselves (*BA* 234; cf. *JP* vi. 6395). Even though in *Two Ethical-Religious Essays*, which was written in 1847 but not published until 1849, the theological conclusion had been reached that Christians do not have the right to make others guilty by allowing themselves to be put to death for the sake of the truth, Kierkegaard predicts that only martyrs will be able to rule the world at a critical time in the future because 'no human being will any longer be able to rule the generation at such a moment; only the divine can do it, assisted by those unconditionally obedient to him, those who are also willing to suffer', namely the martyrs, who would not rule secularly but religiously by suffering (*BA* 235; cf. *JP* iii. 2649). But unlike previous martyrs, who needed only the immediacy of faith and courage to risk their lives, these future martyrs or missionaries will possess superior powers of reflection that will enable them to diagnose the specific sickness of a particular age, how it is to be healed, what kind of mistreatment and persecution they must be exposed to, whether they will fall or not, and if so, where it will happen, so that the survivors are wounded 'in the right spot' by their deaths (*JP* iii. 2649). Contrasting such martyrs to tyrants, especially tyrants in the form of the masses or the crowd, Kierkegaard suggests that, while there is an infinite difference between these two types of rulers, they have one thing in common: *the power to constrain others*. But whereas the tyrant constrains others by using force to rule over them in an egotistical and inhuman fashion, the martyr constrains others by his own sufferings out of love for humankind, thereby educating them in Christianity and 'converting the mass into single individuals' (ibid.; cf. *JP* i. 187).

In suggesting that martyrs or missionaries will become the leaders or rulers of the future, Kierkegaard reflects his religious roots in Moravian piety, which was noted for its missionary zeal and dedication, especially in the eighteenth and early nineteenth centuries, in which foreign missions became 'the hallmark of the Moravian community around the world' and many missionaries lost their lives witnessing to the truth in this way.[14] But whereas their efforts were directed towards the conversion of non-Christians, Kierkegaard envisions the missionaries or martyrs of the future as being deployed to reintroduce Christianity into Christendom (*PV* 123–4). At this point he does not elaborate further on this apocalyptic vision of a movement from worldliness to religiosity, leaving it to a future philosopher-poet who will see close at hand what he has 'only dimly imagined will be carried out sometime in a distant future' (*JP* iii. 2649). The following year, however, he returns to the idea that the present political crisis will turn out to be a religious movement, suggesting this time that *Christian pastors* will be needed to bring it about: '*There* is where the battle will be; if there is to be genuine victory, it must come about through pastors. Neither soldiers nor police nor diplomats nor political planners will achieve it' (*JP* vi. 6256, 6257). This comes as a surprise in light of Kierkegaard's general disdain for the Danish clergy, who in a later journal entry are explicitly blamed for the social breakdown of 1848: 'When a society goes to pieces the way it did in '48, it is not the fault of kings and nobility—but is essentially the fault of the clergy' (*JP* iv. 4193). The kind of Christian pastors Kierkegaard has in mind to lead this religious movement, however, must measure up to some stringent qualifications: They must be educated but also practised in 'spiritual guerrilla skirmishing', 'doing battle not so much with scientific-scholarly attacks and problems as with the human passions'; they should be 'powerfully eloquent', if possible, but 'no less eloquent in keeping silent and enduring without complaining'; they must 'know the human heart' but refrain 'from judging and denouncing'; they must 'know how to use authority through the art of making sacrifices' and be 'disciplined and...prepared to obey and to suffer' in order to 'be able to mitigate, admonish, build up, move, but also to constrain—not with force, anything but, no, constrain by their own obedience, and above all patiently, to suffer all the rudeness of the sick without being disturbed... For the generation is sick, spiritually, sick unto death' (*JP* vi. 6256). Although Kierkegaard does not use the term 'martyr' with reference to these pastors, they clearly fit that description. Perhaps he means to

[14] Burgess (2006: 185).

suggest, then, that Christian pastors should be the martyrs who will lead the modern age to a genuine religious awakening.

Another reason why genuine Christian pastors will be sorely needed to lead the religious movement of the future is to counter the greatest danger with respect to a religious movement, namely the introduction of a demonic religiousness through the rise of 'demonically tainted characters' who 'like mushrooms after a rain' will appear on the scene and presumptuously lay claim to being apostles on a par with the biblical apostles, 'assuming the task of perfecting Christianity' or perhaps becoming 'inventors of a new religion which will gratify the times and the world in a completely different way from Christianity's "asceticism" ' (*JP* vi. 6257). Communism in particular, Kierkegaard suggests, possesses the strength and demonic potential to establish a foothold and prevent the development of true religiousness.

THE RELATION OF RELIGION AND POLITICS

The political turmoil of the time also provided an occasion for Kierkegaard to articulate in a more theoretical fashion his views on the relation between religion and politics or church and state. Reflecting Luther's distinction between the two realms or kingdoms, Kierkegaard's general position is that their viewpoints are worlds apart, as the religious takes its point of departure from above and seeks to transfigure and lift the temporal or earthly to the level of the heavenly, spiritual, or eternal, whereas the political 'begins on earth in order to remain on earth' and 'has nothing to do with *eternal truth*' (*PV* 103, 109–10).[15] Yet they are not wholly unrelated, as Kierkegaard suggests that, with a little patience, the politician will become aware that 'the religious is the transfigured rendition of what a politician, provided he actually loves being a human being and loves humankind, has thought in his most blissful moment, even if he will find the religious too lofty and too ideal to be practical' (103).[16] The political ideal to which Kierkegaard refers here is perfect human equality, which in his estimation, as we have seen, is not attainable in the temporal realm. Politics has to do with the external system of government under which people live, whereas religion, particularly Christianity, is a matter of inwardness, of the individual's personal relationship to God, before whom every individual already enjoys true human equality in the form of spiritual equality. In line with 'the old Christianity', by which he presumably means the original apostolic

[15] On Luther's theory of the two kingdoms, see Cranz (1998: 159–78).

[16] On 'the patient politician', see Perkins (2003*b*).

tradition, Kierkegaard holds that Christianity is fundamentally indifferent towards all forms of government and 'can live equally well under all of them', even 'under the most imperfect conditions and forms', which is what constitutes 'Christianity's perfection' (*JP* iv. 4191, 4193; *COR* 54). It is not Christianity's business, therefore, to be concerned with bringing about external changes in the political realm.

This is not to say, however, that 'Christianity consists purely and simply of putting up with everything in regard to external forms, without doing anything at all' (*COR* 56). On the contrary, Kierkegaard maintains that 'there are situations . . . in which an established order can be of such a nature that the Christian ought not put up with it, ought not say that Christianity means precisely this indifference to the external' (56). He does not spell out what those situations might be, leaving them to be determined by individual conscience in a particular social situation. He also suggests that 'If at a given time the forms under which one has to live are not the most perfect, if they can be improved, in God's name do so', which leaves the door open for a wide range of political action on the part of individual Christians (53).

These remarks were written in response to a book by Andreas G. Rudelbach (1792–1862), a Grundtvigian who took Kierkegaard to be an advocate of the emancipation of the church from the state and wanted to claim him as an ally in the Grundtvigian political campaign to usher in religious freedoms such as civil marriage (*COR* 51). Kierkegaard published *An Open Letter* (1851) in order to clarify his position *vis-à-vis* the established order, both political and ecclesiastical. While admitting to being a hater of 'habitual Christianity', he denies having fought for the emancipation of the church or any other form of external change but only for 'the inward deepening of Christianity' in himself and others (53). In fact, he insists that 'I have overscrupulously seen to it that not a passage, not a sentence, not a line, not a word, not a letter has slipped in suggesting a proposal for external change or suggesting a belief that the problem is lodged in externalities, that external change is what is needed, that external change is what will help us' (53). Expressing suspicion towards the 'politically achieved free institutions' championed by the Grundtvigians and other political parties of the time, 'especially of their saving, renewing power', Kierkegaard states: 'There is nothing about which I have greater misgivings than about all that even slightly tastes of this disastrous confusion of politics and Christianity' (53–4). In the aftermath of the crisis of 1848, therefore, Kierkegaard sees his task as opposing those who want to reform the church in political ways and by political means rather than religiously or inwardly through individual penance before God as a true reformation would require (*JP* vi. 6719–21, 6727; *FSE* 21; *JFY* 130–1, 211–13). He thus declares: '*The evil in our time is not the established order with its many faults. No, the evil in our time is precisely: this evil penchant for reforming, this flirting with wanting to reform,* this sham of wanting to reform without being willing to suffer and to make sacrifices' (*JFY* 212–13). In his view, 'Dabblers in reforming are more corrupting than the most corrupt established order, because reforming is the highest and therefore dabbling in it is the most corrupting of all' (212). Thus, if one is 'not willing to walk *in the character* of being a reformer', one ought to hold one's tongue (212).

These views are amplified by a number of journal entries in this period in which Kierkegaard continually maintains that he has sought to defend the established order, not to attack or do away with it, although that does not mean that he agrees with it (*JP* vi. 6343, 6344, 6693, 6705, 6774, 6778). Politically, we have seen that Kierkegaard's polemic is directed primarily against the crowd, in relation to which he severely criticizes those in charge, both political and ecclesiastical officials, for their failure to govern in the crisis of 1848: 'I saw how the ones who were supposed to rule, both in Church and State, hid themselves like cowards while barbarism boldly and brazenly raged' (*JP* vi. 6444; cf. 6699, 6719). With regard to the established church, Kierkegaard maintains that 'in the highest Christian sense there is no established Church, only a Church Militant', by which he means a church in the process of becoming victorious in the world through struggle in a hostile environment as opposed to a church triumphant in which the time of struggle is over and victory is declared (*JP* vi. 6671, 6672; *CD* 229; *PC* 211).[17] Factually, of course, the established church does exist, although Kierkegaard repeatedly charges in his writings that it has abolished true Christianity and substituted a confused, illusory, 'toned-down approximation of Christianity' that is paganism and worldliness (*PC* 35, 135, 144; *JFY* 212). But at this stage in his authorship he does not call for the overthrow of the church or for a political separation of church and state, although ideally he recognizes that is what Christianity requires: 'There is hardly a person hereabouts who is as cognizant as I of all the objections that can be leveled from a Christian point of view against a state Church, a folk Church, an established Christian Church, and the like, also that in the strictly Christian sense the demand is separation—this is ideality's maximum requirement' (*JP* vi. 6671, 6761). As Kierkegaard sees it, however, such an undertaking would require 'such a qualitatively religious operation that only a qualitatively distinguished religious character' such as an apostle or witness to the truth willing to become a martyr would be able to accomplish it (*JP* vi. 6761; i. 599). Since such a person cannot be found

[17] See also Cranz (1998: 120), and Schmid (1961: 587–8), on the distinction between the church militant and triumphant in Luther and early Lutheran theology.

in the present age and Kierkegaard does not regard himself as physically able or spiritually qualified to assume such a role, he concludes that the established order must be allowed to stand. But at least an admission that the established church does not represent true Christianity is required of the church officials, particularly Primate Bishop J. P. Mynster (*JP* vi. 6699, 6723). Unsurprisingly, Kierkegaard waited in vain for such a statement to be forthcoming.

THE CHURCH MILITANT VERSUS THE CHURCH TRIUMPHANT

Kierkegaard's beef with the established church was so uncompromising that he is often accused of lacking a positive conception of the church, which is not so. To be sure, he did not write much on this topic, the only sustained discussion of it in his published works appearing in *Practice in Christianity* by his Christian pseudonym Anti-Climacus. But his critique of the established church was prompted by a clear understanding of what constitutes the true church in the realm of temporality. As noted above, Kierkegaard associates the true church in the world with a church militant rather than a church triumphant, with which, according to Anti-Climacus, established Christendom illusorily confuses itself (*PC* 211). In making this charge Anti-Climacus may also have in mind the Grundtvigians, who thought of themselves as constituting the one true church in the form of 'the living congregation' of the cultic community, in which Christ is spiritually present in the Apostles' Creed, Lord's Prayer, and sacraments of baptism and holy communion.[18] As Anti-Climacus sees it, however, the triumphant church does not belong to this world, which is heterogeneous to the essentially Christian and has room for Christ's church only if it makes room for itself by struggling to exist in the interim between his ascension and second coming. In assuming that the time of struggle is over, the church triumphant becomes homogeneous and synonymous with the world, as in established Christendom, whereas the church militant seeks to express Christianity in an environment that is the opposite of the essentially Christian, which means that it involves suffering and self-denial in likeness to Christ in his lowliness. In Anti-Climacus's judgement, therefore, 'the Church triumphant or established Christendom resembles the Church militant no more than a square resembles a circle' (212).

The cause of this illusory identification of the established church with the church triumphant, as Anti-Climacus sees it, can be traced to a

[18] See Allchin (1997: 105–14); N. Thulstrup (1984: 220–1); Kirmmse (1990: 212–14).

fundamental confusion concerning the nature of truth, how it is acquired, and what it means to say that Christ is the truth. Anti-Climacus asks whether truth is something that can be summarily appropriated with the help of another person 'without willing oneself to be developed in like manner, to be tried, to battle, to suffer as did the one who acquired the truth for him' (202–3). Is it not an illusion to refuse to understand that there is no abridgement in the acquisition of truth, 'so that every generation and everyone in the generation must essentially begin from the beginning' (203)? These questions are particularly relevant to the nature of truth as it pertains to Christ, who is the truth 'in the sense that to *be* the truth is the only true explanation of what truth is', which means that 'truth in the sense in which Christ is the truth is not a sum of sentences, not a definition etc., but a life' (205). The task of his followers, therefore, is not to *know* the truth but to *be* the truth in the sense that they are to reduplicate or actualize it in their lives in such a way as to express 'approximately the being of the truth in the striving for it' (205). In this understanding of truth, *knowing the truth* is a consequence of *being the truth* rather than vice versa, with the result that knowing the truth becomes an untruth when it is separated from or made a prerequisite to being the truth, for only when the truth 'becomes a life in me', declares Anti-Climacus, 'do I in truth know the truth' (206).

There is a difference, then, between truth understood as *the way*, or the reduplication of the truth in one's own life, and truth understood as a *result*, the final yield that is reached at the end of this journey (*PC* 206–7). If Christianity were the truth in the form of a result, Anti-Climacus admits that triumph would be in order, but 'only the person who has traveled the way can triumphally celebrate' and that can only take place at the end of life when one is no longer in the world but on high with Christ in eternity (209). Similarly, if Christianity were a result in the form of knowledge that could be passed on to later generations without their having to replicate all the steps in the process of acquiring that knowledge, such as the invention of gun powder or printing, then a triumphant celebration by the church would be appropriate in this instance as well. But if Christianity is the truth in the sense of the way, if it is a matter of becoming the truth rather than knowing the truth, there can be no shortening of the way by passing on knowledge of the truth without each individual having personally traversed the whole way.

According to Anti-Climacus, original Christianity held the view that truth is a matter of being rather than knowledge, but the modern age, with its 'comprehending, speculating, observing, etc.', has altered Christianity by defining truth as a matter of knowledge, thus making the 'monstrous mistake' of continually didacticizing Christianity (*PC* 206). Not only has the modern age committed the fallacy of interpreting truth as a result, thereby missing the essence of Christianity, it has also committed another fallacy that has contributed to the illusion of a church triumphant, namely the pretence that everyone is a Christian, for 'if this is taken as given', Anti-Climacus says, then 'a militant Church seems to be an impossibility' (211). The problem with the assumption that everyone is a Christian, as Anti-Climacus sees it, is that being a Christian becomes a matter of *hidden inwardness*, which means that there are no direct, outward signs by which one can be recognized as being a Christian (214). He notes that there was a time (presumably in the Middle Ages) when being a Christian in the church triumphant was directly recognizable by virtue of belonging to a particular order whose task was to represent what it means to be a Christian, while the rest of the world looked on and provided an 'environment of admiration' rather than opposition to Christianity. With the rise of secular, bourgeois society in the modern age, however, Anti-Climacus claims that 'a complete change of scene with regard to being a Christian' took place. The illusion of a church triumphant together with its external trappings was abandoned; being a Christian was relegated to inwardness under the assumption that everyone is a Christian 'in exactly the same sense as it is a given that we are all human beings'; and another form of opposition to Christianity was introduced, namely an 'opposition of indifference' towards being a Christian (215). 'Here we have the conception of established Christendom', Anti-Climacus declares (216). Whereas being a Christian in the church triumphant of old was directly recognizable by the honour and esteem a true Christian enjoyed, being a Christian in the new church triumphant of established Christendom is kept hidden, presumably because everyone is 'too Christian' and pious to want to be honoured and esteemed for being one, he suggests ironically (216–17). With biting satire, Anti-Climacus thus warns the visitor to all those countries with millions of pious Christians: 'Take off your shoes, for the place where you are standing is holy when you are standing in Christendom, where there is no one but true Christians! Let God keep eternity, where all in all he will scarcely get as many true Christians as there are at any moment in established Christendom, where all are Christians' (217).

Of course, it is impossible to determine whether everyone (or anyone) actually is a Christian in hidden inwardness in established Christendom, as no one but God can know the hearts of human beings. In the *Postscript*, in which Christianity is defined essentially as (hidden) inwardness, Climacus leaves open the possibility that everyone in Christendom is a Christian, although he is highly suspicious of the idea (*CUP* i. 236, 475, 510–11). But Anti-Climacus cleverly perceives a way to break open this 'jammed lock' of secretiveness without claiming to be 'a knower of hearts' and without judging others, namely by someone openly deciding 'to confess Christ in the midst of Christendom' in such a way that others will disclose themselves by how this person is judged and treated by them (*PC* 220). In turn, this person would become *inversely* recognizable as a member of the church militant by the degree of external opposition or suffering encountered and endured in this situation (212, 215).

As Anti-Climacus sees it, the illusion of a church triumphant in established Christendom is also linked with the human impatience of wanting to have in advance what only comes later, namely the victory of the eternal, whereas 'God's invention and intention' is to make all existence, temporality, this life a time of struggle and testing (*PC* 211). Christianity's idea, then, is that 'as long as this world lasts, or as long as the Christian Church is to exist in this world, it is and must be a militant Church' (219, 221). But Anti-Climacus also points out that 'Christianly, struggling is always done by single individuals, because spirit is precisely this, that everyone is an individual before God' (223). This means that just as the single individual is higher than the species and the universal, the single individual is also higher than the congregation or fellowship. Even though individuals may struggle conjointly with others, they must struggle individually and give an accounting of themselves on judgement day when their lives as single individuals will be examined. The notion of a congregation, then, is really 'an impatient anticipation of the eternal' in that it 'does not belong in time but belongs first in eternity, where it is, at rest, the gathering of all the single individuals who endured in the struggle and passed the test' (223). To the established church Anti-Climacus thus issues the following ominous warning: 'But woe, woe to the Christian Church when it will have been victorious in this world, for then it is not the Church that has been victorious but the world. Then the heterogeneity between Christianity and the world has vanished, the world has won, and Christianity has lost' (223).

This view of the religious community or congregation is reiterated in Kierkegaard's journals of the period, where he once again suggests that the concept of the congregation 'lies on the other side of "the single individual" ', who must intervene as a middle term 'in order to make sure that "the congregation" is not taken in vain as synonymous with the public, the crowd, etc.' (*JP* i. 595, translation modified). Kierkegaard further contends that 'it is not the single individual's relationship to the congregation which determines his relationship to God, but his relationship to God which determines his relationship to the congregation' (595). This statement nicely sums up his understanding of the relation between the single individual and the church in contrast to the established church and the Grundtvigians. Ideally, in his view there should be 'no established religious order at all', so that everyone will be immediately responsible to

God (*JP* ii. 1415). But since existing continually alone before God is 'too strenuous' and 'almost unendurable' for a human being, religious sociality or an established order has been granted as a 'concession to human weakness' and as a 'middle term' between the single individual and God (*JP* ii. 1377, 1415, 1416). For all his emphasis upon the single individual, then, Kierkegaard does recognize the need not only for community but also for a religious community to temper the strenuousness of the individual's relation to God.

THE FUNCTION AND AUTHORITY OF THE INSTITUTIONAL CHURCH

Kierkegaard also recognized the temporal authority of the institutional church to conduct worship services and to administer the sacraments—at least up until the last year of his life. In his view, all immanent or earthly authority in the 'political, civic, social, domestic, and disciplinary realms' is transitory in nature and vanishes in the essential equality of eternity; only Christ and the apostles possess divine authority, which is given to them by God and thus is eternally valid (*WA* 99; cf. *JP* i. 182–3, 189–90). Moreover, true authority does not reside in profundity of thought or power over others but in being willing to sacrifice oneself for the cause of truth (*JP* i. 183, 187). Within an immanent or conditional context, then, Kierkegaard was prepared to accept the temporal authority of the established church and participated in it without questioning the fundamental validity of the confessional writings, rituals, liturgy, and sacraments that formed the basis of faith and practice in the Evangelical-Lutheran Church of Denmark. He was even prepared to accept infant baptism as required by the Augsburg Confession, conceding in the voice of Johannes Climacus that it is 'defensible and commendable' in that it serves the interests of both the church and pious parents as 'a safeguard against fanatics' and as an expression of parental providential care (*CUP* i. 363–8, 381–2, 601; *JP* i. 494).[19] In Kierkegaard's and Climacus's view, however, one does not become a Christian as a matter of course by being baptized, nor is it decisive for becoming a Christian or for salvation (*CUP* i. 366–7, 372–3, 418 n.; *JP* iii. 3086). At best, baptism provides the possibility for becoming a Christian at a more mature stage of life; at worst, without inward appropriation, which is the decisive mark of being a Christian, it contributes to the fundamental confusion of what Christianity is by associating it with an external act rather than inwardness (*CUP* i. 363–8, 373).

[19] On Kierkegaard's view of baptism, see also Law (1988) and Eller (1968: 309–19).

In contrast to his rather lukewarm endorsement of infant baptism, the sacrament of Holy Communion, together with the service of public confession and absolution of sin that precedes it, was very important to Kierkegaard.[20] Over against Grundtvig's emphasis on the sacrament of baptism as constituting the basis of the church, Kierkegaard regarded the Lord's Supper as 'the originally true center in the Church' and the place where reconciliation and communion with Christ takes place (*JP* v. 5089; *CD* 270–1). The thirteen discourses which he wrote for the communion on Fridays testify to the importance this sacrament had for his life and authorship in that it constitutes the resting point for his authorship as a whole and for his own existential position as a penitent. In the preface to the last set of communion discourses Kierkegaard writes:

> An authorship that began with *Either/Or* and advanced step by step seeks here its decisive place of rest, at the foot of the altar, where the author, personally most aware of his own imperfection and guilt, certainly does not call himself a truth-witness but only a singular kind of poet and thinker who, *without authority*, has had nothing new to bring but 'has wanted once again to read through, if possible in a more inward way, the original text of individual human existence-relationships, the old familiar text handed down from the fathers.' (*WA* 165; cf. *CUP* i. 629–30)

WHAT IS A TRUTH-WITNESS?

If Kierkegaard was not a truth-witness, neither in his view was Bishop Mynster, who died on 30 January 1854 and was eulogized at a memorial service on 5 February by Professor Martensen, who shortly thereafter was named Mynster's successor as Primate Bishop of the Danish People's Church. In his address Martensen claimed that Mynster was one of the 'authentic truth-witnesses' in a long line of glorious personages stretching from the apostles to the present (*TM* 359). Having waited silently for three years for an admission from the old bishop that the Christianity he represented was a mitigated, toned-down version, Kierkegaard took exception to Martensen's claim and used it as the basis for launching a final open attack upon the state church.

The attack came in two phases, first via a series of articles published in a political newspaper, *Fædrelandet* (The Fatherland), followed by a series of self-published pamphlets called *The Moment* because they allowed Kierkegaard to address his contemporaries instantly. Given his disdain for the press, it is perhaps surprising that Kierkegaard resorted to that medium

[20] See also Law (2007); Cappelørn (2006); Plekon (1992).

for initiating the attack. But he had good reason for doing so. By using a popular medium that everyone reads, he was able to compel his contemporaries to take notice. There were other motivations as well. Noting a statement in one of Luther's sermons that 'preaching actually should not be done inside of churches' (although Kierkegaard points out that this was said inside a church and thus was 'nothing more than talk'), he agrees that preaching should take place 'on the street, right in the middle of life, the actuality of ordinary, weekday life' (*JP* vi. 6957). Due to his lack of physical strength, however, Kierkegaard sought to achieve only 'an approximation of preaching in the streets' by using a political newspaper devoted to mundane issues in order to gain a hearing for his views in the context of everyday life (ibid.). It also enabled him to communicate his views in smaller doses for consumption by the general public and to maintain his independence by publishing in a newspaper that was completely unassociated with him and his cause. In this way Kierkegaard believed that he was able to use the press successfully without contradicting his previous objections to it.

In the first newspaper article, written in February 1854 but not published until the following December, well after Martensen's appointment as primate bishop in April, Kierkegaard begins his objection to Martensen's claim that Bishop Mynster was a truth-witness by repeating his previous charge that, in comparison to the New Testament, Mynster's proclamation of Christianity was a toned-down version that 'veils, suppresses, omits some of what is most decisively Christian', namely such inconvenient requirements as dying to the world, voluntary self-denial, and suffering for the doctrine, which would 'make our lives strenuous' and 'prevent us from enjoying life' (*TM* 3–4). But if one considers the extent to which 'the proclaimer's life expresses what he says', which in Kierkegaard's view is 'Christianly decisive', then neither the proclamation nor the man was in character, inasmuch as in the New Testament a truth-witness is someone 'whose life from first to last is unfamiliar with everything called enjoyment' and who witnesses for the truth in poverty, lowliness, and abasement, bringing upon oneself flogging, mistreatment, and finally death by crucifixion, beheading, or burning (4–6). Only by advancing to the final ignominy of martyrdom is one admitted to 'the first class in the *Christian* order of precedence among the authentic truth-witnesses' (6). Denying Martensen's contention in reply (the only time the new bishop deigned to address Kierkegaard's charge in public) that he had made being a truth-witness synonymous with being a martyr, which Mynster admittedly was not, Kierkegaard maintains that he has described the truth-witness as a sufferer 'without in any way whatever asserting that to suffer should mean to suffer death' (9 n.; cf. 360–6). Far from suffering for the truth, however, Bishop Mynster had led a life of self-indulgence and worldly sagacity, having 'attained and enjoyed on the greatest scale every possible benefit and advantage' from his office (10).

The point at issue for Kierkegaard, then, was not only Mynster's proclamation of Christianity, which in his view was an illusion and accommodation to the world that constituted 'high treason against Christianity', but also the character of the man, whose life did not resemble a break or heterogeneity with the world 'in even the remotest way' (*TM* 8, 14, 17). It was clear to Kierkegaard from Martensen's memorial address, however, that the professor and soon-to-be bishop intended to include the clergy in the category of truth-witness as well (12, 20). This was the final straw for Kierkegaard, who exclaims:

> As soon, however, as it is heard that the pastor is also a truth-witness, that what we call a pastor means to be a truth-witness, at that very moment the whole ecclesiastical established order, from the Christian point of view, is a shameless indecency. With this claim the established order can no longer be considered an extreme mitigation that still relates itself to the Christianity of the New Testament, but it is an obvious falling away from the Christianity of the New Testament, and with that claim is, from the Christian point of view, a shameless indecency, an attempt verging on making a fool of God.... (*TM* 20)

'BEWARE OF THE PASTORS'

With this statement the attack shifts from a focus on Mynster to the clergy and established order in general. Earlier Kierkegaard had envisioned the need for pastors who would assume the role of martyrs to bring about a religious awakening and reformation in the land as a result of the triumph of anarchy in society. Now those who hold appointments in the established church, including pastors, deans, and bishops, are viewed not as truth-witnesses but merely as 'teachers, public officials, professors, councilors' who are in their professions primarily for the sake of securing a livelihood, just like any other profession in society (*TM* 26, 31, 60, 162–4). These 'silk-and-velvet pastors', as Kierkegaard disdainfully describes them, are excoriated as 'liars' and 'shameless scoundrels' for betraying Christianity and, like Judas, accepting 'blood-money' procured by the death of Christ (43–4, 195). They are accused of being egotists and parasites out for personal financial gain and power; of being more dishonest than moneylenders and merchants; of misleading people and cheating them not only out of their money but also out of the eternal by the 'gibberish' they preach; of 'skulduggery' for 'knavishly abolishing Christianity'; of 'hypocrisy to the second power' in passing themselves off as earnest and true preachers of Christianity; of being 'huckstering knaves' who 'for the sake of business' have gained millions of Christians by falsifying Christianity; and finally of being 'cannibals' who live off those 'glorious ones' (Christ, the apostles, the truth-witnesses) whose sufferings made it possible for them to enjoy a comfortable life (61, 160, 165–6, 188, 226, 321–3, 340). These epithets and accusations are damning indeed, leading Kierkegaard to advise his readers to 'beware of the pastors!' (197). Yet he claims that he is 'not motivated by any hostility to the clergy' in making these charges; apart from falsely being called truth-witnesses, which they of all social classes are furthest from being, the clergy are in his view just as 'competent, respectable, and worthy a class in society as any other' (53). Nor has he 'taken aim at their making a living in the finite sense'; on the contrary, he claims that he 'would perhaps even be inclined to fight for the clergy' if their livelihoods were attacked (60–1).

THE STATE CHURCH AS A TOXIC JUNK HEAP

Indeed, Kierkegaard holds the state responsible for providing materially for those with whom it has contracted in the event of a church–state separation, which he now regards as necessary: 'The question about what Christianity is, including in turn the question about the state Church, the people's Church, which they now want to call it, the amalgamation or alliance of Church and state, must be brought to the most extreme decision. It cannot and must not go on as it did year after year under the old bishop' (*TM* 53, 75, 164). Whereas earlier Kierkegaard had sought to defend the established order, or more accurately, to urge it to defend itself by confessing its distance from the Christian requirements and thus resorting to grace, he now finds the established order to be utterly indefensible: 'I have completely made up my mind on two things: both that the established order is Christianly indefensible, that every day it lasts it is Christianly a crime; and that in this way one does not have the right to draw on grace' (70). Graphically describing the state church as a toxic 'junk heap' in which 'the religious life is sick or has expired', he concludes that it must be got rid of, along with the royally authorized 'quacks' who pose as physicians of the soul (158).

The fundamental problem with a state church, as Kierkegaard had perceived all along, is that it confuses royal authority with divine authority. He admits that 'a Christian is to be, if possible, His Majesty's best subject. But, *Christianly*, the king is not the authority; he is not and cannot and shall not and will not be the authority in relation to a kingdom that at no price wants to be of this world' (*TM* 113). The problem becomes particularly acute with respect to ordination, through which the clergy receives divine authority from a kingdom that is not of this world, leading Kierkegaard to ask: 'can one be a royally authorized teacher of Christianity, can Christianity (the Christianity of the New Testament) be proclaimed by royally authorized teachers, can the sacraments be administered by them, or does this involve a self-contradiction' (57, cf. 147, 150)? The implied answer, of course, is that it does involve a self-contradiction, which can be resolved only by removing the enormous illusion that Christianity and the state are fused together. In Kierkegaard's view, however, that must be done by the state, which alone has the power to remove it, since pastors serve the state and are not in a position to tell the congregation what Christianity really is without resigning their state offices. The state should therefore release the clergy from one or the other of their oaths swearing loyalty to the New Testament and loyalty to the state as royal officeholders. Kierkegaard's preference was for the state to eliminate the 1,000 royal livelihoods and let the proclamation of Christianity become strictly a matter of private practice, which in his view is 'the only true Christian requirement' as well as 'the only reasonable one' (151, 153). However, since the state had 'enticed' and 'seductively beckoned' young and inexperienced theological graduates to become royal officeholders, tempting them with the promise of a comfortable life, it had the responsibility to provide for them financially in the event that they resigned from office or the 1,000 livelihoods were eliminated (164).

JUST ONE THESIS

Meanwhile, Kierkegaard calls upon ordinary Christians, who have been led to believe that everything is as it should be, to cease participating in 'the public divine service as it now is' because it is 'a forgery, a falsification' of the Christianity of the New Testament (*TM* 73–4). By refusing to participate in public worship, they will thus have one less 'great guilt' to account for, namely 'making a fool of God by calling something New Testament Christianity that is not New Testament Christianity' (73–4). Whereas Luther posted ninety-five theses in his effort to reform the Roman Catholic Church, Kierkegaard contends that the point had been reached in Protestantism, especially in Denmark, where there was only one thesis: 'The Christianity of the New Testament does not exist at all' (39; cf. 519–20; *JP* vi. 6842, 6943, 6947). What official Christianity called Christianity was not true Christianity but a hypocritical 'playing at Christianity' that removed all the dangers from being a Christian (*TM* 6, 32, 119, 133, 168, 178). The only difference between the established church and a theatre, as Kierkegaard sees it, is that 'the theatre honorably and honestly acknowledges being what it is' whereas the church is 'a theatre that in every way dishonestly seeks to conceal what it is' (221). In like manner, he also distinguishes between the atheist (presumably Feuerbach)[21] and official Christianity by suggesting that 'the atheist is an honest man who directly *teaches* that Christianity is fiction, poetry', whereas 'official Christianity is a falsification that solemnly assures that Christianity is something else entirely, solemnly declaims against atheism, and by means of this covers up that it is itself *making* Christianity into poetry and abolishing the imitation of Christ' (129). In a journal entry dating from 1849 Kierkegaard even claims Feuerbach as an ally in his defence of Christianity against Christendom, stating that 'it is wrong of established Christendom to say that Feuerbach is attacking Christianity; it is not true, he is attacking the Christians by demonstrating that their lives do not correspond to the teachings of Christianity' (*JP* vi. 6523).

At this late stage Kierkegaard's attack extends to almost every aspect of the established church and social life in Christendom, including baptism, confirmation, marriage, and family life. Whereas earlier he was prepared to accept infant baptism and confirmation nominally as anticipations of the possibility of becoming a Christian, now they are regarded as nonsensical inventions, with confirmation constituting 'far more extreme nonsense than infant Baptism' because it 'claims to supply what was lacking in infant Baptism: an actual personality who is able consciously to take over a promise pertaining to the decision of an eternal happiness'—as if a boy of 15 were mature enough to make that decision (*TM* 244; cf. *JP* i. 602; iii. 3101)! No, in Kierkegaard's view confirmation is 'a glorious invention' that makes sense only if one assumes that the purpose of divine worship is to make a fool of God and that the ceremony is primarily intended to provide a pleasant occasion for family festivities (*TM* 243). As for marriage, which in Kierkegaard's earlier works, both pseudonymous and signed, is seen as the very embodiment of the ethical and spiritually sanctified by being consciously related to God (cf. *EO* ii. 302; *SLW* 87–184; *TDIO* 43–68; *WL* 112–13, 137–45), Kierkegaard now reminds his readers that celibacy is recommended by Christianity (cf. 1 Corinthians 7: 1, 7–8), whereas marriage, although not forbidden, is a concession to human lust that is displeasing to God (*TM* 245–8). Thus pastors should not take part in weddings at all, as these ceremonies are made 'as criminal as possible' by clerical participation and pronouncements that marriage is well pleasing to God (247). Alluding to a legendary blacksmith associated with performing weddings at a famous place for elopements in Scotland, Kierkegaard suggests instead that 'it is preferable to be married by a blacksmith' (247). Christian family

[21] Cf. Feuerbach (1989: pp. xvi–xxi and *passim*).

life and the upbringing of children are also now seen as being based on a falsehood, inasmuch as '*Christianly* it is anything but the greatest good deed to give a child life' and 'anything but pleasing to God that one engages in begetting children' because of the sinfulness and wickedness of the world into which they would be born and the misery of life awaiting both those who are saved and those who are damned (250–1).

ASSESSING THE ATTACK

These extremely negative viewpoints expressed in Kierkegaard's final attack on Christendom have led many critics, both in his time and ours, to dismiss this last phase of his theological reflection and critique of Christendom altogether. Clearly, in certain respects it does represent a radical departure from some of the views expressed earlier in his authorship. This suggests, however, that these writings do not so much constitute the logical conclusion of Kierkegaard's theological reflection as a relaxing of the dialectical balance that characterizes the large body of religious writings produced during the second period of his literary activity from 1847–51. Theologically, it is primarily this second or middle phase of his authorship that should be regarded as normative for the interpretation of Kierkegaard's theology, although his thought undergoes considerable development even in the course of these writings as a result of his personal encounter with the *Corsair* and the political changes of 1848. But there is also a good deal of continuity between the attack literature and this body of writings. For example, Kierkegaard never departs from the conviction that God is love, evidenced by the fact that shortly before his death in 1855 he published the discourse on the changelessness of God's love written in 1851 (*TM* 263–81; cf. 294). Nor does he repudiate Christianity's leniency and promise of a resort to grace.[22] Moreover, the attack on Christendom itself, which began somewhat covertly in Kierkegaard's early pseudonymous works and continued to gather steam with increasing emphasis and directness in the later religious writings, reaches its culmination in these late writings. Many of the charges lodged against the established order and present age in these writings, such as the spiritlessness and worldliness of both church and society, are not new, but they do become shriller and more specific as Kierkegaard zeros in on the illusions and practices of the state church in dead earnest. What is different is the fact that he has now given up on the church as an institution, finding it completely indefensible and encouraging others to join him in ceasing to participate in it. But he has not given up

22 On Kierkegaard's view of rigour and leniency in Christianity, see Possen (2004).

on Christianity itself, and that is what distinguishes him most profoundly from other nineteenth-century critics of religion such as Feuerbach, Marx, and Nietzsche.

A LITTLE DASH OF CINNAMON

In attempting to disentangle the essentially Christian from its various counterfeit expressions, confusions, and accommodations in church and society, Kierkegaard understood his task as a writer to be that of providing a corrective to the established order. Like a skilled cook, he sought to add 'a little dash of cinnamon' to the mix in order to give it 'a specific taste' (*JP* i. 709). In his view, the task of the corrective is to 'study the weak sides of the established order scrupulously and penetratingly and then one-sidedly present the opposite—with expert one-sidedness' (*JP* vi. 6467, cf. 6693). Thus he warily observes that 'it is an unhappy mistake if the person who is used to introduce the corrective becomes impatient and wants to make the corrective normative for the others, an attempt which will confuse everything' (*JP* i. 709). That is what happened with Luther's corrective, he contends, for by being made the norm or sum total of Christianity for later generations it has produced 'the most refined kind of secularism and paganism'—the exact opposite of the original corrective (*JP* i. 711). It was never Kierkegaard's intention, therefore, to set forth a normative theology for his age or ours. In providing the missing ingredient, namely the demanding, rigorous side of Christianity that had been so sorely abolished and forgotten in his own time, Kierkegaard's legacy as a corrective hopefully will be to enable us and future generations to think Christianly with a more balanced and existentially oriented understanding of what Christianity is and how to become a Christian in the context of our own existential situations and times.

THE RECEPTION OF KIERKEGAARD

Because Kierkegaard's writings had to be translated into other languages before they could become widely available outside Denmark, the initial reception of Kierkegaard in the seventy-odd years following his death was slow in coming.[23] When it did come, it was quite mixed and often coloured by partisan reviews, misconceptions, and a lack of access to his writings other than *The Moment*, which was the first to be translated. This had the deleterious, off-putting effect of making Kierkegaard seem like a religious

[23] For a detailed account see Malik (1997).

fanatic or even anti-Christian in his uncompromising critique of Christendom. When the cart is put before the horse in this manner, severing the critique from its context in the authorship as a whole, it is no wonder that the religious establishment gave him a cold shoulder. Beyond Scandinavia, where Kierkegaard's reputation as a literary writer was helped along by his influence on the Norwegian dramatist Henrik Ibsen (1828–1906) and his Swedish counterpart August Strindberg (1849–1912), the initial interest in him was theological rather than literary or philosophical.[24] The leader in the dissemination of Kierkegaard's theology in Germany was Johann Tobias Beck (1804–78), a professor of systematic theology at Tübingen for whom, according to Barth, Kierkegaard 'was the only distinguished theologian of the time of whom Beck had a good opinion'.[25] Although Beck's impact on German theology was minimal, the introduction of Kierkegaard's writings to Germany was adversely affected by one of Beck's former students, Christoph Schrempf (1860–1944), a Lutheran pastor who was the general editor of the first German edition of Kierkegaard's works. While this translation had the merit of making Kierkegaard's works widely available in German, it was notorious for its errors, editorial excesses, and biased commentary by the disaffected editor, who resigned his pastorate and left the church upon reading the Dane.[26] This disservice to Kierkegaard's legacy was counteracted by the translation of excerpts from some of Kierkegaard's writings by the Catholic writer and cultural critic Theodor Haecker (1879–1945) in the Austrian cultural periodical *Der Brenner*, which was widely read and respected by German-speaking intellectuals before and after the First World War, including Kafka, Heidegger, Husserl, Jaspers, and Wittgenstein.[27] Acquaintance with Kierkegaard's writings in the rest of Europe was gained largely through these and other German translations and scholarship of the early twentieth century.[28]

Among the excerpts from Kierkegaard's writings translated by Haecker was 'The Present Age' in *Two Ages*, the second instalment of which appeared in *Der Brenner* just two weeks before the First World War broke out in 1914.[29] It was thus at a time of great political crisis that the serious reception of Kierkegaard in Europe was taking place in modern theology, philosophy, and literature. This crisis was soon followed by a second one with the outbreak of the Second World War in 1939. Protestant theologians who felt Kierkegaard's influence during these critical times included Karl Barth, Emil Brunner, Paul Tillich, Rudolf Bultmann, Dietrich Bonhoeffer,

[24] Malik (1997: 220). [25] Barth (1972: 618). [26] Malik (1997: 311–15, 332–8).
[27] Ibid., 367–92; see also Janik (1984).
[28] Malik (1997: 353). See also Thulstrup and Thulstrup (1981*b*, 1987).
[29] Malik (1997: 379).

Friedrich Gogarten, P. T. Forsyth, and Reinhold Niebuhr, among others. Catholic thinkers such as Erich Przywara, Romano Guardini, Cornelio Fabro, Hans Urs von Balthazar, and Henri de Lubac felt his impact as well.[30] While many German theologians opposed the Nazi regime, some, such as Gogarten (briefly) and the distinguished Kierkegaard scholar Emmanuel Hirsch, supported National Socialism and its Protestant and Catholic sympathizers, thereby perhaps contributing to a misperception of Kierkegaard in some quarters.[31] I cannot at this stage enter into an extensive discussion of Kierkegaard's contributions to twentieth-century theology, but a few words about his reception by some of these thinkers will at least give an indication of the kind of impact he had.

Although perhaps not as decisive an influence upon Karl Barth (1886–1968) as once generally believed, Kierkegaard clearly made a strong impact on the 'theology of crisis' or dialectical theology introduced in the 2nd edition of Barth's *The Epistle to the Romans* (1922).[32] Barth admitted as much in an address delivered in Copenhagen in 1963 in which he states that Kierkegaard 'was for us one of the cocks whose crowing seemed to proclaim from near and far the dawn of a really new day' and that he had 'remained faithful to Kierkegaard's *reveille*' throughout his theological life.[33] Not only does Barth appropriate key Kierkegaardian terminology and concepts in his commentary on Romans, he asserts that the revelation of God in Jesus Christ is a paradox that 'is not, and never will be, a self-evident truth' because it is inaccessible to historical and psychological experience, sense perception, imagination, and contemplation and therefore must be believed in faith, which is accessible to all, regardless of education, intelligence, temper of mind and heart, and economic status.[34] Barth thus rejects all forms of natural religion and theology, especially post-Enlightenment liberal theologies of the nineteenth century, in the conviction that there is no way from humanity to a knowledge of God but only the way from God to humanity via the special revelation of God in Christ. But Barth later repudiated his association with Kierkegaard, concluding that the Dane 'was bound more closely to the nineteenth century than we at that time wanted to believe' inasmuch as the 'new anthropocentric system' he announced was, in Barth's revised judgement, a continuation of the liberal programme of Schleiermacher.[35] Adopting the Anselmian

[30] Thulstrup and Thulstrup (1981*b*); Roos (1954).

[31] See Ericksen (1985); Law (2002); Gorringe (1999: 117–23, 129–30); Shiner (1966: 204–16).

[32] McCormack (1995: 216–17, 235–40). [33] Barth (1965: 5).

[34] Barth (1968: 97–9, 116, 120–1).

[35] Barth (1965: 6). Barth's reading of Kierkegaard was apparently quite limited, as he owned only an abridged edn. of Kierkegaard's journals, *Practice in Christianity*, and the Schrempf translation of *The Moment* (see McCormack 1995: 235–6). There is no evidence that he read

principle of 'faith seeking understanding' in his *Church Dogmatics*, Barth also identifies Christian faith with a rational knowledge of God, reverting to the sort of objective theology that Kierkegaard had contested.[36] The most mystifying thing about Barth's later rejection of Kierkegaard, however, is that he is not included in Barth's great historical work, *Protestant Theology in the Nineteenth Century*. This exclusion was certainly not justified and, given Barth's enormous status as a theologian, may well have had an adverse effect on the reception of Kierkegaard as a theological thinker in the twentieth century. In the foreword to the English translation of this work Barth warns that the reader 'will find all sorts of gaps that I would not leave open today'.[37] Presumably Kierkegaard was one of those gaps, inasmuch as in his Copenhagen address Barth states: 'I consider him to be a teacher into whose school every theologian must go once. Woe to him who has missed it! So long as he does not remain in or return to it!'[38]

Emil Brunner (1889–1966), a close associate of Barth until a sharp controversy erupted between them over the relation of religion and natural theology to Christian faith, continued to reflect a Kierkegaardian perspective in his understanding of faith as a personal encounter with the revelation of God in Christ.[39] Like Barth, Brunner denies the ability of natural theology to arrive at a genuine knowledge of God, but he distinguishes natural theology from the general revelation of God given in the creation of humanity in the image of God, which in his view provides a point of contact between God and humanity that is perverted but not erased by sin.[40] For Brunner, therefore, theological anthropology in the form of an eristic or polemical theology against natural theology is a legitimate propaedeutic to dogmatic theology in that it compels one to abandon a theoretical or speculative attitude towards one's existence in the realization that true self-knowledge is attained only when one understands oneself 'in the light of faith in the Creator revealed in Christ'.[41] Brunner views Kierkegaard as having devoted his intellectual genius to the relation between Christian and non-Christian thought. Calling him 'the greatest Christian thinker of modern times', Brunner credits Kierkegaard and, under his influence, dialectical theology with bringing about a dissolution of the classical synthesis

Philosophical Fragments and *Concluding Unscientific Postscript*, the two most important texts relating to the question of whether there is an anthropological or immanent point of contact between human beings and God, which Schleiermacher affirms but Kierkegaard denies on the basis of original sin.

36 Barth (1949: 22–7); cf. Gouwens (1996: 20).

37 Barth (1972: 11).

38 Barth (1965: 7).

39 Brunner (1946: 9, 399). See also McGrath (1994: 148–53); Nicholls (1969: 139–44).

40 Brunner (1946: 58–80).

41 Brunner (1952: 72); see also McCormack (1995: 403–4).

between philosophy and theology, reason and revelation, but he rightly points out that Kierkegaard did not intend 'to discredit the use of reason' in opposing reason and faith.[42] On the contrary, Brunner maintains that 'Kierkegaard himself is an example of a truly great thinker who was a Christian, and, indeed, a very great Christian who was a thinker, and not only a theological but a philosophical thinker . . . who used his great philosophical powers in the service of his faith.'[43]

Unlike Barth, Paul Tillich (1886–1965) includes Kierkegaard in his *Perspectives on Nineteenth and Twentieth Century Protestant Theology* and refers to him sporadically in his systematic theology and other writings. For Tillich, Kierkegaard's importance lies in his critique of Hegel's theology of mediation and in his analyses of anxiety, despair, the stages of life, and the dialectic between Religiousness A (the coincidence of the infinite and the finite in every human being) and Religiousness B (the revelation of the gap between the divine and human due to sin or estrangement in Christianity).[44] Tillich identifies this dialectic as being important in his own theology, which contains an existentialist analysis of the estrangement between God and human beings that is indebted to Kierkegaard's analysis of the human condition.[45] Tillich also embraces the notion of paradox with reference to Jesus as the Christ but rejects the traditional understanding of the incarnation as God becoming man, which in his view is nonsensical and pagan in connotation.[46] For Tillich Christ is the 'New Being' who is the bearer of essential humanity or the re-established unity of God and man in the form of an 'Eternal God-Manhood', which is precisely what Kierkegaard opposed in his critique of the Hegelian Christologies of his day.[47] Tillich's method of correlation, in which the content of the Christian faith is explained theologically by correlating the existential questions implied in the human situation with the ontological answers implied in divine revelation, may also be seen from a Kierkegaardian perspective as another version of the Hegelian attempt to translate Christian concepts into another conceptual framework in order to make them more understandable and digestible to modern culture.[48]

Focusing on the problem of the historical Jesus in relation to the existential decision of faith, Rudolf Bultmann (1884–1976) developed a full-fledged existentialist theology of the New Testament that owes much to Kierkegaard but also differs from him in some important respects.[49] Bultmann was introduced to Kierkegaard through the dialectical theology

[42] Brunner (1946: 310, 376). [43] Ibid. 377. [44] Tillich (1967: 162–80).
[45] Tillich (1951–63: ii. 19–78; 1952: 86–154). [46] Tillich (1951–63: ii. 90–5).
[47] Ibid. 94–5, 148–9; see also Nicholls (1969: 254).
[48] Tillich (1951–63: i. 59–66); see also Gouwens (1996: 11–12).
[49] See Wolf (1965: 61–92), for a comparative study.

of Barth, but the Dane's influence upon him was also mediated through the philosophy of Martin Heidegger, whose analysis of the structure of human existence is deeply indebted to Kierkegaard. Seeking to demythologize or reinterpret the New Testament kerygma (proclamation of Christ) in Heideggerian existentialist terms that supposedly clarify its anthropological meaning and open up the possibility of authentic existence for modern individuals through an existential encounter with Christ in the kerygma, Bultmann is subject to the same charge of philosophical mediation and cultural accommodation as Tillich.[50] In the spirit of Kierkegaard, however, Bultmann rejects the objectification of the kerygma in theology because in his view it distorts the gospel for contemporary hearers by presenting existential truths in objectivist terms that allow them to evade the existential decision of faith.[51]

Of all the twentieth-century theologians influenced by Kierkegaard, none embraced and embodied his view of Christian discipleship and martyrdom as did Dietrich Bonhoeffer (1906–45). Although Barth was the leader of the German Confessing Church's theological opposition to the Nazi political regime, Bonhoeffer was imprisoned and executed for his involvement in the German resistance movement.[52] Kierkegaard's influence on Bonhoeffer is most evident in *Discipleship* (*Nachfolge*), in which Bonhoeffer, reminiscent of Kierkegaard's attack on Christendom, indicts the 'cheap grace' offered by the secularized, bourgeois church of his time in contrast to the 'costly grace' of the incarnation and Christian discipleship, which involves obedience, suffering, rejection, and bearing one's cross in likeness to Christ.[53] Like Kierkegaard, Bonhoeffer believes that the only way to follow Jesus is by living in the world—a view that is radicalized in his prison writings as he reflects on who Christ is for us today, namely the man for others in a world come of age that has no need of an omnipotent, transcendent God in the form of a false and other-worldly *deus ex machina* (mechanical god) who comes when called.[54] Just before his death Bonhoeffer began working out a secular interpretation of biblical concepts in the form of a religionless Christianity and non-metaphysical view of God as a this-worldly transcendence encountered in the weakness, humiliation, suffering, and cross

50 See Gouwens (1996: 11–12), contra Wolf (1965: 67).

51 Nicholls (1969: 179–81).

52 On Barth's role in the struggle against fascism see Gorringe (1999: 117–23, 158–63). See also Nicholls (1969: 109–16 on Barth and 202–12 on Bonhoeffer).

53 Bonhoeffer (2001). Bonhoeffer used an anthology of selections from Kierkegaard's later journals and notebooks—incorrectly identified in the new English edn. as a 'book' by Kierkegaard titled *Der Einzelne und die Kirche: Über Luther und den Protestantismus* (The Individual and the Church: On Luther and Protestantism)—as a source for this work, previously translated under the title *The Cost of Discipleship*.

54 Bonhoeffer (1997: 281–2, 286, 325–7, 341, 360–1).

of Christ.[55] Although Bonhoeffer's embrace of secularism runs the danger of collapsing into the very autonomy, immanence, and aesthetic forms of worldliness that Kierkegaard opposed, he appeals to a 'secret discipline' that presumably will preserve and protect the spiritual content of Christianity until it can be reinterpreted in an idiom that speaks to a godless age.[56]

Like Tillich and Bultmann, Reinhold Niebuhr (1892–1971), the foremost American political theologian of the twentieth century, reflects Kierkegaard's analysis of anxiety, sin, human freedom, and selfhood in his theological anthropology. In his magnum opus, *The Nature and Destiny of Man*, Niebuhr unabashedly claims that 'Kierkegaard's analysis of the relation of anxiety to sin is the profoundest in Christian thought'.[57] Placing his focus primarily on the social and political existence of human beings, Niebuhr takes aim at secular and Christian liberalism in America, countering the sociopolitical optimism and utopianism of the social gospel of the 1930s with a dialectical analysis of the biblical account of original sin in the individual and society which in his view provides a more realistic assessment of the human condition and the prospects for love and justice in human history.

Among Catholic theologians influenced by Kierkegaard, Erich Przywara, SJ (1889–1972) stands out for his classic study of Kierkegaard's relationship to Catholicism, *Das Geheimnis Kierkegaards* (The Mystery of Kierkegaard, 1929), in which Kierkegaard is seen as transcending Lutheranism in the direction of Catholicism in his emphasis upon authority and ordination and in his mystical affinity with St John of the Cross concerning 'the abandonment of Christ and the uncertainty of life's darkness'.[58] Przywara also finds in Kierkegaard's life, if not also in his writings, an appreciation of women and the feminine that anticipates a positive interpretation of Kierkegaard's view of women in some contemporary Catholic feminist studies.[59]

It is too early to determine how the theology of Kierkegaard will be received in the present century, although he is already being hailed in some quarters as a proto-postmodernist whose ethical and religious insights are being appropriated for the purpose of deconstructing traditional metaphysics or ontotheology and negative or apophatic theology in the name of *différence* or the *tout autre* (absolutely other or the impossible) that presumably makes possible a 'demystified, deconstructed' Christianity.[60] But if we are to think theologically or Christianly in an existential manner

[55] Ibid. 279–81, 285–6, 360–1, 381–2. [56] Ibid. 281, 286.

[57] Niebuhr (1951: 182). [58] Roos (1954: p. xii); O'Meara (2002: 127–8).

[59] O'Meara (2002: 128); Keeley (2002).

[60] Caputo (1995: 233; 1997); see also Derrida (1995); Dooley (2001); Westphal (1997); Cupitt (1997).

as Kierkegaard enjoins us to do, it is important to read his works first of all on their own terms, that is, as indirect communications to the reader, 'that single individual', for the sake of personal appropriation, rather than as theological fodder that must be translated into some other conceptual framework in order to have contemporary relevance. Only then will Kierkegaard be truly read for the first time, even though we may have read him many times previously.

References

Adams, Noel (2003), 'How is an Existence-Communication Possible?' in P. Houe and G. D. Marino (eds.), *Søren Kierkegaard and the Word(s)* (Copenhagen: C. A. Reitzel), 160–70.

Adorno, Theodor W. (1940), 'On Kierkegaard's Doctrine of Love', *Studies in Philosophy and Social Studies*, 8: 413–29.

Allchin, A. M. (1997), *N. F. S. Grundtvig: An Introduction to his Life and Work* (Aarhus, DK: Aarhus University Press).

Althaus, Paul (1966), *The Theology of Martin Luther*, tr. Robert C. Schultz (Philadelphia, Pa.: Fortress Press).

Anselm, St (1962), *Saint Anselm: Basic Writings*, tr. S. W. Deane (La Salle, Ill.: Open Court Publishing Co).

Aristotle (1984), *The Complete Works of Aristotle*, i–ii, ed. Jonathan Barnes (Princeton: Princeton University Press).

Aulén, Gustaf (1950), *Christus Victor: An Historical Study of the Three Main Types of the Idea of the Atonement* (London: SPCK).

Axt-Piscalar, Christine (2007), 'Julius Müller: Parallels in the Doctrines of Sin and Freedom in Kierkegaard and Müller', in J. Stewart (ed.), *Kierhegaard and his German Contemporaries* (Burlington, Vt.: Ashgate), ii. 143–59.

Barrett, Lee C. (1985), 'Kierkegaard's "Anxiety" and the Augustinian Doctrine of Original Sin', in R. L. Perkins (ed.), *International Kierhegaard Commentary* (Macon, Ga.: Mercer University Press), viii. 35–61.

——(1997), 'Subjectivity is (Un)Truth: Climacus's Dialectically Sharpened Pathos' in ibid. xii. 291–306.

——(1999), 'The Neighbor's Material and Social Well-Being in Kierkegaard's *Works of Love*: Does it Matter?', ibid. xvi. 137–65.

——(2002), 'Faith, Works, and the Uses of the Law: Kierkegaard's Appropriation of Lutheran Doctrine', ibid. xxi. 77–109.

——(2006), 'Kierkegaard on the Problem of Witnessing While Yet Being a Sinner', ibid. xviii. 147–75.

——(2007), 'Bretschneider: The Tangled Legacy of Rational Supernaturalism' in J. Stewart (ed.), *Kierkegaard and his German Contemporaries* (Burlington, Vt.: Ashgate), ii. 39–52.

——(2007), 'Christ's Efficacious Love and Human Responsibility: The Lutheran Dialectic of "Discourses at the Communion on Fridays" ', in R. L. Perkins (ed.), *International Kierkegaard Commentary* (Macon, Ga.: Mercer University Press), xvii. 251–72.

Barth, Karl (1949), *Dogmatics in Outline*, tr. G. T. Thomson (New York: Philosophical Library).

——(1965), 'A Thank You and a Bow: Kierkegaard's Reveille', *Canadian Journal of Theology*, 11/1: 3–7.

Barth, Karl (1968), *The Epistle to the Romans*, 6th edn. [reprint of 2nd edn.], tr. Edwyn C. Hoskyns (Oxford: Oxford University Press).

—— (1972), *Protestant Theology in the Nineteenth Century: Its Background and History* (London: SCM Press).

Beabout, Gregory R. (1996), *Freedom and its Misuses: Kierkegaard on Anxiety and Despair* (Milwaukee, Wis.: Marquette University Press).

Beiser, Frederick C. (1987), *The Fate of Reason: German Philosophy from Kant to Fichte* (Cambridge, Mass.: Harvard University Press).

—— (1993) (ed.), *The Cambridge Companion to Hegel* (Cambridge, Mass.: Cambridge University Press).

Bøgeskov, Benjamin Olivares (2007), 'Can We Joyfully Will One Thing? The Place of Joy in the Present Life According to "The Purity of Heart" ', in Cappelørn *et al.* (eds.), *Kierkegaard Studies Yearbook 2007* (Berlin and NewYork: de Gruyter), 137–49.

Bonhoeffer, Dietrich (1997 [1971]), *Letters and Papers from Prison: The Enlarged Edition*, ed. Eberhard Bethge (New York: Simon & Schuster).

—— (2001), *Discipleship*, Dietrich Bonhoeffer Works, 4, tr. Barbara Green and Reinhard Krauss, ed. Geffrey B. Kelly and John D. Godsey (Minneapolis, Minn.: Fortress Press).

Boyd, George Nolan (1970), 'The Doctrine of Original Sin and the Fall in the Theology of Friedrich Schleiermacher', Th.D. thesis (Union Theological Seminary, NY).

Brazill, William J. (1970), *The Young Hegelians* (New Haven, Conn.: Yale University Press).

Breckman, Warren (1999), *Marx, the Young Hegelians, and the Origins of Radical Social Theory* (Cambridge: Cambridge University Press).

Brunner, Emil (1939), *Man in Revolt: A Christian Anthropology*, tr. Olive Wyon (London and Redhill, UK: Lutterworth Press).

—— (1946), *Revelation and Reason: The Christian Doctrine of Faith and Knowledge*, tr. Olive Wyan (Philadelphia, Pa.: Westminster Press).

—— (1952), *The Christian Doctrine of Creation and Redemption: Dogmatics*, ii (London: Lutterworth Press).

Bukdahl, Jørgen (2001), *Søren Kierkegaard and the Common Man*, tr. and ed. Bruce H. Kirmmse (Grand Rapids, Mich., and Cambridge: Eerdmans).

Bultmann, Rudolf (1958 [1934]), *Jesus and the Word*, tr. Louise Pettibone Smith and Erminie Huntress Lantero (New York: Charles Scribner's Sons).

Burgess, Andrew J. (1994), 'Forstand in the Swenson–Lowrie Correspondence and in the "Metaphysical Caprice" ', in R. L. Perkins (ed.), *International Kierkegaard Commentary* (Macon, Ga.: Mercer University Press), vii. 109–28.

—— (2004), 'Kierkegaard, Brorson, and Moravian Music', in ibid. xx. 11–43.

—— (2006), 'Kierkegaard, Moravian Missions, and Martyrdom', ibid. xviii. 177–201.

Cappelørn, Niels Jørgen (2004), 'The Movements of Offense Toward, Away From, and Within Faith: "Blessed is he who is not offended at me" ' in R. L. Perkins (ed.), *International Kierkegaard Commentary* (Macon, Ga.: Mercer University Press), xx. 95–124.

——(2006), 'Søren Kierkegaard at Friday Communion in the Church of Our Lady', tr. K. Brian Söderquist, ibid. xviii. 255–94.

—— (2007), 'Longing for Reconciliation with God: A Fundamental Theme in "Friday Communion Discourses"' in Cappelørn *et al.* (eds.), *Kierkegaard Studies Yearbook 2007* (Berlin and NewYork: de Gruyter), 318–36.

——and Hermann Deuser (1996) (eds.), *Kierkegaard Studies Yearbook 1996* (Berlin and New York: Walter de Gruyter).

——and——(1998) (eds.), *Kierkegaard Studies Yearbook 1998* (Berlin and New York: Walter de Gruyter).

——and——(1999) (eds.), *Kierkegaard Studies Yearbook 1999* (Berlin and New York: Walter de Gruyter).

————and Jon Stewart (2000) (eds.), *Kierkegaard Studies Yearbook 2000* (Berlin and New York: Walter de Gruyter).

——————(2001) (eds.), *Kierkegaard Studies Yearbook 2001* (Berlin and New York: Walter de Gruyter).

——————(2004) (eds.), *Kierkegaard Studies Yearbook 2004* (Berlin and New York: Walter de Gruyter).

————and K. Brian Söderquist (2006) (eds.), *Kierkegaard Studies Yearbook 2006* (Berlin and New York: Walter de Gruyter).

——————(2007) (eds.), *Kierkegaard Studies Yearbook 2007* (Berlin and New York: Walter de Gruyter).

——Richard Crouter, Theodor Jørgensen, and Claus Osthövener (eds.) (2006), *Schleiermacher und Kierkegaard: Subjektivität und Wahrheit/Subjectivity and Truth* (Berlin and New York: Walter de Gruyter).

Caputo, John D. (1995), 'Instants, Secrets, and Singularities: Dealing Death in Kierkegaard and Derrida' in M. J. Matuštík and M. Westphal (eds.), *Kierkegaard in Post/Modernity* (Bloomington, Ind.: Indiana University Press), 216–38.

——(1997), *The Prayers and Tears of Jacques Derrida: Religion without Religion* (Bloomington, Ind.: Indiana University Press).

Cole, Preston (1971), *The Problematic Self in Kierkegaard and Freud* (New Haven, Conn.: Yale University Press).

Come, Arnold B. (1997), *Kierkegaard as Theologian: Recovering my Self* (Montreal: McGill-Queen's University Press).

Conant, James (1993), 'Kierkegaard, Wittgenstein and Nonsense', in Ted Cohen, Paul Guyer, and Hilary Putnam (eds.), *Pursuits of Reason* (Lubbock, Tex.: Texas Tech University Press), 195–224.

Connell, George B., and C. Stephen Evans (1992) (eds.), *Foundations of Kierkegaard's Vision of Community: Religion, Ethics, and Politics in Kierkegaard* (Atlantic Highlands, NJ: Humanities Press).

Copleston, Frederick, SJ (1953–1975), *A History of Philosophy*, i–ix (Westminster, Md.: Newman Press).

Cranz, F. Edward (1998 [1987]), *An Essay on the Development of Luther's Thought on Justice, Law, and Society*, 2nd edn., ed. Gerald Christianson and Thomas M. Izbicki (Mifflintown, Pa.: Sigler Press).

Crites, Stephen (1998), *Dialectic and Gospel in the Development of Hegel's Thinking* (University Park, Pa.: Pennsylvania State University Press).

Crouter, Richard (2005), *Friedrich Schleiermacher: Between Enlightenment and Romanticism* (Cambridge: Cambridge University Press).

——(2007), 'Schleiermacher: Revisiting Kierkegaard's Relationship to Him', in J. Stewart (ed.), *Kierkegaard and his German Contemporaries* (Burlington, Vt.: Ashgate), ii. 197–231.

Cupitt, Don (1988 [1984]), *The Sea of Faith* (Cambridge: Cambridge University Press).

——(1997), *After God: The Future of Religion* (New York: Basic Books).

Czakó, István (2007), 'Feuerbach: A Malicious Demon in the Service of Christianity', in J. Stewart (ed.), *Kierkegaard and his German Contemporaries* (Burlington, Vt.: Ashgate), i. 25–46.

Davenport, John J. (2000), '"Entangled Freedom": Ethical Authority, Original Sin, and Choice in Kierkegaard's *Concept of Anxiety*', *Kierkegaardiana*, 21: 131–51.

——(2001), 'Towards an Existential Virtue Ethics: Kierkegaard and MacIntyre', in John J. Davenport and Anthony Rudd (eds.), *Kierkegaard After MacIntyre: Essays on Freedom, Narrative, and Virtue* (Chicago and LaSalle, Ill.: Open Court), 265–323.

Derrida, Jacques (1995), *The Gift of Death*, tr. David Wills (Chicago: University of Chicago Press).

Descartes, René (1951), *Meditations on First Philosophy*, tr. Laurence J. LaFleur (New York: Macmillan).

Dewey, Bradley R. (1968), *The New Obedience: Kierkegaard on Imitating Christ* (Washington, DC, and Cleveland, Ohio: Corpus Books).

Dooley, Mark (2001), *The Politics of Exodus: Søren Kierkegaard's Ethics of Responsibility* (New York: Fordham University Press).

Eller, Vernard (1968), *Kierkegaard and Radical Discipleship: A New Perspective* (Princeton: Princeton University Press).

Elrod, John W. (1981), *Kierkegaard and Christendom* (Princeton: Princeton University Press).

Ericksen, Robert P. (1985), *Theologians under Hitler: Gerhard Kittel, Paul Althaus and Emanuel Hirsch* (New Haven, Conn., and London: Yale University Press).

Evans, C. Stephen (1983), *Kierkegaard's 'Fragments' and 'Postscript': The Religious Philosophy of Johannes Climacus* (Atlantic Highlands, NJ: Humanities Press).

——(1990), *Søren Kierkegaard's Christian Psychology* (Grand Rapids, Mich.: Zondervan Publishing House).

——(1992), *Passionate Reason: Making Sense of Kierkegaard's 'Philosophical Fragments'* (Bloomington and Indianapolis, Ind.: Indiana University Press).

——(1996), *The Historical Christ and the Jesus of Faith: The Incarnational Narrative as History* (Oxford: Clarendon Press).

——(2004), *Kierkegaard's Ethic of Love: Divine Commands and Moral Obligations* (Oxford: Oxford University Press).

——(2006*a*) (ed.), *Exploring Kenotic Christology: The Self-Emptying of God* (Oxford: Oxford University Press).

——(2006*b*), *Kierkegaard on Faith and the Self: Collected Essays* (Waco, Tex.: Baylor University Press).

Evans, Jan E. (2005), *Unamuno and Kierkegaard: Paths to Selfhood in Fiction* (Lanham, Md.: Lexington Books).

Fairweather, Eugene R. (1956) (ed. and tr.), *A Scholastic Miscellany: Anselm to Ockham* (Philadelphia, Pa.: Westminster Press).

Fenger, Henning (1980), *Kierkegaard, The Myths and their Origins: Studies in the Kierkegaardian Papers and Letters*, tr. George C. Schoolfield (New Haven, Conn., and London: Yale University Press).

Ferreira, M. Jamie (1991), *Transforming Vision: Imagination and Will in Kierkegaardian Faith* (Oxford: Clarendon Press).

—— (2001), *Love's Grateful Striving: A Commentary on Kierkegaard's 'Works of Love'* (Oxford: Oxford University Press).

Feuerbach, Ludwig (1989), *The Essence of Christianity*, tr. George Eliot (Amherst, NY: Prometheus Books).

Frawley, Matthew J. (2003), 'The Existential Role of the Holy Spirit in Kierkegaard's Biblical Hermeneutic', in P. Houe and G. D. Marino (eds.), *Søren Kierkegaard and the Word(s)* (Copenhagen: C. A. Reitzel), 93–104.

—— (2006), 'Human Nature and Fall in Schleiermacher and Kierkegaard' in Cappelørn *et al.* (eds.), *Schleiermacher und Kierkegaard* (Berlin and New York: de Gruyter), 145–58.

Funk, Robert W., and the Jesus Seminar (1998), *The Acts of Jesus: The Search for the Authentic Deeds of Jesus* (San Francisco: HarperSanFrancisco).

—— Roy W. Hoover, and the Jesus Seminar (1993), *The Five Gospels: The Search for the Authentic Words of Jesus* (San Francisco: HarperSanFrancisco).

Garff, Joakim (2005), *Søren Kierkegaard: A Biography*, tr. Bruce H. Kirmmse (Princeton: Princeton University Press).

Gavrilyuk, Paul (2004), *The Suffering of the Impassible God: The Dialectics of Patristic Thought* (Oxford: Oxford University Press).

Gorringe, Timothy J. (1999), *Karl Barth: Against Hegemony* (Oxford: Oxford University Press).

Gouwens, David J. (1996), *Kierkegaard as Religious Thinker* (Cambridge: Cambridge University Press).

Green, Ronald M. (1985), 'The Limits of the Ethical in Kierkegaard's *The Concept of Anxiety* and Kant's *Religion within the Limits of Reason Alone*', in R. L. Perkins (ed.), *International Kierkegaard Commentary* (Macon, Ga.: Mercer University Press), vii. 63–87.

—— (1992), *Kierkegaard and Kant: The Hidden Debt* (Albany, NY: State University of New York Press).

Grillmeier, Aloys, SJ (1965), *Christ in Christian Tradition: From the Apostolic Age to Chalcedon (451)*, tr. J. S. Bowden (New York: Sheed & Ward).

Hall, Amy Laura (2002), *Kierkegaard and the Treachery of Love* (Cambridge: Cambridge University Press).

Hannay, Alastair (2001), *Kierkegaard: A Biography* (Cambridge: Cambridge University Press).

—— and Gordon D. Marino (1998) (eds.), *The Cambridge Companion to Kierkegaard* (Cambridge: Cambridge University Press).

Harrison, Carol (2000), *Augustine: Christian Truth and Fractured Humanity* (Oxford: Oxford University Press).

Harvey, Van A. (1995), *Feuerbach and the Interpretation of Religion* (Cambridge: Cambridge University Press).

Hegel, G. W. F. (1948), *Early Theological Writings*, tr. T. M. Knox (Chicago: University of Chicago Press).

——(1955), *Hegel's Lectures on the History of Philosophy*, i–iii, tr. E. S. Haldane (London: Routledge & Kegan Paul).

——(1969), *Hegel's Science of Logic*, tr. A. V. Miller (London: George Allen & Unwin).

——(1977), *Phenomenology of Spirit*, tr. A. V. Miller (Oxford: Clarendon Press).

——(1984–7), *Lectures on the Philosophy of Religion*, i–iii, ed. Peter C. Hodgson and tr. R. F. Brown, P. C. Hodgson, and J. M. Stewart (Berkeley, Calif.: University of California Press).

——(1991*a*), *Elements of the Philosophy of Right*, ed. Allen W. Wood and tr. H. B. Nisbet (Cambridge: Cambridge University Press).

——(1991*b*), *The Encyclopedia Logic (with the Zusätze)*, tr. T. F. Geraets, W. A. Suchtung, and H. S. Harris (Indianapolis, Ind.: Hackett).

——(2007), *Hegel's Philosophy of Mind*, tr. W. Wallace and A. V. Miller, with revisions and commentary by M. J. Inwood (Oxford: Clarendon Press).

Heiberg, Johann Ludvig (2005), *On the Significance of Philosophy for the Present Age and Other Texts*, ed. and tr. Jon Stewart (Copenhagen: C. A. Reitzel's Publishers).

Hinkson, Craig (2001), 'Luther and Kierkegaard: Theologians of the Cross', *International Journal of Systematic Theology*, 3/1: 27–45.

——(2002), 'Will the Real Martin Luther Please Stand up! Kierkegaard's View of Luther vs. the Evolving Perceptions of the Tradition', in R. L. Perkins (ed.), *International Kierkegaard Commentary* (Macon, Ga.: Mercer University Press), xxi. 37–73.

Hoberman, John M. (1987), 'Kierkegaard on Vertigo', in R. L. Perkins (ed.), *International Kierkegaard Commentary* (Macon, Ga.: Mercer University Press), xix. 185–208.

Hodgson, Peter C. (2005), *Hegel and Christian Theology: A Reading of the 'Lectures on the Philosophy of Religion'* (Oxford: Oxford University Press).

Houe, Poul, and Gordon D. Marino (2003) (eds.), *Søren Kierkegaard and the Word(s): Essays on Hermeneutics and Communication* (Copenhagen: C. A. Reitzel).

———— and Sven Hakon Rossel (2000) (eds.), *Anthropology and Authority: Essays on Søren Kierkegaard* (Amsterdam and Atlanta, Ga.: Rodopi).

Hovde, B. J. (1943), *The Scandinavian Countries, 1720–1865: The Rise of the Middle Classes*, i–ii (Boston, Mass.: Chapman & Grimes).

Howland, Jacob (2006), *Kierkegaard and Socrates: A Study in Philosophy and Faith* (Cambridge: Cambridge University Press).

Hume, David (1988), *An Enquiry Concerning Human Understanding*, ed. Antony Flew (La Salle, Ill.: Open Court).

Jackson, Timothy (1998), 'Arminian Edification: Kierkegaard on Grace and Free Will', in A. Hannay and G. D. Marino (eds.), *The Cambridge Companion to Kierkegaard* (Cambridge: Cambridge University Press), 235–56.

Jaeschke, Walter (1990), *Reason in Religion: The Foundations of Hegel's Philosophy of Religion* (Berkeley, Calif.: University of California Press).

James, David, and Douglas Moggach (2007), 'Bruno Bauer: Biblical Narrative, Freedom and Anxiety', in J. Stewart (ed.), *Kierkegaard and his German Contemporaries* (Burlington, Vt.: Ashgate), ii. 1–18.

Janik, Allan (1984), 'Haecker, Kierkegaard, and the Early Brenner: A Contribution to the History of the Reception of *Two Ages* in the German-Speaking World', in R. L. Perkins (ed.), *International Kierkegaard Commentary* (Macon, Ga.: Mercer University Press), xiv. 189–222.

Kähler, Martin (1964), *The So-Called Historical Jesus and the Historic, Biblical Christ*, tr. and ed. Carl E. Braaten (Philadelphia, Pa.: Fortress).

Kangas, David (2005), 'The Very Opposite of Beginning with Nothing: Guilt Consciousness in Kierkegaard's "The Gospel of Sufferings" IV', in R. L. Perkins (ed.), *International Kierkegaard Commentary* (Macon, Ga.: Mercer University Press), xv. 287–313.

——(2007), *Kierkegaard's Instant: On Beginnings* (Bloomington and Indianapolis, Ind.: Indiana University Press).

——(2008), 'Kierkegaard', in *The Oxford Handbook of Religion and Emotion*, ed. John Corrigan (Oxford: Oxford University Press), 380–403.

Kant, Immanuel (1956), *Critique of Pure Reason*, tr. Norman Kemp Smith (London: Macmillan).

——(1963), *On History*, tr. Lewis White Beck, Robert E. Anchor, and Emil L. Fackenheim (Indianapolis, Ind.: Bobbs-Merrill Co.).

——(1978), *Anthropology from a Pragmatic Point of View*, tr. Victor Lyle Dowdell, rev. and ed. Hans H. Rudnick (Carbondale, Ill.: Southern Illinois University Press).

——(1990), *Foundations of the Metaphysics of Morals*, 2nd edn., tr. Lewis White Beck (New York: Macmillan).

——(1996), *Religion and Rational Theology*, ed. and tr. Allen Wood and George di Giovanni (Cambridge: Cambridge University Press).

——(1998), *Religion within the Boundaries of Mere Reason and Other Writings*, tr. and ed. Allen Wood and George Di Giovanni (Cambridge: Cambridge University Press).

Keeley, Louise Carroll (2002), 'Silence, Domesticity, and Joy: The Spiritual Life of Women in Kierkegaard's *For Self-Examination*', in R. L. Perkins (ed.), *International Kierkegaard Commentary* (Macon, Ga.: Mercer University Press), xxi. 223–57.

Kelly, J. N. D. (1968), *Early Christian Doctrines*, 4th edn. (London: Adam & Charles Black).

Kierkegaard, Søren (1968 [1954]), *Fear and Trembling and The Sickness unto Death*, tr. Walter Lowrie (Princeton: Princeton University Press).

Kirmmse, Bruce H. (1990), *Kierkegaard in Golden Age Denmark* (Bloomington, Ind.: Indiana University Press).

——(2001), 'Socrates in the Fast Lane: Kierkegaard's *The Concept of Irony* on the University's *Velocifère*. Documents, Context, Commentary, and Interpretation', in R. L. Perkins (ed.), *International Kierkegaard Commentary* (Macon, Ga.: Mercer University Press), ii. 17–99.

Kirmmse, Bruce H. (1996) (ed.), *Encounters with Kierkegaard: A Life as Seen by his Contemporaries*, tr. Bruce H. Kirmmse and Virginia R. Laursen (Princeton: Princeton University Press).

Knappe, Ulrich (2004), *Theory and Practice in Kant and Kierkegaard* (Berlin and New York: Walter de Gruyter).

Koch, Hal (1952), *Grundtvig*, tr. Llewellyn Jones (Yellow Springs, Ohio: Antioch Press).

Kosch, Michelle (2006), *Freedom and Reason in Kant, Schelling, and Kierkegaard* (Oxford: Clarendon Press).

Koslowski, Peter (2007), 'Baader: The Centrality of Original Sin and the Difference of Immediacy and Innocence', in J. Stewart (ed.), *Kierkegaard and his German Contemporaries* (Burlington, Vt.: Ashgate), i. 1–16.

Lausten, Martin Schwarz (2002), *A Church History of Denmark*, tr. Frederick H. Cryer (Burlington, Vt.: Ashgate).

Law, David R. (1988), 'Kierkegaard on Baptism', *Theology*, 91/740 (Mar.): 114–22.

——(1993), *Kierkegaard as Negative Theologian* (Oxford: Clarendon Press).

——(1997), 'Resignation, Suffering, and Guilt in Kierkegaard's *Concluding Unscientific Postscript to "Philosophical Fragments"*' in R. L. Perkins (ed.), *International Kierkegaard Commentary* (Macon, Ga.: Mercer University Press), xii. 263–89.

——(2002*a*), 'Cheap Grace and the Cost of Discipleship in Kierkegaard's *For Self-Examination*', ibid. xxi. 111–42.

——(2002*b*), 'Christian Discipleship in Kierkegaard, Hirsch, and Bonhoeffer', *Downside Review*, 120: 293–306.

——(2005), 'Wrongness, Guilt, and Innocent Suffering in Kierkegaard's *Either/Or*, Part Two and *Upbuilding Discourses in Various Spirits*', in R. L. Perkins (ed.), *International Kierkegaard Commentary* (Macon, Ga.: Mercer University Press), xv. 315–48.

——(2007), 'Kierkegaard's Understanding of the Eucharist in *Christian Discourses*, Part Four', ibid. xvii. 273–98.

Leibniz, Gottfried Wilhelm von (1965), *Monadology and Other Philosophical Essays*, tr. Paul Schrecker and Anne Martin Schrecker (Indianapolis, Ind.: Bobbs-Merrill).

Léon, Céline, and Sylvia Walsh (1997) (eds.), *Feminist Interpretations of Søren Kierkegaard* (University Park, Pa.: Pennsylvania State University Press).

Lessing, Gotthold Ephraim (2005), *Philosophical and Theological Writings*, tr. H. B. Nisbet (Cambridge: Cambridge University Press).

Lindström, Valter (1982), 'The First Article of the Creed in Kierkegaard's Writings', *Kierkegaardiana*, 12: 38–50.

Lippitt, John (2000), 'On Authority and Revocation: Climacus as Humorist', in P. Houe *et al.* (eds.), *Anthropology and Authority* (Amsterdam and Atlanta, Ga.: Rodopi), 107–17.

——(2003), *Guidebook to Kierkegaard and 'Fear and Trembling'* (London: Routledge).

Loewenich, Walther von (1976), *Luther's Theology of the Cross*, tr. Herbert J. A. Bouman (Minneapolis, Minn.: Augsburg).

Løgstrup, Knud Ejler (1997), *The Ethical Demand*, ed. Hans Fink and Alasdair MacIntyre (Notre Dame, Ind.: Notre Dame University Press).

Lowrie, Walter (1962), *Kierkegaard*, i–ii (New York: Harper & Brothers).

Luther, Martin (1978 [1807]), *A Commentary on St. Paul's Epistle to the Galatians*, ed. Philip S. Watson (Cambridge: James Clarke & Co.)

——(1989), *Martin Luther's Basic Theological Writings*, ed. Timothy F. Lull (Minneapolis, Minn: Fortress Press).

McCarthy, Vincent (1978), *The Phenomenology of Moods in Kierkegaard* (The Hague and Boston, Mass.: Martinus Nijhoff).

——(1985), 'Schelling and Kierkegaard on Freedom and Fall', in R. L. Perkins (ed.), *International Kierkegaard Commentary* (Macon, Ga.: Mercer University Press), viii. 89–109.

McCormack, Bruce L. (1995), *Karl Barth's Critically Realistic Dialectical Theology: Its Genesis and Development, 1909–36* (New York: Oxford University Press).

McGrath, Alister E. (1994), *The Making of Modern German Christology 1750–1990*, 2nd edn. (Eugene, Oreg.: Wipf & Stock).

McKinnon, Alastair (1971), *Fundamental Polyglot Konkordans til Kierkegaards Samlede Værker* (Leiden: E. J. Brill).

Magurshak, Dan (1985), 'The Concept of Anxiety: The Keystone of the Kierkegaard–Heidegger Relationship', in R. L. Perkins (ed.), *International Kierkegaard Commentary* (Macon, Ga.: Mercer University Press), viii. 167–95.

——(1987), 'Despair and Everydayness: Kierkegaard's Corrective Contribution to Heidegger's Notion of Fallen Everydayness', ibid. xix. 209–37.

Mahn, Jason (2006), 'Felix Fallibilitas: The Benefit of Sin's Possibility in Kierkegaard's *The Concept of Anxiety*', *Faith and Philosophy*, 23/3: 254–78.

Malantschuk, Gregor (1980), *The Controversial Kierkegaard*, tr. Howard V. Hong and Edna H. Hong (Waterloo, Ont.: Wilfrid Laurier University Press).

Malik, Habib C. (1997), *Receiving Søren Kierkegaard: The Early Impact and Transmission of his Thought* (Washington, DC: Catholic University of America Press).

Marcel, Gabriel (2006), *Man and Mass Society* (South Bend, Ind.: St Augustine's Press).

Marcuse, Herbert (1964), *One-Dimensional Man* (Boston, Mass.: Beacon).

Mariña, Jacqueline (2005*a*), 'Christology and Anthropology in Friedrich Schleiermacher', in Mariña (ed.), *The Cambridge Companion to Friedrich Schleiermacher* (Cambridge: Cambridge University Press), 151–70.

——(2005*b*) (ed.), *The Cambridge Companion to Friedrich Schleiermacher* (Cambridge: Cambridge University Press).

Marino, Gordon (1998), 'Anxiety in *The Concept of Anxiety*', in A. Hannay and G. D. Marino (eds.), *The Cambridge Companion to Kierkegaard* (Cambridge: Cambridge University Press), 308–28.

Martens, Paul (2002), 'The Emergence of the Holy Spirit in Kierkegaard's Thought: Critical Theological Developments', in R. L. Perkins (ed.), *International Kierkegaard Commentary* (Macon, Ga.: Mercer University Press), xxi. 199–222.

Martensen, Hans Lassen (1866), *Christian Dogmatics*, tr. William Urwick (Edinburgh: T. & T. Clark).

Martensen, Hans Lassen (1997), *The Autonomy of Human Self-Consciousness in Modern Dogmatic Theology*, tr. Curtis Thompson, in *Between Hegel and Kierkegaard*, tr. C. Thompson, and D. Kangas (Atlanta, Ga.: Scholars Press), 73–147.

——(2004), 'Rationalism, Supernaturalism and the *principium exclusi medii*', tr. Jon Stewart in Cappelørn *et al.* (eds.), *Kierkegaard Studies Yearbook 2004* (Berlin and New York: de Gruyter), 587–98.

Marx, Karl (1963), *Karl Marx: Early Writings*, tr. and ed. T. B. Bottomore (New York: McGraw-Hill).

——(1972), *Karl Marx: Early Texts*, tr. and ed. David McLellan (New York: Barnes & Noble).

Matuštík, Martin J., and Merold Westphal (1995) (eds.), *Kierkegaard in Post/Modernity* (Bloomington, Ind.: Indiana University Press).

May, Rollo (1977), *The Meaning of Anxiety*, rev. edn. (New York: Norton).

Mooney, Edward F. (1991), *Knights of Faith and Resignation: Reading Kierkegaard's 'Fear and Trembling'* (Albany, NY: State University of New York Press).

Mulhall, John (1994), *Faith and Reason* (London: Duckworth).

Müller, Julius (1852–3 [1849]), *The Christian Doctrine of Sin*, i–ii, 3rd edn., tr. William Pulsford (Edinburgh: T. & T. Clark).

Mynster, Jakob Peter (2004), 'Rationalism, Supernaturalism', tr. Jon Stewart in Cappelørn *et al.* (eds.), *Kierkegaard Studies Yearbook 2004* (Berlin and New York: de Gruyter), 570–82.

Nelson, Christopher A. P. (2007), 'The Joy of it' in R. L. Perkins (ed.), *International Kierkegaard Commentary* (Macon, Ga.: Mercer University Press), xvii. 119–41.

Nicholls, William (1969), *Systematic and Philosophical Theology* (Baltimore, Md.: Penguin Books).

Niebuhr, Reinhold (1951), *The Nature and Destiny of Man: A Christian Interpretation* (New York: Charles Scribner's Sons).

Niebuhr, Richard R. (1964), *Schleiermacher on Christ and Religion: A New Introduction* (New York: Charles Scribner's Sons).

Nordentoft, Kresten (1973), *'Hvad Siger Brand-Majoren?': Kierkegaards Opgør Med Sin Samtid* (Copenhagen: Gad).

——(1978), *Kierkegaard's Psychology*, tr. Bruce H. Kirmmse (Pittsburgh, Pa.: Duquesne University Press).

Nygren, Anders (1954), *Agape and Eros*, tr. Philip S. Watson (London: SPCK).

O'Meara, Thomas F., OP (2002), *Erich Przywara, S.J.: His Theology and his World* (Notre Dame, Ind.: University of Notre Dame Press).

Osborn, Eric (1997), *Tertullian, First Theologian of the West* (Cambridge: Cambridge University Press).

Paget, James Carleton (2001), 'Quests for the Historical Jesus', in *The Cambridge Companion to Jesus*, ed. Markus Bockmuehl (Cambridge: Cambridge University Press).

Pattison, George (1992), *Kierkegaard: The Aesthetic and the Religious* (London: Macmillan).

——(1999), *'Poor Paris!' Kierkegaard's Critique of the Spectacular City* (Berlin and New York: Walter de Gruyter).

—— (2002*a*), *Kierkegaard, Religion and the Nineteenth-Century Crisis of Culture* (Cambridge: Cambridge University Press).

—— (2002*b*), *Kierkegaard's Upbuilding Discourses: Philosophy, Theology, Literature* (London and New York: Routledge).

—— (2005), *The Philosophy of Kierkegaard* (Chesham: Acumen Publishing).

—— (2007), 'D. F. Strauss: Kierkegaard and Radical Demythologization', in J. Stewart (ed.), *Kierkegaard and his German Contemporaries* (Burlington, Vt.: Ashgate), ii. 233–57.

—— and Steven Shakespeare (1998) (eds.), *Kierkegaard: The Self in Society* (London and New York: Macmillan and St Martin's Press).

Pedersen, Jørgen (1980), 'Credo ut intelligam', in N. Thulstrup and M. M. Thulstrup (eds.), *Theological Concepts in Kierkegaard* (Copenhagen: C. A. Reitzels Boghandel), 113–16.

Perkins, Robert L. (1981) (ed.), *Søren Kierkegaard's 'Fear and Trembling': Critical Appraisals* (Tuscaloosa, Ala.: University of Alabama Press).

—— (1984) (ed.), *International Kierkegaard Commentary: Two Ages*, xiv (Macon, Ga.: Mercer University Press).

—— (1985) (ed.), *International Kierkegaard Commentary: The Concept of Anxiety: A Simple Psychologically Orienting Deliberation on the Dogmatic Issue of Hereditary Sin*, viii (Macon, Ga.: Mercer University Press).

—— (1987) (ed.), *International Kierkegaard Commentary: The Sickness unto Death*, xix (Macon, Ga.: Mercer University Press).

—— (1990) (ed.), *International Kierkegaard Commentary: The Corsair Affair*, xiii (Macon, Ga.: Mercer University Press).

—— (1993) (ed.), *International Kierkegaard Commentary: Fear and Trembling and Repetition*, vi (Macon, Ga.: Mercer University Press).

—— (1994) (ed.), *International Kierkegaard Commentary: Philosophical Fragments and Johannes Climacus*, vii (Macon, Ga.: Mercer University Press).

—— (1995) (ed.), *International Kierkegaard Commentary: Either/Or, Part II*, iv (Macon, Ga.: Mercer University Press).

—— (1997) (ed.), *International Kierkegaard Commentary: Concluding Unscientific Postscript to 'Philosophical Fragments'*, xii (Macon, Ga.: Mercer University Press).

—— (1999*a*) (ed.), *International Kierkegaard Commentary: Early Polemical Writings*, i (Macon, Ga.: Mercer University Press).

—— (1999*b*) (ed.), *International Kierkegaard Commentary: Works of Love*, xvi (Macon, Ga.: Mercer University Press).

—— (1999*c*), 'Language, Social Reality, and Resistance in the Age of Kierkegaard's Review of *Two Ages*', in Cappelørn and Deuser (eds.), *Kierkegaard Studies Yearbook 1999* (Berlin and New York: de Gruyter), 164–81.

—— (1999*d*), 'Power, Politics, and Media Critique: Kierkegaard's First Brush with the Press', in Perkins (ed.), *International Kierkegaard Commentary* (Macon, Ga.: Mercer University Press), i. 27–44.

—— (2001) (ed.), *International Kierkegaard Commentary: The Concept of Irony*, ii (Macon, Ga.: Mercer University Press).

Perkins, Robert L. (2002) (ed.), *International Kierkegaard Commentary: For Self-Examination and Judge for Yourself!*, xxi (Macon, Ga.: Mercer University Press).

——(2003*a*) (ed.), *International Kierkegaard Commentary: Eighteen Upbuilding Discourses*, v (Macon, Ga.: Mercer University Press).

——(2003*b*), 'Upbuilding as a Propaedeutic for Justice', ibid. v. 325–56.

——(2004*a*), 'Habermas and Kierkegaard: Religious Subjectivity, Multiculturalism, and Historical Revisionism', *International Philosophical Quarterly*, 44/4: 481–96.

——(2004*b*) (ed.), *International Kierkegaard Commentary: Practice in Christianity*, xx (Macon, Ga.: Mercer University Press).

——(2004*c*), 'Kierkegaard's Anti-Climacus in his Social and Political Environment', ibid. xx. 275–302.

——(2005) (ed.), *International Kierkegaard Commentary: Upbuilding Discourses in Various Spirits*, xv (Macon, Ga.: Mercer University Press).

——(2006*a*) (ed.), *International Kierkegaard Commentary: Without Authority*, xviii (Macon, Ga.: Mercer University Press).

——(2006*b*), '*Kierkegaard's Relations to Hegel Reconsidered* by Jon Stewart', *The Owl of Minerva*, 37/2 (Spring/Summer), 199–209.

——(2007) (ed.), *International Kierkegaard Commentary: Christian Discourses and The Crisis and a Crisis in the Life of an Actress*, xvii (Macon, Ga.: Mercer University Press).

Plato (1997), *Complete Works*, ed. John M. Cooper (Indianapolis, Ind., and Cambridge: Hackett).

Plekon, Michael (1992), 'Kierkegaard and the Eucharist', *Studia Liturgica*, 22: 214–36.

Poole, Roger (2001), ' "Dizziness, Falling ... Oh (dear)! ... ": Reading *Begrebet Angest* for the Very First Time', in Cappelørn *et al.* (eds.), *Kierkegaard Studies Yearbook 2001* (Berlin and New York: de Gruyter), 199–219.

Possen, David D. (2004), 'The Voice of Rigor', in R. L. Perkins (ed.), *International Kierkegaard Commentary* (Macon, Ga.: Mercer University Press), xx. 161–85.

Quinn, Philip L. (1990), 'Does Anxiety Explain Original Sin?' *Noûs* 24: 227–44.

——(1998), 'Kierkegaard's Christian Ethics', in A. Hannay and G. D. Marino (eds.), *The Cambridge Companion to Kierkegaard* (Cambridge: Cambridge University Press), 349–75.

Rae, Murray A. (1997), *Kierkegaard's Vision of the Incarnation* (Oxford: Clarendon Press).

——(2002), 'Kierkegaard, Barth, and Bonhoeffer: Conceptions of the Relation between Grace and Works' in R. L. Perkins (ed.), *International Kierkegaard Commentary* (Macon, Ga.: Mercer University Press), xxi. 143–67.

Richardson, Alan (1976) (ed.), *A Dictionary of Christian Theology* (Philadelphia, Pa.: Westminster Press).

Ringleben, Joachim (2006), 'Søren Kierkegaard as a Reader of Hamann' in Cappelørn *et al.* (eds.), *Kierkegaard Studies Yearbook 2006* (Berlin and New York: de Gruyter), 207–18.

Roberts, Robert C. (1986), *Faith, Reason, and History: Rethinking Kierkegaard's 'Philosophical Fragments'* (Macon, Ga.: Mercer University Press).

——(1997), 'Dialectical Emotions and the Virtue of Faith', in R. L. Perkins (ed.), *International Kierkegaard Commentary* (Macon, Ga.: Mercer University Press), xii. 73–93.

——(1998), 'Existence, Emotion, and Virtue: Classical Themes in Kierkegaard', in A. Hannay and G. D. Marino (eds.), *The Cambridge Companion to Kierkegaard* (Cambridge: Cambridge University Press), 177–206.

Rohde, H. P. (1967) (ed.), *Auktionsprotokol over Søren Kierkegaards Bogsamling* (Copenhagen: Det Kongelige Bibliotek).

Roos, H., SJ (1954), *Søren Kierkegaard and Catholicism*, tr. Richard M. Brackett, SJ (Westminster, Md.: Newman Press).

Rose, Tim (2001), *Kierkegaard's Christocentric Theology* (Burlington, Vt.: Ashgate).

Rudd, Anthony John (2000), 'On Straight and Crooked Readings: Why the *Postscript* Does Not Self-Destruct', in P. Houe *et al.* (eds.), *Anthropology and Authority* (Amsterdam and Atlanta, Ga.: Rodopi), 119–27.

Rumble, Vanessa (1992), 'The Oracle's Ambiguity: Freedom and Original Sin in Kierkegaard's *The Concept of Anxiety*', *Soundings*, 75/4: 605–25.

Saxbee, John (2003), 'The Golden Age in an Earthen Vessel: The Life and Times of Bishop J. P. Mynster', in J. Stewart (ed.), *Kierkegaard and his Contemporaries* (Berlin and New York: de Gruyter), 149–63.

Schelling, F. W. J. (2006), *Philosophical Investigations into the Essence of Human Freedom*, tr. Jeff Love and Johannes Schmidt (Albany, NY: State University of New York Press).

Schjørring, J. H. (1982), 'Martensen', in N. Thulstrup and M. M. Thulstrup (eds.), *Kierkegaard's Teachers* (Copenhagen: C. A. Reitzels Forlag), 177–207.

Schleiermacher, Friedrich (1956), *The Christian Faith*, ed. H. R. Mackintosh and J. S. Stewart (Edinburgh: T. & T. Clark).

——(1996), *On Religion: Speeches to its Cultured Despisers*, ed. and tr. Richard Crouter (Cambridge: Cambridge University Press).

Schmid, Heinrich (1961 [1899]), *Doctrinal Theology of the Evangelical Lutheran Church*, 3rd edn., tr. Charles A. Hay and Henry E. Jacobs (Minneapolis, Minn.: Augsburg).

Schulz, Heiko (2007*a*), 'Marheineke: The Volatilization of Christian Doctrine', in J. Stewart (ed.), *Kierkegaard and his German Contemporaries* (Burlington, Vt.: Ashgate), ii. 117–42.

——(2007*b*), 'Rosenkranz: Traces of Hegelian Psychology and Theology in Kierkegaard', ibid. ii. 161–96.

Schweitzer, Albert (1961), *The Quest of the Historical Jesus* (New York: Macmillan).

Sextus Empiricus (2000), *Outlines of Scepticism*, ed. Julia Annas and Jonathan Barnes (Cambridge: Cambridge University Press).

Shiner, Larry (1966), *The Secularization of History: An Introduction to the Theology of Friedrich Gogarten* (Nashville, Tenn.: Abingdon).

Siggins, Ian D. Kingston (1970), *Martin Luther's Doctrine of Christ* (New Haven, Conn.: Yale University Press).

Söderquist, K. Brian (2003), 'Kierkegaard's Contribution to the Danish Discussion of Irony', in J. Stewart (ed.), *Kierkegaard and his Contemporaries* (Berlin and New York: de Gruyter), 78–105.

Søgard, Ib (2007), 'What does the Doctor Really Know? Kierkegaard's Admission to Frederik's Hospital and his Death There in 1855', in Cappelørn *et al.* (eds.), *Kierkegaard Studies Yearbook 2007* (Berlin and New York: de Gruyter), 381–400.

Sorainen, Kalle (1981), 'Brøchner' in N. Thulstrup and M. M. Thulstrup (eds.), *The Legacy and Interpretation of Kierkegaard* (Copenhagen: C. A. Reitzel's Boghandel), 198–203.

Spinoza, Benedict de (1951), *The Chief Works of Benedict de Spinoza*, i–ii, tr. R. H. M. Elwes (New York: Dover).

Sponheim, Paul (2004), 'Relational Transcendence in Divine Agency', in R. L. Perkins (ed.), *International Kierkegaard Commentary* (Macon, Ga.: Mercer University Press), xx. 47–68.

Stewart, Jon (2003*a*), *Kierkegaard's Relations to Hegel Reconsidered* (Cambridge: Cambridge University Press).

——(2003*b*) (ed.), *Kierkegaard and his Contemporaries: The Culture of Golden Age Denmark* (Berlin and New York: Walter de Gruyter).

——(2004*a*), 'Mynster's "Rationalism, Supernaturalism"' in Cappelørn *et al.* (eds.), *Kierkegaard Studies Yearbook 2004* (Berlin and New York: de Gruyter), 565–9.

——(2004*b*), 'Martensen's "Rationalism, Supernaturalism and the *principium exclusi medii*"', ibid. 583–7.

——(2007), 'Werder: The Influence of Werder's Lectures and *Logik* on Kierkegaard's Thought', in J. Stewart (ed.), *Kierkegaard and his German Contemporaries* (Burlington, Vt.: Ashgate), i. 335–72.

——(2007*a*) (ed.), *Kierkegaard and his German Contemporaries*, i. *Philosophy* (Burlington, Vt.: Ashgate).

——(2007*b*) (ed.), *Kierkegaard and his German Contemporaries*, ii. *Theology* (Burlington, Vt.: Ashgate).

Strauss, David Friedrich (1973), *The Life of Jesus Critically Examined*, ed. Peter C. Hodgson (London: SCM Press).

——(1983), *In Defense of 'My Life of Jesus' Against the Hegelians*, tr. and ed. Marilyn Chapin Massey (Hamden, Conn.: Archon Books).

Tanner, John S. (1992), *Anxiety in Eden: A Kierkegaardian Reading of 'Paradise Lost'* (New York and Oxford: Oxford University Press).

Taylor, Mark C. (1975), *Kierkegaard's Pseudonymous Authorship: A Study of Time and the Self* (Princeton: Princeton University Press).

——(1980), 'Christology' in N. Thulstrup and M. M. Thulstrup (eds.), *Theological Concepts in Kierkegaard* (Copenhagen: C. A. Reitzels Boghandel), 167–206.

Tennant, F. R. (1946), *The Sources of the Doctrines of the Fall and Original Sin* (New York: Schocken Books).

Tertullian (2004), *On the Flesh of Christ* (Whitefish, Mont.: Kessinger Publishing).

The Book of Concord: The Confessions of the Evangelical Lutheran Church (2000), ed. Robert Kolb and Timothy J. Wengert (Minneapolis, Minn.: Fortress Press).

The New Oxford Annotated Bible (2001), 3rd edn., ed. Michael D. Coogan (Oxford: Oxford University Press).

Theissen, Gerd, and Annette Merz (1998), *The Historical Jesus: A Comprehensive Guide* (Minneapolis, Minn.: Fortress Press).

Theunissen, Michael (2005), *Kierkegaard's Concept of Despair*, tr. Barbara Harshav and Helmut Illbruck (Princeton: Princeton University Press).

Thompson, Curtis L., and David J. Kangas (1997) (tr.), *Between Hegel and Kierkegaard: Hans L. Martensen's Philosophy of Religion* (Atlanta, Ga.: Scholars Press).

Thompson, Thomas R. (2006), 'Nineteenth-Century Kenotic Christology: The Waxing, Waning, and Weighing of a Quest for a Coherent Orthodoxy', in C. S. Evans (ed.), *Exploring Kenotic Christology* (Oxford: Oxford University Press), 74–111.

Thulstrup, Marie Mikulová (1981), 'Pietism', in N. Thulstrup and M. M. Thulstrup (eds.), *Kierkegaard and Great Traditions* (Copenhagen: C. A. Reitzels Boghandel), 173–222.

Thulstrup, Niels (1978), 'Theological and Philosophical Studies' in N. Thulstrup and M. M. Thulstrup (eds.), *Kierkegaard's View of Christianity* (Copenhagen: C. A. Reitzels Boghandel), 38–60.

——(1980*a*), 'Adam and Original Sin' in N. Thulstrup and M. M. Thulstrup (eds.), *Theological Concepts in Kierkegaard* (Copenhagen: C. A. Reitzels Boghandel), 122–56.

——(1980*b*), 'Dogma and Dogmatics', ibid. 82–8.

——(1980*c*), 'The Formula of Concord', ibid. 105–12.

——(1980*d*), *Kierkegaard's Relation to Hegel*, tr. George L. Stengren (Princeton: Princeton University Press).

——(1982), 'H. N. Clausen', in N. Thulstrup and M. M. Thulstrup (eds.), *Kierkegaard's Teachers* (Copenhagen: C. A. Reitzels Forlag), 158–69.

——(1984), *Kierkegaard and the Church in Denmark*, Bibliotheca Kierkegaardiana, 13, ed. Niels Thulstrup and Marie Mikulová Thulstrup (Copenhagen: C. A. Reitzels Forlag A/S).

——and M. Mikulová Thulstrup (1978) (eds.), *Kierkegaard's View of Christianity*, Bibliotheca Kierkegaardiana, 1 (Copenhagen: C. A. Reitzels Boghandel).

——and——(1980) (eds.), *Theological Concepts in Kierkegaard*, Bibliotheca Kierkegaardiana, 5 (Copenhagen: C. A. Reitzels Boghandel).

——and——(1981*a*) (eds.), *Kierkegaard and Great Traditions*, Bibliotheca Kierkegaardiana, 6 (Copenhagen: C. A. Reitzels Boghandel), 173–222.

——and——(1981*b*) (eds.), *The Legacy and Interpretation of Kierkegaard*, Bibliotheca Kierkegaardiana, 8 (Copenhagen: C. A. Reitzels Boghandel).

——and——(1982) (eds.), *Kierkegaard's Teachers*, Bibliotheca Kierkegaardiana, 10 (Copenhagen: C. A. Reitzels Forlag).

——and——(1987) (eds.), *Kierkegaard Research*, Bibliotheca Kierkegaardiana, 15 (Copenhagen: C. A. Reitzels Forlag).

Tice, Terrence N. (2006), *Schleiermacher* (Nashville, Tenn.: Abingdon Press).

Tillich, Paul (1951–63), *Systematic Theology*, i–iii (Chicago: University of Chicago Press).

——(1952), *The Courage to Be* (New Haven, Conn.: Yale University Press).

——(1967), *Perspectives on Nineteenth and Twentieth Century Protestant Theology*, ed. Carl E. Braaten (New York: Harper & Row).

Toews, John Edward (1980), *Hegelianism: The Path Toward Dialectical Humanism, 1805–1841* (Cambridge: Cambridge University Press).

——(1993), 'Transformations of Hegelianism, 1805–1846' in F. C. Beiser (ed.), *The Cambridge Companion to Hegel* (Cambridge: Cambridge University Press), 378–413.

Tolstrup, Christian Fink (2004), ' "Playing a Profane Game with Holy Things": Understanding Kierkegaard's Critical Encounter with Bishop Mynster', in R. L. Perkins (ed.), *International Kierkegaard Commentary* (Macon, Ga.: Mercer University Press), xx. 245–74.

Tornøe, Caspar Wenzel (2006), 'The Changeless God of Schleiermacher and Kierkegaard', in Cappelørn *et al.* (eds.), *Kierkegaard Studies Yearbook 2006* (Berlin and New York: de Gruyter), 265–78.

Tudvad, Peter (2004), *Kierkegaards København* (Copenhagen: Politiken).

Tuttle, Howard N. (2005), *The Crowd is Untruth: The Existential Critique of Mass Society in the Thought of Kierkegaard, Nietzsche, Heidegger, and Ortega y Gasset* (New York: Peter Lang).

Walsh, Sylvia (1987), 'On "Feminine" and "Masculine" Forms of Despair', in R. L. Perkins (ed.), *International Kierkegaard Commentary* (Macon, Ga.: Mercer University Press), xix. 121–34; repr. in C. Léon and S. Walsh (1997) (eds.), *Feminist Interpretations of Søren Kierkegaard* (University Park, Pa.: Pennsylvania State University Press), 203–15.

——(1994), *Living Poetically: Kierkegaard's Existential Aesthetics* (University Park, Pa.: Pennsylvania State University Press).

——(2000), 'When "That Single Individual" is a Woman', in Cappelørn, *et al.* (eds.), *Kierkegaard Studies Yearbook 2000* (Berlin and New York: de Gruyter), 1–18; repr. in R. L. Perkins (ed.), *International Kierkegaard Commentary* (Macon, Ga.: Mercer University Press, 2003), v. 31–50.

——(2005), *Living Christianly: Kierkegaard's Dialectic of Christian Existence* (University Park, Pa.: Pennsylvania State University Press).

——(2006), 'Prototypes of Piety: The Woman Who was a Sinner and Mary Magdalene', in R. L. Perkins (ed.), *International Kierkegaard Commentary* (Macon, Ga.: Mercer University Press), xviii. 313–42.

Watkin, Julia (1995), 'Judge William: A Christian?', ibid. iv. 113–37.

——(1999), 'Serious Jest? Kierkegaard as Young Polemicist in "Defense" of Women', ibid. i. 7–25.

Welch, Claude (1965), *God and Incarnation in Mid-Nineteenth Century German Theology* (New York: Oxford University Press).

——(1972), *Protestant Thought in the Nineteenth Century*, i. *1799–1870* (New Haven, Conn., and London: Yale University Press).

Weston, Michael (1999), 'Evading the Issue: The Strategy of Kierkegaard's *Postscript*', *Philosophical Investigations*, 22/1 (Jan.): 35–64.

Westphal, Merold (1991), *Kierkegaard's Critique of Reason and Society* (University Park, Pa.: Pennsylvania State University Press).

——(1996), *Becoming a Self: A Reading of Kierkegaard's 'Concluding Unscientific Postscript'* (West Lafayette, Ind.: Purdue University Press).

——(1997), 'Kierkegaard's Climacus: A Kind of Postmodernist', in R. L. Perkins (ed.), *International Kierkegaard Commentary* (Macon, Ga.: Mercer University Press), xii. 53–71.

Widenmann, Robert J. (1982), 'Sibbern', in N. Thulstrup and M. M. Thulstrup (eds.), *Kierkegaard's Teachers* (Copenhagen: C. A. Reitzels Forlag), 70–88.

Williamson, Raymond Keith (1984), *Introduction to Hegel's Philosophy of Religion* (Albany, NY: State University of New York Press).

Wolf, Herbert C. (1965), *Kierkegaard and Bultmann: The Quest of the Historical Jesus* (Minneapolis, Minn.: Augsburg).

Wood, Allen W. (1990), *Hegel's Ethical Thought* (Cambridge: Cambridge University Press).

——(1993*a*), 'Hegel and Marxism', in F. C. Beiser (ed.), *The Cambridge Companion to Hegel* (Cambridge: Cambridge University Press), 414–44.

——(1993*b*), 'Hegel's Ethics', ibid. 211–33.

Woszek, Norbert (1987), 'Eduard Gans on Poverty: Between Hegel and Saint-Simon', *The Owl of Minerva*, 18/2 (Spring): 167–78.

Wyman, Walter E., Jun. (2005), 'Sin and Redemption', in J. Mariña (ed.), *The Cambridge Companion to Friedrich Schleiermacher* (Cambridge: Cambridge University Press), 129–49.

Index